LOURMARIN
IN THE
EIGHTEENTH
CENTURY

THE JOHNS HOPKINS UNIVERSITY STUDIES IN HISTORICAL AND POLITICAL SCIENCE

EIGHTY-EIGHTH SERIES (1970)

1. Fashoda Reconsidered: The Impact of Domestic Politics
on French Policy in Africa, 1893–1898
BY ROGER GLENN BROWN

2. Lourmarin in the Eighteenth Century:
A Study of a French Village
BY THOMAS F. SHEPPARD

THOMAS F. SHEPPARD

LOURMARIN IN THE EIGHTEENTH CENTURY

A STUDY OF A FRENCH VILLAGE

THE JOHNS HOPKINS PRESS
BALTIMORE AND LONDON

B.2170

The Johns Hopkins Press, Baltimore, Maryland 21218
The Johns Hopkins Press Ltd., London

Library of Congress Catalog Card Number 79-126803

ISBN 0-8018-1132-5

TO DONNA LYN

ACKNOWLEDGMENTS

THIS STUDY OF A FRENCH VILLAGE in the eighteenth century owes a great deal to Professors Noël Coulet and Michel Vovelle, of the University of Aix-Marseilles, who introduced me to the mysteries of the French archives and who guided me through the voluminous literature on Provence. Professor André Bourde, also of the University of Aix-Marseilles, made several helpful suggestions. My thanks also to the archivists and their assistants in Aix-en-Provence, Marseilles, and Avignon. I would also like to thank Messieurs Henri Barthelemy, mayor, and Edgar Valton, secretary-general of Lourmarin, for their help and courtesy. M. Valton was particularly kind in allowing me to browse through the municipal archives. Madame Juliette Lisle, curator of the chateau of Lourmarin, was very generous with her advice and allowed me to consult the notarial archives in the chateau. Laurence Wylie's sociological study of Roussillon in the twentieth century, *Village in the Vaucluse*, encouraged me to see the villagers of eighteenth-century Lourmarin as individuals and helped me appreciate the strength and beauty of Provence.

I would like to thank Professor Richard M. Brown of the College of William and Mary, Professor Jeremy Jackson of Syracuse University, and Professor John Cameron, Jr., of the University of Southwestern Louisiana for their critical judgment on individual chapters. I would also like to acknowledge the advice and continuing encouragement of Professor Charles Delzell of Vanderbilt University. Both at the University of

Nebraska and at The Johns Hopkins University, Professor Robert Forster has given freely of his time and his wise counsel. Finally I wish to acknowledge the constant help of my wife who has worked along with me on this book from the first days in the archives to the final manuscript. Through it all she has not only been an inspiration but a constant companion along the byways of France.

CONTENTS

TABLES AND FIGURES

TABLES

ABBREVIATIONS

A.D.	Archives Départementales
M.C.	Musée Calvet, Avignon
A.Not.	Archives Notariales, Lourmarin
A.M.	Archives Municipales, Lourmarin
D.M.	Délibérations Municipales
R.P.Cath.	Registre Paroisse Catholique
R.P.Prot.	Registre Paroisse Protestant
Cont.Fon.	Contribution Foncière
Cont.Mob.	Contribution Mobilière

INTRODUCTION

THE PROVENÇAL VILLAGE of Lourmarin lies in a long, narrow valley between the Luberon Mountain to the north and a series of steep hills to the south which gradually diminish until they reach the Mediterranean 30 miles away. The landscape does not have the verdant lushness found nearer the Mediterranean, but it is green and fertile. The valley is strikingly beautiful in the spring and fall, first when there are white blossoms on every grape vine and later when the leaves turn a brilliant golden red.

Approaching from the south, the visitor follows a narrow road which slowly winds its way toward the crest of the hill. From the summit one can see the whole panorama of the Luberon valley. Below lies the village where perhaps two hundred buff or gray stucco houses, each with the red tile roof indigenous to the south of France, are jumbled together. Slightly apart from the village are the soccer field, the Protestant church, severely plain except for a single bell tower, and the impressive chateau, its turreted magnificence ringed by stately cypress trees. Finally one sees the cemetery with white granite crosses and tombs reflecting the bright sunlight. But above all one is aware of the Luberon Mountain.

Brooding over the landscape all stark gray granite with a sparse growth of scrubby pines, the Luberon is the color of ages-old moss even on the brightest summer day. Down from its heights rushes the winter *mistral* with an icy breathtaking intensity. In the spring, rainclouds wreathe its summit with vapor. No, the Luberon is not classically beautiful as is Aix's Mont Sainte Victoire, favorite subject of Cézanne, but the raw strength of its beauty is strangely primitive and awe-inspiring. Something of the Luberon's brute force also pervades the valley to which it gave its name.

From the highest tower of the chateau, a pattern of land utilization is clearly evident—here a few neat rows of grape vines, there a cherry orchard, beyond land planted in grain, while a few brown cows contentedly graze on the green meadowland at the foot of the chateau wall. Much of Lourmarin's land is devoted to vineyards, small in size but carefully cultivated. Often the tiny fields are separated by low walls of loosely piled rock near which spring wildflowers bloom in profusion. And everywhere one sees olive trees with their fine, slender leaves glowing a soft gray when they ripple in the wind. There are also tall gray-green cypresses and cedars and occasionally a huge pine, or *sapin,* long-needled and bearing clusters of cones.

Although the population is much smaller today than in the eighteenth century, the land, houses, and other buildings have changed little, and a stroll along Lourmarin's narrow streets or across its vineyards makes one feel a kinship with the past. The people who live in the village of Lourmarin or in the farmhouses nearby are typical of the rural population of Provence. The men, clad in faded trousers and shirts or smocks, bend from the waist as they cultivate their vines. The women are neatly dressed, usually in black, as they draw water from the village fountains or go about their marketing, basket on their arm. The children wear the nylon smocks and high stockings one sees everywhere in France as they walk back and forth to school or play in the narrow streets. But Lourmarin has become a village of the young and the elderly. I happened to be in the town hall one cold, windy morning in early March when the church bell began tolling a funeral. All of the villagers joined the walking procession which carried the casket to the cemetery. The old men, many of them wearing their war decorations, came first, followed by the black-clad women and the children. There were very few young faces.

Clustered close to the narrow streets and arcades, the houses of Lourmarin usually have three stories. All windows are protected by heavy wooden shutters to keep out the *mistral* and the hot summer sun. The buildings have a bleak, worn appearance, especially when the weather-

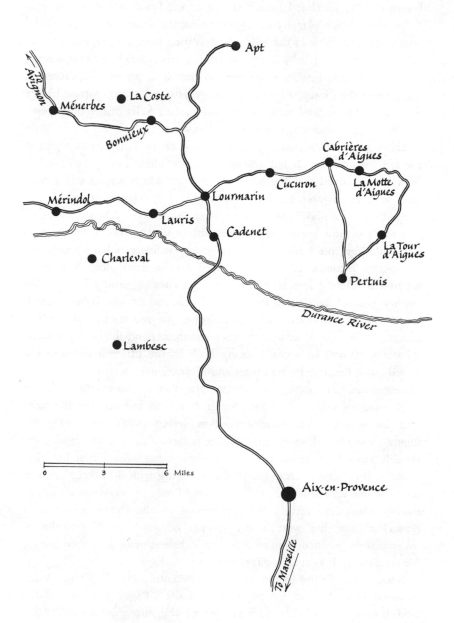

beaten shutters are closed, since there are no window boxes or flowers; only a few weary green plants grow in the casements. Water constantly trickles from three fountains in the village and is used both for washing and for drinking. One fountain is located in front of the Catholic church, a small building in the center of town next to the clock tower. The Protestant church is at the western edge of the village, adjacent to the chateau. Unlike the parish church, its interior, with whitewashed walls and wooden pews, has no sculpture, paintings, or stained glass windows.

The chateau, erected on a knoll northwest of the village, was begun in the fifteenth century. Of buff-colored stone, the oldest tower is guarded by ferocious gargoyles and has narrow slits from which arrows might have been shot, but it was not erected primarily for defensive purposes and the walls are not high. There is a large garden whose walks are shaded by ancient pines and a spacious terrace with a well-stocked goldfish pond surrounded by rose bushes and ornate stone jardineres filled with fuschia and purple petunias. Above the massive wooden front door is a carved inscription offering free water but no other alms to passing beggars. On the first floor of the chateau are a large kitchen and storage rooms. Ascending the ornate, curved Renaissance staircase, one reaches the salon which houses a collection of antique musical instruments and the library with its collection of notarial records dating back to the fifteenth century. The carved stone fireplace in the library shows an eighteenth-century interest in the Americas since some unknown sculptor flanked the mantle with two large caryatids said to represent South American Indians. On the third floor are several small bedrooms where young artists stay during the summer months. Although the chateau is beautiful, it is far from comfortable from October through March since it has neither heat nor electricity in the rooms open to the public. Working with the notarial records often became an endurance contest, enlivened only by occasional groups of tourists who were usually more interested in the shivering American researcher than they were in the elegant surroundings. The wealth of material to be gleaned from records in the chateau more than compensated for occasional physical discomfort however.

What was daily life like in an eighteenth-century French village? What could be learned about the population of the village? Who owned the land, how was it utilized, and what type of obligations did it bear? What was the relationship between the village and other institutions—royal, seigneurial, and ecclesiastical? How was the village government organized and to what extent did the community leaders regulate Lourmarin's political life? What was the role of the church? What effect did the Revolution have on this village, and did the Revolution and its attendant changes ultimately prove to be a blessing or a curse for village life? Finally, what long-range changes occurred in Lourmarin from 1680 to the early nineteenth century?

It was to answer such questions that I went to France in the fall of 1967, hoping to find in the archives of Aix-en-Provence data relevant to the social, economic, and political life of a rural village during the *ancien régime*. I was aided in my search by Professors Coulet and Vovelle, who suggested that Lourmarin, a predominantly Protestant village with an embryonic textile industry and an absentee lord, might prove a productive subject for research. Located 20 miles north of Aix-en-Provence, the commune of Lourmarin now has a population of 612, but it was a thriving village of about 1,500 persons at the time of the Revolution. The village officials of Lourmarin were most helpful and allowed full access to their municipal archives located in the town hall in a small room which is nearly filled with street signs, shovels, sawhorses, and other useful objects. Against the back wall stands a large armoire filled to overflowing with record books, letters, and various other documents. Stacked under the work table are the *cadastres*, the community tax records, along with old maps of the village. Much to his secretary's amazement, I discovered the parish registers carefully stored in the back of a large closet in the mayor's private office.

The data gleaned from the municipal deliberations, parish registers, tax rolls, and other records helped me gain an idea of village life in the eighteenth century. The parish registers enabled me to follow population trends and to reconstitute many of the village families. From the municipal deliberations I learned how the community was governed and how the village government coped with the myriad of problems confronting it, many of them fiscal in nature, while the tax records showed how the village property was divided and assessed. Other records in the departmental archives at Avignon and Marseilles as well as in the Musée Calvet at

Avignon provided information about the seigneur and supplemented the data available in village records.

One of the most fascinating aspects of a village study is the opportunity afforded the researcher to learn about the villagers' lives, sometimes in the most minute detail. It is possible to see that divisions occurred along social, economic, religious, and political lines, and that occasionally feuds erupted and threatened to disrupt community life. One learns with interest something of how the *travailleurs, ménagers*, artisans, and village *bourgeois* lived, how they met crises, and how they celebrated their *fêtes*. As one becomes familiar with the villagers, as one reconstitutes their families through several generations and reads about their political activities in the municipal council minutes, as one strolls along Lourmarin's narrow streets, the past becomes less remote and the village as it was in the eighteenth century lives again.

From an examination of the complete Catholic and Protestant parish registers from 1680 to 1830 we may see the patterns emerging. Analyzing the choice of marriage partners, we can discover how often mates were chosen from outside the village. Using the parish registers, family reconstitution will enable us to record the age at marriage, number of children born, and the interval between marriage and the birth of the first child. Indirectly such statistics will also give us an insight into village mores: does the evidence indicate that the Lourmarinois made a conscious attempt to limit the size of their families? We can also measure the frequency of premarital conception and illegitimacy which, if they occurred often, testify as to the villagers' attitudes toward sexual behavior and might also indicate a change in their religious orientation.

It will be our task to attempt to measure the political sophistication of the villagers as well as the amount of participation in local affairs and the degree to which the village was free to act without interference from either civil officials or the seigneur. The political organization of the village will be explained and related to the making and implementing of decisions at the local level.

To the Lourmarinois, as to us, one of the most important issues was the expenditure of their money. We shall examine the taxes paid to the three governmental units—district (*viguerie*), province, and crown—as well as the seigneurial dues and the church *dîme* (tithe). An important part of this study will investigate how the villagers, both collectively and on an individual basis, met their fiscal responsibilities. Since the primary source of wealth was real property, this will necessitate an examination of the land, its use, and its distribution among the villagers, as well as speculation about the amount of property held by the various segments of the population.

We shall also examine the relations of the villagers with their seigneur, who was both a Catholic and an absentee lord. It is interesting to discover how the community cared for its poor and reacted to the crisis engendered by the plague in 1720. It will also be important to learn how the Protestants managed to survive and, it would appear, prosper, when their existence was not even recognized after 1685.

This study will conclude with an examination of the effects of the Revolution on all facets of life in Lourmarin in an attempt to determine what, if any, lasting changes were introduced into the village after 1789.

Ultimately, of course, the end result of a village study depends on what sources are available. Although there are some blind spots and some areas which are illuminated only faintly, I feel fortunate that the data available answered many questions about one Provençal village in the eighteenth century.

I

THE LAND

STATISTICS AND QUANTIFICATION assume an important role as one attempts to analyze the pattern of land distribution and utilization in eighteenth-century Lourmarin. Although figures for per capita income and land ownership were used mainly as a measurement of an individual's wealth vis-à-vis his neighbor and thus were employed primarily to ascertain a villager's tax payment, a great amount of data pertaining to the economy of eighteenth-century Lourmarin has survived. This extant data enables us to examine in detail a village whose economy was based on agriculture but which also was in the process of developing an embryonic textile industry.

Reflecting the primacy of the land, the most accurate and detailed figures compiled by the village are found in Lourmarin's tax roll (*cadastre*).[1] The *cadastre* listed in minute detail all real property, including houses and other structures, in the village.[2] Taxes were levied on the basis of the

---

[1] This judgment is based on the fact that the *cadastre* was drafted by expert surveyors and was checked by Lourmarin's notables and verified by all taxpayers. See Chapter IV for a more detailed discussion of the drafting of the *cadastre*.

[2] During the eighteenth century in other areas of France, it was the practice to include such items as household furnishings and animals in each individual's evaluation, but this practice had been ended in Provence and the *cadastre* listed only land of all types as well as every structure on or improvement to the land. Raoul Busquet, "Les cadastres et les 'unites cadastrales' en Provence du XVe au XVIIIe siècle," *Annales de Provence*, VII (April, June, 1910), 119–34, 161–84.

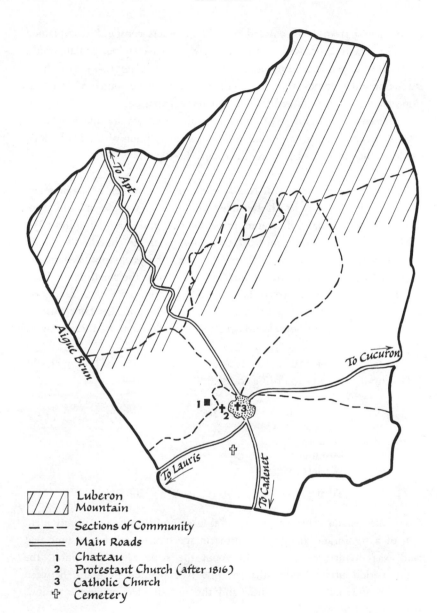

To Apt

To Cucuron

Aigue Brun

1 ■
+ 2 † 3

✙

To Lauris

To Cadenet

Luberon Mountain

Sections of Community

Main Roads

1 Chateau
2 Protestant Church (after 1816)
3 Catholic Church
✙ Cemetery

COMMUNITY OF LOURMARIN

cadastre, and from 1680 onward the village elders constantly complained that their tax roll, drawn up about 1640, was hopelessly out of date, but a new *cadastre* was not commissioned until 1770. Comprising two huge leather-bound volumes, this document is an invaluable source of information about the land, its utilization, and its distribution. A second tax roll was drafted in 1791 and, used in conjunction, these two documents provide a fairly accurate although not entirely precise description of the land which made up the territory of eighteenth-century Lourmarin.

The territory of Lourmarin had an area of 4,722 acres, or about seven and one-half square miles. If the irregular shape of the parish were regularized, it would have measured three by two and one-half miles. The village proper, containing most of the houses plus the church, town hall, clock tower, and the artisans' shops, was near the geographic center and adjacent to the chateau. The territory also contained the small, badly built cottages of the poorest peasants as well as a few comfortable country homes belonging to the gentlemen farmers. Most of the Lourmarinois lived in the village in houses and apartments clustered along the extremely narrow streets.

The land of Lourmarin was recorded in the 1770 *cadastre* with the following distribution according to use.[3]

Grain land	48.1%
Vineyard	18.0
Orchard	9.4
Meadow	8.6
Wasteland	15.9
Total	100.0%

Given the general conservatism of rural areas and the absence of any mention of a significant change at Lourmarin specifically, one can assume that land was divided by cultures in about the same ratio throughout the entire period under study—that is, one half planted in grain, between one-fifth and one-sixth in vines, and the rest divided between meadow, orchard, and wasteland.

[3] *A.M., Cadastre,* 1770.

According to a detailed report drawn up in 1790, the village produced about equal amounts of wheat, rye, and *maslin* (a mixture of wheat and rye known locally as *conségal* or *méteil*).[4] Lourmarin, as well as most of Provence, used both the two- and the three-field system of crop rotation.[5] Existing leases are not very informative because the lessee was instructed only to plant the land "in the usually prescribed manner." Occasionally leases were more explicit, as occurred in 1762 when Louis Lajon, *travailleur*, agreed to plant "one-third in wheat, one-third in rye, and leave one-third fallow."[6] The second field was sometimes planted in vegetables rather than rye while livestock, primarily sheep, were grazed on the fallow.

An examination of Appendix A indicates that there were few oxen in Lourmarin in 1790; there is no reason to believe that this figure was ever higher earlier in the century. The existence of few draft animals combined with the small plots supports the conclusion that Lourmarin's agriculture was essentially a hoe-culture, a conclusion that agrees with Marc Bloch's description of Provence as a region of "irregular open-fields" where "fields were almost as broad as they were long and were scattered almost at random over the village lands."[7] Bloch also notes an unusual feature still evident in Lourmarin today, that is, wheat and grape vines are often grown on the same parcel of land.[8]

Yields averaged about five to one, or ten bushels per acre, and after seed was set aside each fall for the next spring's planting, only about one-half the grain necessary to feed Lourmarin's population remained.[9]

[4] See Appendix A for the complete *État* of the Community in 1790.

[5] René Baehrel, *Une croissance: La Basse-Provence, fin du XVIᵉ siècle—1789* (Paris, 1961), pp. 154–58; Octave Festy, *L'agriculture pendant la Révolution française: Les conditions de production et de récolte* (Paris, 1947), pp. 13–15.

[6] *A.Not.*, Ailhaud, October 20, 1762.

[7] Marc Bloch, *French Rural History: An Essay on Its Basic Characteristics*, trans. by Janet Sondheimer (Berkeley, 1966), pp. 49, 221.

[8] *Ibid.*, p. 23.

[9] Lourmarin's yield of about five to one was typical in the eighteenth century. The actual yield, according to Appendix A, was wheat, six to one, *maslin*, five to one, and rye, four to one. Festy has examined the diversity of yields in France and concludes that four or five to one was not uncommon. Leroy-Ladurie and Baehrel have found the same fluctuation in Languedoc and Provence, depending upon the quality of soil, seeds, implements, etc. Paul Masson has found the five to one figure applicable to Provence as a whole. Michel Morineau has investigated, and provisionally rejected, the idea of an agricultural revolution in eighteenth-century France. What does appear evident to Morineau is that agricultural innovation never came from the south. Festy, *L'agriculture pendant la Révolution française*,

11

The grain deficit was chronic although the amount which had to be purchased elsewhere depended upon the harvest; there was no possibility of a
surplus. Cash needed to purchase grain in neighboring markets was
obtained by selling the excess olive oil produced in Lourmarin since the
yield of oil in an average year was about twice that consumed by the
villagers. Severe winters, dry summers, and heavy rains adversely affected
the grain harvest, but the effect on the olive trees was much more devastat-
ing. Extreme cold might destroy 90 percent of the olive trees, a loss which
would continue for several years until the new saplings began to bear
fruit. The extreme variability in the olive crop was demonstrated by the
harvest of 1789 when the orchards produced only two percent of a normal
year's yield because of the severe winter of 1788–89.[10] When poor years
occurred, not only was there not enough olive oil for domestic needs, there
was no surplus to alleviate the deficit in grain. The tillable land also produced a variety of fruits, vegetables, and nuts, primarily almonds, all of
which were consumed in the village.

Just over one-sixth of the land was devoted to the growing of grapes.
Wine was a popular beverage and according to the 1790 report Lourmarin
annually produced 20 percent more wine than was consumed, the excess
being sold outside the village.[11] Meadowland constituted slightly less than
one-tenth of the territory of Lourmarin, a small amount barely adequate to
support a few livestock. The irrigation and maintenance of the meadow
was regulated by a board of governors made up of local residents who
owned property watered by the Aigue Brun, the only creek flowing through
the territory of Lourmarin. These property holders assessed themselves a
special levy for repairs to the culverts of the Aigue Brun and met periodically to supervise the system. A lengthy 72-page document drawn up

---

pp. 36–37; Emmanuel Leroy-Ladurie, *Les paysans de Languedoc* (Paris, 1966),
pp. 533–37, and *passim;* Baehrel, *Une croissance*, pp. 152–54; Paul Masson, *La
Provence au XVIIIᵉ siècle* (Paris, 1936), p. 615; Michel Morineau, "Y a-t-il eu
une révolution agricole en France au XVIIIᵉ siècle?" *Revue Historique*, CCXXXIX
(January–June, 1968), 299–326.

[10] *A.M., D.M.*, May 10, 17, 24, 1789. See also Appendix A, *État* of the Community, 1790.

[11] See Appendix A.

January 26, 1685, reiterated a 1616 agreement designed to preserve the system.[12]

Since Provence was a region of the *taille réelle*, its taxes were paid to the royal government in a lump sum.[13] Each Provençal village's *cadastre* was very important because the provincial government in Aix apportioned the tax burden among the various cities and towns on the basis of the tax rolls. But a serious problem arose in Provence because each community evaluated its property differently, making an equitable division of the tax burden virtually impossible. In an attempt to remedy this deficiency, a royal declaration of July 9, 1715, ordered the drafting of new *cadastres* in which property was to be "evaluated at its true value."[14] In 1724 the General Assembly of the Communities of Provence announced its intention to implement this reform throughout the province, but resolve seemed to be lacking. Furthermore, a staff of expert surveyors would have been required to insure that property actually was evaluated at its true value. It is therefore not surprising that many communities continued to undervalue their holdings when they drafted a new *cadastre*. Raoul Busquet, former archivist of the department of Bouches-du-Rhône, has found that 13 of 22 village *cadastres* drafted shortly after the announced regulation was promulgated were undervalued by at least 25 percent; some by as much as 60.[15] Busquet felt that because of increased supervision, *cadastres* drafted after 1750 tend to reflect more accurately the true value of property, especially land.[16]

When Lourmarin finally drafted a new *cadastre* in 1770, it was assumed that property would be recorded at its true value; however, the actual evaluation used was never mentioned. Busquet says that houses and other structures were always listed at a fraction of their real value and that the evaluation varied from community to community.[17] An examination of Lourmarin's *cadastre* indicates that the various types of land were evaluated

---

[12] *A.M., Copie d'extrait des registres du greffe de Lourmarin*, January 26, 1685, 72 pages.

[13] In the south the *taille réelle* was a land-tax on the revenue from landed property whereas the *taille personnelle* in the north was a tax on all revenue. Albert Soboul, *Précis d'histoire de la Révolution française* (Paris, 1962), p. 74.

[14] Busquet, "Les cadastres," p. 175.

[15] *Ibid.*, pp. 176–77.

[16] *Ibid.*

[17] *Ibid.*

at slightly below their market value while the different types of buildings were seriously undervalued.[18]

There were 365 individual entries in the 1770 *cadastre*, one for each landowner. Of course 365 is not the precise figure of the number of families living in Lourmarin since some families owned no property at all while others who owned property in Lourmarin lived elsewhere, usually in a neighboring village. The total evaluation of real property in Lourmarin was 249,250 livres, a figure that certainly was too low. The average evaluation was 683 livres; the median was 249 livres. If the small property holdings of the "outsiders" who owned land in Lourmarin were excluded, both the average and the median figures above would be slightly higher.[19] The median figure is also lowered by the large number of small holdings since 109 entries, or 30 percent, included property evaluated at less than 100 livres while 67 individuals owned property valued at less than 50 livres (see Table I–1).

TABLE I–1. CAPITAL EVALUATION OF PROPERTY IN LOURMARIN IN THE 1770 CADASTRE

Property Evaluation	Number
0–100 livres	109
101–200	52
201–300	40
301–400	36
401–500	19
501–600	12
601–700	14
701–800	8
801–900	4
901–1,000	11
1,001–2,000	29
2,001–3,000	16
3,001–4,000	6
4,001–5,000	1
5,001–6,000	3
6,001–7,000	2
over 7,000 livres	3
Total	365

SOURCE: *A.M., Cadastre*, 1770.

[18] *A.M., Cadastre*, 1770.

[19] There were 60 individuals who owned property evaluated at 1,000 livres or more in 1770, all of whom were native Lourmarinois. In 1791 there were only 14 landholders classed as "outsiders" or "unidentified" and their holdings were all small. Because of the difficulty of identification in the 1770 *cadastre*, the 1791 figure was used for "outsiders." It is very probable that the number of "outsiders" in 1770 was about the same as in 1791. *A.M., Cadastre*, 1770; *Cont.Fon.*, 1791.

Georges Lefebvre has estimated that in Flanders, a reasonably fertile area, a minimum of about 13 acres (5 ha.) was needed in order that a peasant might be self-sufficient.[20] Pierre Goubert has put forward the figure of between ten and 12 acres in the Beauvais.[21] However, because of the extreme variation in the land even within a fairly well-defined area, these figures cannot, by their very nature, be precise, and of course a much higher acreage figure is needed in areas less favored. What does seem clear, however, is that even in the best agricultural areas, the majority of the inhabitants had less land than that required for self-sufficiency.

If the total amount of land in Lourmarin, excluding that of the seigneur, were divided by the number of landholders, the average would be slightly more than ten acres, divided into several small pieces scattered throughout the village. Since 60 Lourmarinois, about 16 percent of the total population, had land evaluated at over 1,000 livres, well over one-half of the villagers owned less than ten acres. Those who owned less than ten acres probably supplemented their income by farming as tenants and on shares. The income derived from the handicraft of the artisans and from the local textile industry, coupled with supplementary farming, spelled the real difference between starvation and subsistence to those who owned little or no land.[22] The 109 Lourmarinois whose land was evaluated at less than 100 livres included 28 artisans, of whom seven were weavers engaged almost exclusively in the textile industry. Another 68 were *travailleurs* who also farmed land owned by others. Although no precise figures are available, one may speculate that most of these land-poor *travailleurs* supplemented their income by performing certain essential services in the textile industry, particularly during the winter.

Property belonging to Lourmarin's seigneur and largest landholder, François de Bruny, of course was not included in the 1770 *cadastre*, and

[20] Georges Lefebvre, "Repartition de la propriété et de l'exploitation foncières à la fin de l'ancien régime," in *Études sur la Révolution française* (Paris, 1954), pp. 210–11.

[21] Pierre Goubert, *Beauvais et le beauvaisis de 1600 à 1730* (Paris, 1960), pp. 158–73.

[22] Henri Sée, *Economic and Social Conditions in France during the Eighteenth Century*, trans. by Edwin H. Zeydel (New York, 1927), pp. 34–36; Paul Masson, *Les Bouches-du-Rhône encyclopédie départementale*, Vol. III, *Les temps modernes* (n.p., 1931), pp. 235–54. This entry will be referred to henceforth as Masson, *Les temps modernes*. See also Appendix A for a discussion of the rather extensive income derived from the local textile industry.

consequently is not listed in Table I–1. Unfortunately it is impossible to determine the seigneur's exact holdings in 1770. However, we do possess the entry for Jean-Baptiste Jérôme Bruny, François's son, in the 1791 *Contribution Foncière* as well as an inventory of Bruny's property in 1800.[23] Bruny's holdings in these two documents were the same, and since there is no record of any purchases in Lourmarin after 1770, one may project the seigneur's holdings in 1770 by referring to the two documents discussed above. The seigneur owned about 150 acres of land, one half of it meadowland, plus a chateau, two ovens, grain mill, olive press, and assorted other buildings in 1770. It is impossible to know the exact value of this property, but by comparing the income from the seigneur's property in 1791 with the income from the property of Pierre Henri Joseph de Girard, the largest *roturier* landholder in Lourmarin, we see that the evaluation of Bruny's landed property in 1770 would have been about twice that of Girard's, or about 25,000 livres.[24]

Sieur Pierre Henri Joseph de Girard used the title *écuyer* although there is no record of his ever having received it officially. The Girard family originally came from Grenoble in the seventeenth century. Although almost all the large landowners were Protestant, the Girards were an exception. Like the few other wealthy Catholic families in Lourmarin who began as, and sometimes remained, officials of the government or the seigneur, Girard's great-grandfather served as the seigneur's agent. Girard's father, who died in 1765, was mayor of Lourmarin for 11 years, including ten consecutive years from 1748 to 1757 when the community's rules calling for annual elections and forbidding successive terms were ignored. Girard *fils* took an active interest in village politics and was elected mayor in 1783. He also served on the village council for 12 years and as auditor for three. By a judicious marriage in 1693 to Magdelene Ailhaud, daughter of a wealthy local *bourgeois*, by astute purchases, and by the happy accident that there had been only one surviving son in each generation, Pierre Henri Joseph de Girard owned property valued at 12,863 livres in 1770.

<hr/>

[23] *A.M., Cont.Fon.*, 1791; *M.C.*, 4580, fo. 132, January 12, 1800.
[24] *A.M., Cont.Fon.*, 1791. This figure, of course, does not include the seigneur's 1770 income from the various seigneurial monopolies and dues. See Chapter VI for a discussion of the seigneur and his income.

Pierre Henri Joseph de Girard was 41 years old in 1770 and was the father of one son, François Henri Joseph, and four daughters, all under seven years old. By 1775 he was the father of three more sons, Cézar François Henri, Henri Camille, and Philippe Henri. Like their older brother, the other sons were educated in Marseilles. The eldest, François Henri Joseph, became subprefect of Bouches-du-Rhône in the nineteenth century and was elected to the *corps législatif* under Napoleon and to the Chamber of Deputies after the Restoration. Henri Camille led the abortive Federalist movement in Lourmarin in 1793.

Philippe Henri, the youngest son, became Lourmarin's most famous citizen as inventor of a mechanical flax-spinning mill and a steam engine.[25] He went to Paris shortly after 1800 to pursue a teaching career in physics and chemistry begun in Marseilles six years before at the age of 19. Affected by the vicissitudes of Napoleonic policy, he worked with moderate success in Paris and although he had perfected his mechanical spinning mill, it went virtually unnoticed in the last days of the Empire. When the Austrians entered Paris in 1815, they were so impressed with his invention that they coaxed Girard to Vienna. He took most of his inventions with him and spent the next few years in Austria, Saxony, and Silesia until, in the early 1820's, he found the village of Girardow in Poland and erected a giant spinning mill there. In 1825 he was named Chief Engineer of Mines in Poland. Philippe Henri Girard returned to Paris in the late 1830's, wrote several articles about his inventions, and died there penniless in 1845.[26] A statue of him was later erected in front of the railroad station at Avignon, *chief-lieu* of the Department of the Vaucluse. At present the Guide Michelin lists three things to see in Lourmarin—the restored chateau, the grave of Albert Camus, and the house where Philippe Girard was born, now housing Lourmarin's public school on the first floor and a museum containing some of Girard's inventions on the second.

[25] For information on Philippe Henri Girard see Jules Courtet, *Dictionnaire, géographique, historique, archéologique et biographique des communes du département de Vaucluse* (Avignon, 1876), pp. 216–17; M. Bancol, *Monographies communales, arrondissement d'Apt* (n.p., 1896), pp. 122–23; C. F. H. Barjavel, *Dictionnaire historique, biographique et bibliographique du département de Vaucluse*, Vol. I (Carpentras, 1841), pp. 24–28.

[26] Barjavel, *Dictionnaire historique*, I, 24–28.

The Girards were active in community affairs. In 1784 Pierre Henri Joseph and his sister contributed 800 livres to double the principal of a charitable foundation, the interest being used for poor relief.[27] Girard was on friendly terms with the Marquis de Sade, a landowner in the neighboring village of Lacoste, donated considerable amounts of money to buy grain in the hard years of 1789 and 1790, did not openly oppose the Revolution, and died, a venerable senior statesman, in 1811 at the age of 82.[28]

Girard owned 21 pieces of property comprising about 100 acres, including 50 acres planted in grain and 25 in meadowland.[29] The remainder included orchards, vineyards, and a small amount of wasteland. He owned five houses, each of which had a courtyard and stable. Girard's comfortable house in the village had 12 rooms, a balcony, and a terrace. Seigneur Bruny usually stayed there on his infrequent trips to Lourmarin rather than in his own chateau. Girard also owned two of the eight small buildings in the village where silk was spun, along with a sheepfold, a pigsty, a chicken coop, a poultry yard, and 14 other assorted buildings. After Girard, Lourmarin's largest property holder was Sieur Jean Corgier, *bourgeois*, who owned property valued at 12,399 livres. His son, Jean Paul, had the unenviable position of mayor in 1789.

The median property evaluation in Lourmarin was 249 livres according to the 1770 *cadastre*. Barthelemy Reymond, *travailleur*, had property valued at exactly 249 livres. Reymond was 67 years old in 1770 and had been married for 42 years to Magdelene Chauvin. They were the parents of five daughters and one son, none of whom was living at home in 1770. Reymond had a small house in town and owned nine separate fields amounting to about three acres planted in grain, one of vineyard, one of wasteland, and one-sixth of an acre of orchard.[30] His only son, also named Barthelemy, was 38 years old and owned slightly less land and an even smaller house. Holdings of this size could barely have provided a subsistence standard of living to their owners; about half of the villagers owned even less. Peasants like Reymond would have had to work on other land in order to survive.

[27] *A.M.*, *D.M.*, November 21, 1784.
[28] Marquis de Sade, *Oeuvres complètes*, ed. by Gilbert Lely, Vol. XII (Paris, 1964), p. 29.
[29] This information is based on Girard's entry in the 1770 *cadastre*.
[30] This information is based on Reymond's entry in the 1770 *cadastre*.

Altogether more than 3,100 pieces of land were listed in the 1770 *cadastre*. If one subtracts from the total area of Lourmarin the amount of land held by the seigneur, the average size of each piece of land was slightly less than one and one-half acre. And the average size was this large only because of the relative consolidation of property by the larger land-holders such as Girard and Corgier. The average size of Reymond's nine parcels was about one-half acre.

There were 266 houses (*maisons*) in the village ranging in size from Girard's comfortable town house to the cramped apartments of the poor and the small combination shops and apartments of the artisans. There were also 88 farm houses, including Girard's villa, which was only slightly less elegant than his town house. Many of the farm houses, however, were small hovels where the poor peasant family shared their daily life with a few tools, some chickens, and occasionally a pig. There were also 14 sheds (*bastidons*) normally used as storehouses, but housing on occasion the poorest peasants. In 1770 the total of 354 houses of all kinds in Lourmarin was supplemented by 150 stables, 91 pigstys, and 32 sheepfolds, plus a melange of various other structures. The care given to the drafting of the 1770 *cadastre* is obvious; when the experts scrutinized every staircase, terrace, and chicken coop, it must have been extremely difficult to hide even the smallest sign of real wealth.

Manufacturing in Lourmarin was important and was related to the village's embryonic textile industry, which in the eighteenth century had not progressed much beyond the cottage industry stage; certainly no factories as we understand the term had been built.[31] In 1790 the *Etat* of the Community listed the annual income from raw materials produced in Lourmarin and from the village's manufacturing endeavors.[32] The numerous flocks of sheep in the village produced about 3,000 pounds of wool annually which sold for 36 livres per hundred-weight (1,080 livres) while the 1,200 pounds of silk spun from cocoons brought 1,700 livres per hundred-

---

[31] Listed in the 1770 *cadastre* were eight small buildings in which silk was spun, and a 1764 report noted that there were "10 or 12 stocking frames" in Lourmarin. Despite frequent references to the textile industry throughout the eighteenth century, there is no other quantitative information regarding the actual machinery used. *A.M., D.M.*, July 15, 1764; *Cadastre*, 1770.

[32] Appendix A, *État* of the Community, 1790.

weight (20,400 livres).[33] The wool was woven into heavy and light woolen serge to be used for dresses and suits. Lourmarin's tailors and dressmakers retained a small quantity of serge for domestic consumption but most was exported and brought about 2,880 livres each year. Some wool was used locally in the manufacture of hats, worth 750 livres annually.[34]

Lourmarin's most important manufacturing enterprise, valued at 12,050 livres in 1790, was the spinning of silk floss and the making of silk stockings by village weavers.[35] Most of the thread, however, was exported in a rough state to Aix, Marseilles, Avignon, or Lyons where it was woven into the finished product.[36] The value of flax produced in Lourmarin was estimated at 850 livres annually which, when made into linen, brought an additional income of 3,600 livres. Lourmarin's one lacemaker produced lace for the luxury trade valued at 600 livres.[37]

The income from these varied manufacturing pursuits, combined with the smaller surplus from the sale of wine and olive oil, could be used to purchase grain in the markets of Pertuis, Aix, and Marseilles. The detailed figures in the 1790 report indicate that in a typical year Lourmarin's income would have been adequate to cover its expenditures for grain. Thus

[33] There is an unfortunate lack of precise information on the silk industry in Lourmarin. For one thing it is difficult to measure the growth of this industry after 1680. We know from scattered references that there were several weavers in 1680 who were organized into an association that elected a syndic to oversee their operations in Lourmarin. There were mulberry trees in the village and the women were engaged in feeding the silk worms while the men were weavers. We also know that there were looms and stocking frames in Lourmarin, but no details of these operations have survived.

[34] See Appendix A, *État* of the Community, 1790.

[35] *Ibid*.

[36] The value, which must have been an estimate, of the raw silk produced annually in Lourmarin was 20,400 livres, while the silk and silk products exported from Lourmarin brought only 12,050 livres. It is certainly probable, although not certain, that some of the silk remained in the village in the form of silk stockings for the Girards, Savornins, Sambucs, etc. This, however, does not explain a discrepancy of 8,350 livres. It is more likely explained by the fact that the higher figure is an estimate of silk produced "in an average year" while the lower figure is the value of silk exported in 1789, a year which must have been below average in yield because of the damage to the mulberry trees during the winter of 1788–89. But after all this has been said, it must be emphasized that in making out reports such as this, which did not directly affect them as did the drafting of the *cadastre*, the Lourmarinois were prone to make rather crude estimates.

[37] *A.M.*, *D.M.*, March 1, 1790.

the income accruing from manufacturing was essential in providing at least a subsistence standard of living to the villagers.

Responding to the changes effected by the Revolution, in 1791 the National Assembly ordered each village in France to divide its territory into sections and to appoint officials who would record the type and extent of all real property within each section. Jacques Godechot has concluded that this was too much to ask because "it was a complicated operation for the ignorant municipalities, sometimes composed entirely of illiterates."[38] Whatever the situation might have been elsewhere in France, the Lourmarin council was conscientious, relatively competent, and remarkably literate. The resulting *Contribution Foncière* thus listed annual net revenue, based on a 15-year average, of each parcel of real property in the village.[39] A General Council meeting, open to all heads of families, was held in Lourmarin on two successive Sundays in February, 1791, to consider how best to comply with the edict of the National Assembly. The General Council decided to divide the village into six sections and selected the mayor and five municipal officers to supervise committees to evaluate the property in each section. Each of the six committees was augmented by three additional members elected by the General Council. Each man was assigned to the section with which he was most familiar. Although the General Council might have chosen anyone in the village, all of the men elected to the committees were independent peasants or *bourgeois*—the same men who probably would have been chosen *before* the Revolution. All property owners in each section were given two weeks to appear before the committee in order to agree upon the value and net revenue of their property.[40] It was at this point, of course, that the proprietor tried to see that the net revenue of his property was undervalued if at all possible.

Essentially the same process was followed with regard to the new tax on personal property, the *Contribution Mobilière*.[41] Antoine André Bernard was named village treasurer and was responsible for collecting these two taxes. In return he received five percent of the total tax he collected.[42]

[38] Jacques Godechot, *Les institutions de la France sous la Révolution et l'empire* (Paris, 1951), pp. 134–35.

[39] *Ibid.*, pp. 134–36; *A.M., D.M.*, February 20, 1791; *A.M., Cont.Fon.*, 1791.

[40] *A.M., D.M.*, February 13, 20, 1791.

[41] Godechot, *Institutions*, pp. 136–38; *A.M., Cont.Mob.*, 1791.

[42] *A.M., D.M.*, February 13, 20, March 6, May 1, July 31, 1791.

Bernard, a *bourgeois*, had been treasurer before the Revolution as had his father and grandfather. The five percent return (*gages*) he received was about equal to the amount his ancestors had received earlier in the eighteenth century.

Fortunately the revolutionary tax rolls are still in the village archives and provide much useful information about the value of property owned by the Lourmarinois in 1790. With the exception of the seigneur, who was now titled citizen Bruny, the villagers are listed in Table I–2 by profession according to the percentage of net revenue which each group possessed.

TABLE I–2. OCCUPATIONS AND REVENUES OF THE INHABITANTS OF LOURMARIN IN 1791

No.	Profession	Total Net Revenue by Profession (Livres)	Average Net Revenue by Profession (Livres)	Profession as % of 360	% of Net Revenue by Profession
1	Former Seigneur	4,696	4,696	0.3	12.95
15	*Bourgeois*	10,988	732	4.2	30.31
60	*Ménagers*	10,394	173	16.7	28.67
153	*Travailleurs*	3,987	26	42.4	11.00
81	Artisans	2,419	30	22.4	6.67
4	*Négociants*	1,066	266	1.1	2.94
1	Clockmaker	619	619	0.3	1.71
5	Merchants	411	82	1.4	1.13
1	Surveyor-Teacher	356	356	0.3	.98
12	Women-widows	297	24	3.3	.82
5	Innkeepers	195	39	1.4	.54
3	Barbers	346	115	0.8	.95
1	Former Tax Collector	24	24	0.3	.07
1	Community land	22	22	0.3	.06
2	Shepherds	3	2	0.6	.02
1	Priest	3	3	0.3	.01
4	Unidentified	35	9	1.1	.10
10	Residents Outside Lourmarin	400	40	2.8	1.10
360		36,261	101	100.0	100.03

SOURCE: *A.M., Cont.Fon.*, 1791.

Although the Revolution and its effects will be discussed later, one of the most significant facts which emerged from this period is that Jean-Baptiste Jérôme Bruny, the former seigneur, survived the 1790's with all of the property he owned at the time of the Revolution intact. Of course he did not retain any of the seigneurial dues and monopolies which had provided him with a sizable income, but an extract from the tax rolls for 1800 showed that his real holdings were exactly the same as in the 1791 *Contribution Foncière*.[43] Although the lucrative seigneurial monopolies had been abrogated, Bruny continued to own two grain mills, two ovens, and an olive press, as well as the chateau and the irrigated meadowland surrounding it.[44]

Included in Table I–2 are only four unidentified individuals, none of whom owned much land, and ten property owners who resided outside of Lourmarin. In the absence of other evidence it will be assumed that these holdings were cancelled out by the holdings of Lourmarinois in neighboring villages so that, for purposes of analysis, the *Foncière* is relatively complete. This is also true of the tax roll listing personal property, the *Contribution Mobilière*, which showed that one male and 29 female domestics were employed in Lourmarin in 1791. Among those individuals paying an additional one livre, ten sous in taxes because they had a servant was Messire Fauchier, the Catholic priest. Most of the domestics were either daughters of poor peasants from Lourmarin or came from outside the village.[45]

The term *bourgeois* was used rather loosely in eighteenth-century Lourmarin, but the *Foncière* restricted its use to the generally accepted definition of the class—those who did not engage in manual labor and who lived from their rents.[46] The *bourgeois*'s house was well furnished and his existence was comfortable by eighteenth-century standards.[47] Comprising one-sixth of the landholders, the *ménagers* were the upper class among the peasants. In general they owned enough land to subsist and worked it themselves, aided by their sons. Any excess land was rented, either for money

[43] *M.C.*, 4580, fo. 132, January 14, 1800; *A.M., Cont.Fon.*, 1791.

[44] *Ibid.*

[45] *A.M., Cont.Mob.*, 1791.

[46] After extensive examination of eighteenth-century records for Lourmarin it appears that a *bourgeois* was often a gentleman farmer with large landholdings who occasionally farmed some of his land himself.

[47] See Appendix B for an inventory of the household furnishings owned by Pierre Vial, *bourgeois*, at his death in 1685. Notice also the number of public and private promissory notes owed to Vial, all but one of which was owed by men in Lourmarin. This may indicate that a mutually supportive network of rural credit existed.

or on shares.[48] It was not unusual, however, for a *ménager* also to be a tenant farmer or share-cropper on the land of other owners.

A *travailleur* is much harder to define, but the one factor common to all *travailleurs* was that they did not possess enough land of their own to make a living. Although virtually everyone in Lourmarin owned some land, many holdings were ridiculously small; the *travailleurs* therefore worked their own land in addition to other land which they either rented (*arrente-ment*) or cultivated on a share-cropping basis. Contracts governing land rentals and share-cropping agreements were usually for a four- to six-year period and stipulated how much money was to be paid annually and what care was to be given the land and buildings.[49] In addition to caring for the land, "leaving it in the same condition at the end of his lease as he had found it at the beginning," a tenant farmer usually was subject to a number of small obligations, payable in either produce or labor.[50]

Share-cropping, known throughout most of France as *métayage*, was called *mégerie* in Provence; the share-cropper was a *méger*. Unlike other parts of France, in Provence a person was not known as a share-cropper by profession and regardless of what percentage of his income came from this arrangement, he was titled either a *ménager* or a *travailleur*.[51] A share-cropper's contract was, in general, more restrictive than that of a tenant farmer and was more likely to spell out exactly what the *méger* could and could not do. The principle of a share-cropping contract was that the crop, after deduction had been made for the next year's seed, was to be equally divided between the owner of the property and the lessee. In addition to dividing the crop, the share-cropper was often required annually to make a small, supplementary money payment or a payment in kind, a few dozen eggs or several chickens, and he was usually required to furnish some cartage service. The owner of the land paid the taxes on his property.[52] The share-cropper was allowed to use meadowland for pasturing animals,

---

[48] For a discussion of the *ménager* in Provence, see Masson, *Provence*, p. 591.

[49] *A.Not.*, *passim*; René Baehrel, in his study of Basse-Provence, found the median lease to be five years. Baehrel, *Une croissance*, p. 133.

[50] *A.Not.*, Ailhaud, October 26, 1759, Borrelly, October 22, 1787, and *passim*.

[51] Masson, *Provence*, pp. 374, 591–93.

[52] *A.Not.*, Ailhaud, October 26, 1759, Borrelly, January 30, 1779, and *passim*. See also Masson, *Provence*, pp. 591–92.

but the owner retained the exclusive use of the manure for his fields.[53] *Mégerie* arrangements could also be applied to animals, primarily sheep. On October 17, 1759, Guilhaume Paris, *ménager*, signed a *mégerie* contract with Jean Barthelemy, *travailleur*. Paris agreed to provide 11 sheep to Barthelemy, who accepted the responsibility for guarding and pasturing them for five years. Paris and Barthelemy shared the expense of winter feed with each man receiving one-half of the wool. Any losses would be divided equally.[54]

After examining the extreme complexities of the *Foncière*, which listed those who actually worked the land as well as those who owned it, one must conclude that the great majority of peasants owned at least a small amount of land, rented some on a tenant-farmer basis, and worked still other land as share-croppers.[55]

To further confuse the traditional eighteenth-century vocabulary, no peasant in Lourmarin was designated as a day-laborer, although obviously they existed. There were occasional references to *travailleurs à la journée*, but more often all members of this group were simply called *travailleurs* and in the *Foncière* no attempt was made to distinguish between the two. Indeed, such a distinction would probably have been as difficult for contemporaries to make as it is for us, because most of the *travailleurs* supplemented their income with day work, especially in the spring and fall.

If the former seigneur's holdings are included with those of the *bourgeois* in 1791 in Table I–2, less than five percent of the population would have owned 43 percent of the land. If the *bourgeois* and *ménagers*, the wealthier peasants, are added together, they form 21.2 percent of the population but they held almost three-fourths of the land in the village. The peasants (*ménagers* and *travailleurs*) held about 40 percent of the land, but this would be increased to nearly 50 percent if the miscellaneous entries in Table I–2 are added to the peasant holdings. Michel Vovelle has surveyed the distribution of property in 24 Provençal communities at the end of the *ancien régime*. In eleven of these communities the peasants

[53] *A.Not.*, Rey, December 5, 1775, and *passim*.

[54] *Ibid.*, Ailhaud, October 27, 1759.

[55] This observation is admittedly impressionistic. Without an examination of the tenant holdings of each piece of land it is impossible to give a precise figure. *A.M., Cont.Fon.*, 1791.

(*ménagers* plus *travailleurs*) held more than one-half of the property.[56] There is no evidence that these ratios in Lourmarin changed much throughout the eighteenth century, nor did substantial changes occur during the more radical stages of the Revolution. There were no large blocks of church land to distribute and the seigneur became "citizen" Bruny and was accepted as such by the villagers.

One other large segment of the population must be analyzed. The artisan class, constituting 22.4 percent of Lourmarin's population, is listed in Table I–3 by occupation.

TABLE I–3. AVERAGE NET REVENUE OF REAL PROPERTY
OWNED BY LOURMARIN ARTISANS IN 1791

Number	Occupation	Total Net Revenue (Livres)	Average Net Revenue (Livres)
27	Weavers	686	25
12	Shoemakers	385	32
6	Masons	246	41
5	Bakers	260	52
5	Blacksmiths	145	29
4	Tailors	59	14
4	Turners	50	12
3	Butchers	196	65
3	Carpenters	71	24
3	Quarrymen	61	20
2	Dyers	50	25
1	Hatmaker	71	71
1	Lacemaker	50	50
1	Ropemaker	49	49
1	Locksmith	23	23
1	Muleteer	17	17
1	Cartwright	1	1
1	Cooper	1	1
81		2,421	30

SOURCE: *A.M., Cont.Fon.,* 1791.

[56] For an excellent survey of the latest work on the agrarian structure of Provence see Michel Vovelle, "État présent des études de structure agraire en Provence à la fin de l'ancien régime," *Provence Historique,* XVIII (October–December, 1968). 450–84.

Reflecting the importance of textiles in Lourmarin, one-third of the artisans were weavers (*tisserands*). The remaining artisans represent the usual occupations providing goods and services to a typical eighteenth-century French village. The average net income from real property for all 81 artisans was 30 livres; no single occupation group received income from property much higher than the average.[57] Many of the craftsmen owned no land at all and their only entry in the *Foncière* was their shop in town, which probably included their living quarters as well. Since the *Foncière* did not list an artisan's tools, skill, or—most important—the income received for his services, it is obvious that his average net income must have been considerably higher than 30 livres.

There were no guilds in Lourmarin although the master artisans did have apprentices. On September 12, 1759, an apprenticeship agreement was recorded by the local notary. Sieur Pierre Fauchier, who made and sold silk hose, agreed to take the son of Jacques Anastay, aged 14, as his apprentice for two years. Fauchier agreed to teach the boy the trade of weaver in return for a cash payment of 80 livres. The father also assumed financial responsibility for any damages done by his son and agreed to continue providing him with board and room; the young boy simply went to Fauchier's shop each morning.[58] These arrangements were common in the eighteenth century and were financially advantageous to the master craftsmen, who received a welcome supplement to their income as well as a willing, if inexperienced helper.

It would appear from an examination of Table I–2 that, even excluding the former seigneur, the distribution of land within the third estate was very uneven with only the *bourgeois* as well as most *ménagers* and some artisans, or probably not more than one-third of the village population, owning enough for a secure existence. But we know from an examination of the village minutes that there was little extreme poverty. Fortunately the poor *travailleurs* and artisans could supplement their income by working in the textile industry or by day work in the fields.

---

[57] The probable reason for the discrepancy between the 81 artisans listed in the 1791 *Contribution Foncière* and the 65 in the 1790 *État* of the Community is that the 1790 report counted only full-time artisans while the 1791 tax roll recorded a person's primary occupation and therefore discounted the fact that some artisans were also farmers.

[58] *A.Not.*, Ailhaud, September 12. 1759.

An examination of the distribution and utilization of land in eighteenth-century Lourmarin clearly shows that, when the traditional division of land into small, scattered parcels was combined with rudimentary agricultural practices, the result was a land shortage in the village. Little land was uncultivated, and although Jean-Baptiste Jérôme de Bruny, seigneur after 1772, was interested in agricultural reform, no attempt was made to alter the traditional eighteenth-century pattern of exploitation to provide for the increase in population which will be examined in Chapter II.

II

THE PEOPLE

HERE ARE MANY extant documents which help the reader understand the villagers of Lourmarin as individuals, but only the parish
registers enable the historian to see the village as a whole and to
attempt to measure any population changes which occurred. Fortunately
Lourmarin's parish registers have survived. Until 1685 separate Protestant
and Catholic registers were kept, but after the Revocation of the Edict of
Nantes all Protestants became, at least theoretically, new converts, and the
Protestant register ended. Even though technically outlawed, the Protestants
again began to keep a parish register in 1747 which continued until 1792.
The Catholic register is complete for the entire period up to 1792 when
the civil authorities assumed responsibility for the registration of vital
statistics. These latter records, called *état-civil*, are on printed forms that
were filled in by the recorder elected by the community and reflect the
central government's growing interest in population data.[1] Until 1792 the
Catholic priest and the Protestant minister recorded baptisms, burials, and
marriages consecutively in the registers and no attempt was made to separate the different types of entries.[2] Although there are entries for each year,

[1] See *A.M.*, *D.M.*, November 11, 1792, for the election of the first recorder.
[2] Both Catholic and Protestant registers were begun in 1610. Baptismal entries
gave the child's name, mother's maiden name, father's name and sometimes profession, godparents, and date of birth and of baptism. There was seldom a difference
of more than two or three days between these two dates. Marriage entries listed the
date, the marriage partners with ages and place of birth, usually the profession of

there are periods during which underregistration, especially of deaths, must be suspected and in attempting to calculate family size or infant mortality, one cannot hope for certitude. Despite the deficiencies of the parish registers, they are the best source available and, along with evidence from other documents, offer the best avenue toward understanding the people of Lourmarin.[3]

Any attempt to estimate Lourmarin's population in the eighteenth century is unfortunately subject to much confusion. In 1765 Abbé Expilly claimed that Lourmarin's population was 1,389.[4] In the 1790 report dis-

---

the groom's father, both sets of parents or guardians (including maiden names), and the witnesses at the ceremony, usually five or six. If the marriage had not been preceded by a reading of the bans on three consecutive Sundays or if the partners were within the prohibited degree of consanguinity, the source of dispensation was given. Burial entries gave the name of the person buried, age, names of the closest living relatives, place of birth, and the names of at least two persons who witnessed the interment. Often, especially for those Protestant deaths recorded in the Catholic register, the reason for denying the dead person burial in consecrated ground was given—he had died in the "Reputed Reformed Religion" or he had "failed to perform his Catholic duties." Some entries were, of course, less complete than these examples. For burials, the age, except for very young children, was at best an estimate, and the older the deceased, the less accurate the age. Also, attempts to reconstitute families by using the parish registers were complicated because of the large number of Lourmarinois with the same surname. Jacques Cavallier, son of Pierre Cavallier, is not very specific when there were several other Jacques and Pierre Cavalliers living in Lourmarin at the same time.

[3] Especially useful for technical information on demography are Michel Fleury and Louis Henry, *Nouveau manuel de dépouillement et d'exploitation de l'état civil ancien* (Paris, 1965) and Edward A. Wrigley, ed., *An Introduction to English Historical Demography* (New York, 1966). For the master plan of the demographic study of France see Michel Fleury and Louis Henry, "Pour connaître la population de la France depuis Louis XIV. Plan de travaux par sondage," *Population*, XIII (October–December, 1958) and Jean-Noël Biraben, Michel Fleury, and Louis Henry, "Inventaire par sondage des registres paroissiaux de France," *Population*, XV (January–March, 1960). See also Louis Henry and Etienne Gautier, *La population de Crulai paroisse normandie: étude historique* (Paris, 1958). For a review of current research see J. Dupaquier, "Sur la population française au XVIIe et au XVIIIe siècle," *Revue Historique*, CCXXXIX (January–June, 1968), 43–79.

[4] Abbé Jean Joseph Expilly, *Dictionnaire géographique, historique et politique des Gaules et de la France* (6 vols.; Paris, 1762–1770), V, 930–31. Expilly traveled extensively in Europe and lived at Tarascon in Provence as well as at Avignon where he published his most famous work, the *Dictionnaire géographique*, between 1762 and 1770. Comprising six volumes and more than 5,000 pages, it was essentially a modernization of earlier works of this type although it included one important new topic, a study of the population of France, which he estimated by village as well as by province. See especially pages 863–1008 (vol. V) for the

cussed in Chapter I, the village officials reported Lourmarin's population at "about 1,500."[5] Municipal deliberations of early 1794 record the population as 1,430 plus an "additional 100 men" who were serving as volunteers in the army.[6] The first official census extant, taken in 1804, listed every individual by name, age, and profession and put the population at 1,456.[7] It would therefore seem that the 1790 estimate of "about 1,500" was approximately true. Lourmarin's population began to decline in the third and fourth decades of the nineteenth century and by 1896 the population had dropped to 950. The population of Lourmarin in 1968 was 612. With Marseilles, Avignon, Lyons, Grenoble, and Paris to attract its youth, Lourmarin's population, like that of villages throughout the western world, is predominantly elderly today.

A specific problem is to analyze the population growth from 1680 to the Revolution, the difficulty of which is compounded because the first estimate available is that of Expilly in 1765. The only earlier figure available would have to be drawn from the fact that there were about 1,000 Protestants living in Lourmarin together with an undetermined number of Catholics when the Edict of Nantes was revoked in 1685.[8] Logically we should be able to take the surplus of births over deaths after 1680 and subtract that from the 1765 population to obtain a rough approximation of the population in 1680.[9] Unfortunately, because of the apparent under-

---

article on "Provence" in which, by using tax rolls, he lists the population for each village in Provence. Later population figures for Provence have confirmed the essential accuracy of Expilly's figures. The Abbé's most important contribution was to demonstrate that the population of France in the eighteenth century was increasing instead of diminishing as the physiocrats argued. On this subject see Edmond Esmonin, "L'abbé Expilly et ses travaux de statistique," in *Études sur la France des XVIIe et XVIIIe siècles*. ed. by Edmond Esmonin (Paris, 1964), pp. 273–313.

[5] See Appendix A, *État* of the Community, 1790.

[6] *A.M., D.M.*, February 23, 1794. After a complete examination of the council minutes I feel that figures such as "100 men" are at best rough estimates and must not be taken as accurate.

[7] *A.D., Vaucluse*, "Recensement de l'an XII," March 10, 1804.

[8] *A.Not.*, Chastroux and Pacot, October 21, 1685 to February 23, 1686, *passim*. See also Chapter VI.

[9] This is assuming a static population with no emigration from, or immigration to, Lourmarin. Although the composition of Lourmarin's population seems fairly stable, this method of arriving at Loumarin's population in 1680 cannot be used for reasons discussed below.

registration of deaths in the parish registers, it is impossible to arrive at precise population figures for any given year.[10] Despite this deficiency it is still possible to extract some meaningful information about Lourmarin's population from 1680 to 1830.

The curve of Lourmarin's vital statistics by five-year averages appears in Appendix C.[11] The number of births was the lowest in the five-year period from 1706 to 1710 when only 27 births per year occurred, then increased to a high of 62 from 1760 to 1765, remained relatively stable until 1795 and then began to decline in the early nineteenth century. It is difficult to draw any conclusions from the burial curve, but it is worth noting that the highest average of burials after 1700, 54 per year, occurred from 1786 to 1790. Other evidence, such as the council minutes, indicates that such a high figure was caused by increased disease and epidemics rather than by the violence of the Revolution or by actual starvation, although the shortage and high price of grain may have been a contributing factor. The last great plague in France began in Marseilles in 1720 and had spread to much of Provence by 1721 despite all efforts of royal and Provençal officials to contain it. Drastic measures were taken by the city fathers of Lourmarin to seal off their village from any outside contamination. Evidently they were successful because there were fewer burials in 1720 and 1721 than in 1719, while the number of baptisms declined only slightly in the same period.[12] The five-year average for burials from 1721 to 1725 is

---

[10] Underregistration is most apparent from 1755 to 1785. See Appendix C. During this 30-year period the number of burials decreased so far as to be suspicious. After an examination of both the Catholic and Protestant parish registers it appears that by the mid-1750's most of the Protestants had ceased to observe even the formalities of Catholicism and were having their babies baptised and their marriages recorded by the Protestant minister. However, because the Protestant minister often traveled throughout other parts of Provence, Protestants who died while the minister was away were buried immediately with no entry made in the parish register. Prior to this time Protestant burials were recorded in the Catholic register with a notation that the dead person had been denied burial in consecrated ground because of "his heresy" or because "he did not perform the duties of a Catholic" or with similar explanations.

[11] The five-year averages were calculated from entries in the parish registers and état-civil. A.M., R.P.Cath., R.P.Prot., Etat-Civil, 1681–1830.

[12] See Appendix D which lists baptisms, marriages, and burials annually for the period 1681–1830.

higher than the preceding five years because of a rise in 1722. But there is no reason to attribute this exclusively, or even primarily, to the plague.[13]

Since Lourmarin was relatively small and geographically isolated, it is interesting to examine the place of origin of those persons married in the village. For 150 years, from 1681 to 1830, the pattern in the choice of marriage partners remained fairly constant as demonstrated in Table II–1 *a* and *b*.

Examining a more limited sample which covered the period 1780–84, Charles Tilly has found that in 18 rural communities of the Vendée, an area usually looked upon as isolated and inbred, the bride and groom were both from the local community in 61.1 percent of the marriages.[14]

TABLE II–1*a*. ORIGIN OF INDIVIDUALS
MARRIED IN LOURMARIN, 1681–1830

Years by Decade	Marriages Total	Grooms from Lourmarin		Brides from Lourmarin	
		No.	%	No.	%
1681–1690	109	69	63.1	95	87.2
1691–1700	79	58	73.4	74	93.7
1701–1710	87	63	72.4	81	93.1
1711–1720	110	77	70.0	96	87.3
1721–1730	100	70	70.0	93	93.0
1731–1740	68	46	67.6	65	95.6
1741–1750	51	39	76.5	43	84.3
1751–1760	132	93	70.5	108	81.8
1761–1770	106	76	71.7	86	81.1
1771–1780	92	62	67.4	76	82.6
1781–1790	127	88	69.3	109	85.8
1791–1800	119	93	78.2	97	81.5
1801–1810	106	86	81.8	96	90.6
1811–1820	133	102	76.7	117	85.0
1821–1830	137	89	65.0	107	78.1
	1,556	1,111	71.4	1,343	86.3

SOURCE: *A.M., R.P. Cath., R.P. Prot., Etat-Civil*, 1681–1830.

[13] It is also worth mentioning that in 1709–10, a notorious time of crisis throughout France, the number of burials actually went down in Lourmarin. There was some discussion in the council minutes of the bad weather, poor crops, etc., but the situation was not as critical as in the 1690's or later in the eighteenth century.

[14] Charles Tilly, *The Vendée* (Cambridge, Mass., 1964), pp. 88–90.

TABLE II–1b. ORIGIN OF COUPLES
MARRIED IN LOURMARIN, 1681–1830

Years by Decade	Marriages Total	From Lourmarin							
		Both Partners		Groom Only		Bride Only		Neither partner	
		No.	%	No.	%	No.	%	No.	%
1681–1690	109	59	54.1	10	9.2	36	33.0	4	3.7
1691–1700	79	54	68.4	4	5.1	20	25.3	1	1.2
1701–1710	87	59	67.8	4	4.6	22	25.3	2	2.3
1711–1720	110	65	59.1	12	10.9	31	28.2	2	1.8
1721–1730	100	63	63.0	7	7.0	30	30.0	0	—
1731–1740	68	43	63.2	3	4.4	22	32.4	0	—
1741–1750	51	34	66.7	5	9.8	9	17.6	3	5.9
1751–1760	132	72	54.5	21	15.9	37	28.0	2	1.6
1761–1770	106	59	55.7	17	16.0	27	25.5	3	2.8
1771–1780	92	49	53.3	14	15.2	28	30.4	1	1.1
1781–1790	127	75	59.1	13	10.2	34	26.8	5	3.9
1791–1800	119	75	63.0	18	15.1	22	18.5	4	3.4
1801–1810	106	77	72.6	9	8.5	19	17.9	1	1.0
1811–1820	133	88	66.2	14	10.5	29	21.8	2	1.5
1821–1830	137	68	49.6	21	15.3	39	28.5	9	6.6
	1,556	940	60.5	172	11.1	405	25.8	39	2.6

SOURCE: *A.M., R.P. Cath., R.P. Prot., Etat-Civil*, 1681–1830.

This rate corresponds closely with the data in Table II–1b for Lourmarin, both for the entire 150-year period (60.5 percent) and for the decade of the 1780's (59.1 percent).

Table II–1a, b also shows that 71 percent of the grooms and 86 percent of the brides came from Lourmarin, while in three-fifths of all marriages both partners were from Lourmarin. The decade 1821–30 seems to have witnessed a change in these percentages as more "outsiders" married a partner from Lourmarin, although the figures are not so unusual if those who lived in adjacent villages and married in Lourmarin are not classified as "outsiders." If the 150-year averages are corrected to include those marriage partners from adjacent villages, 79 percent of the grooms and 90 percent of the brides are included.[15] Since the decades after 1830 were not examined, it is not clear whether the 1820's marked a unique departure from the

[15] Adjacent villages are defined here as those whose territory touched some part of the *terroir* of Lourmarin.

norm or whether this decade represented the beginning of a new trend. One imagines, however, that the latter was the case, since the 1830's marked the beginning of a real migration from countryside to city.

When one of the marriage partners was from outside the village, it was expected that the marriage would take place in the bride's parish. Hence in 26 percent of the recorded marriages only the bride was from Lourmarin while in 11 percent of the marriages only the groom was from Lourmarin. These percentages would be even farther apart were it not for a phenomenon which occurred between the 1740's and the Revolution. This was the period when Lourmarin had a Protestant minister and, despite the fact that it was illegal, a Protestant girl from another village who married a young Protestant from Lourmarin would be more likely to travel to the groom's parish for the wedding rather than being married by the Catholic priest in her village. Thus the number of marriages in which only the bride was from Lourmarin declined from 81 percent in the period 1691–1740 to 66 percent in the years 1741–90 (see Table II–2).

TABLE II–2. MARRIAGES IN WHICH ONE PARTY ONLY WAS FROM LOURMARIN

Years	Marriages Total No.	Grooms from Lourmarin		Brides from Lourmarin	
		No.	%	No.	%
1691–1740	155	30	19	125	81
1741–1790	205	70	34	135	66
	360	100	28	260	72

SOURCE: *A.M., R.P. Cath., R.P. Prot.*, 1691–1790.

Since there are no other changes in the data during this period, it is reasonable to postulate that Lourmarin's Protestant minister attracted some couples who might otherwise have been married elsewhere. Except for this the pattern of the origin of marriage partners remained relatively constant from 1681 to 1830. One may conclude that Lourmarin followed the pattern of an endogenous community.

An examination of the bride's age at marriage and the average number of children born in completed families was made by a process of family reconstitution. The figures which resulted, however, are merely indications of change and do not include all marriages performed or all children born in Lourmarin.[16] A total of 608 families were reconstituted fully enough to be useful in these calculations. So that the age of marriage might be known during the earlier period, and in order that only complete families be considered, the period used was 1696 to 1815, divided into four 30-year periods.

The 608 brides studied were followed throughout their child-bearing years in order to obtain an idea of family size. Families in which one partner died before the end of the wife's child-bearing years and families in which the time elapsed between the birth of children obviously was abnormal were not analyzed.[17] Table II–3 gives an indication of the age of brides at marriage and Table II–4 of family size.

A comparison of Tables II–3 and II–4, given in Table II–5 by using the mean, median, and mode to discover age at marriage and family size, is very interesting. It is possible that, even for those families reconstituted, children were born outside the village or that some born in Lourmarin were not recorded; consequently, the figures for family size may be lower than they actually were. However, if errors of this sort did occur in the parish registers and the *état-civil,* we have no choice but to assume they were constant throughout the period examined. It is apparent that the bride's age decreased, regardless of which of the three measurements in Table II–5 is used. Contrasted to ages 25 and 24 in the periods 1696–1725 and 1726–55, the most popular age for marriage decreased to 19 after 1756. Using the mean and median age, it appears that it is in the second period (1726–

---

[16] For an excellent essay on the mechanics of family reconstitution by using parish registers see Wrigley, "Family Reconstitution," in *Introduction to English Historical Demography,* pp. 96–159. See also Wrigley, "Mortality in Pre-Industrial England: The Example of Colyton, Devon, over Three Centuries," *Daedalus* XCVII (Spring, 1968), 546–80.

[17] This procedure may seem somewhat arbitrary, but it was felt that the discrepancies which occurred with some reconstituted families who, for example, had four children early in their marriage, followed by a 10- or 12-year period when there were no baptismal entries, followed by the birth of additional children, could be explained most logically by the absence of one or both marriage partners from the village. The unreliability of the burial records, particularly for Protestants, often makes it difficult to tell whether a couple whose marriage was registered but neither of whose burials was recorded, had had no children or had simply left Lourmarin after their marriage. Consequently, only those reconstituted families were studied where it was felt that the couple had been observed from marriage until dissolution of the marriage by the death of one of the partners.

TABLE II-3. AGE OF BRIDE AT MARRIAGE, 1696–1815

Age at Marriage	1696–1725	1726–1755	1756–1785	1786–1815	Total 1696–1815
15	0	1	2	1	4
16	2	1	2	4	9
17	0	5	0	2	7
18	1	11	10	14	36
19	5	13	20	22	60
20	3	11	18	20	52
21	3	13	14	18	48
22	5	8	13	11	37
23	5	12	19	20	56
24	7	16	15	12	50
25	7	4	13	10	34
26	6	10	16	12	44
27	6	4	4	8	22
28	5	10	3	7	25
29	3	8	6	6	23
30	2	5	1	6	14
31	2	4	2	5	13
32	1	2	3	3	9
33	1	3	2	5	11
34	1	2	3	5	11
35	1	0	4	1	6
36	1	2	1	1	5
37	2	1	1	1	5
38	1	3	2	1	7
39	0	0	2	2	4
40	1	1	3	2	7
41	3	0	3	3	9
	74	150	182	202	608
Total marriages performed	223	241	307	362	1,133
Brides in Table II-3 as percentage of total brides	33	63	57	56	53.6

SOURCE: *A.M., R.P. Cath., R.P. Prot., Etat-Civil*, 1696–1815.

55) that one can witness a decrease in the age at marriage. Over the 120-year period both the mean age and the median age decreased by two years.

Family size decreased slightly, especially after 1756. For example, Table II–5 shows that the mean number of children increased slightly in the second period (1726–55) to 4.9, but that after 1756 the mean num-

TABLE II-4. FAMILY SIZE OF BRIDES IN TABLE II-3, 1696–1815

Number of Children	1696–1725	1726–1755	1756–1785	1786–1815	Total 1696–1815
0	11	18	33	24	86
1	5	6	15	13	39
2	4	13	13	25	55
3	8	15	15	34	72
4	10	13	19	27	69
5	10	22	21	28	81
6	4	21	27	22	74
7	9	13	11	10	43
8	4	11	10	7	32
9	2	4	8	9	23
10	3	8	3	3	17
11	2	4	6	0	12
12	2	1	1	0	4
13	0	1	0	0	1
	74	150	182	202	608

SOURCE: *A.M., R.P. Cath., R.P. Prot., Etat-Civil*, 1696–1815.

TABLE II-5. MEAN, MEDIAN, AND MODAL AGE AT MARRIAGE AND FAMILY SIZE

Years	Mern	Median	Mode
	Age at marriage (years)		
1696–1725	26.3	25	24 and 25
1726–1755	24.3	23.5	24
1756–1785	24.4	23	19
1786–1815	24.2	23	19
	Family size (children)		
1696–1725	4.6	4	—
1726–1755	4.9	5	5
1756–1785	4.2	4	—
1786–1815	3.9	4	3

SOURCE: *A.M., R.P. Cath., R.P. Prot., Etat-Civil*, 1696–1815.

ber declined to 4.2 (1756–85) and then to 3.9 (1786–1815). Also, from 1756 to 1785, 15 percent of the families reconstituted included eight or more children, while from 1785 to 1815 the figure declined to nine percent. It is therefore clear that although the bride's age at the time of her marriage decreased, which in turn increased the period of marriage during which she could expect to be fertile, the mean size of a completed family also decreased.

FIGURE II-1. MEDIAN INTERVAL BETWEEN MARRIAGE AND FIRST CHILD, 1681–1830

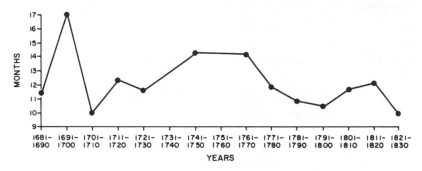

SOURCE: *A.M., R.P. Cath., R.P. Prot., Etat-Civil*, 1681–1830.

Figure II–1 plots the birth of first children to only those mothers whose date of marriage is known. The interval shown represents time between marriage and the birth of her first child and the date is the date of marriage, not the date of birth. Figure II-1 represents 880 first children, spaced fairly regularly over the 150-year period.[18] The decade with the longest interval between marriage and baptism of the first child, 17 months, was from 1691 to 1700 and occurred at a time when the mother's age at marriage was high compared to a century later. Because of the severe weather and high incidence of epidemics during this decade, newly married couples may have voluntarily postponed beginning a family, or the number of abortions caused by the mother's ill health may have increased. After two years of marriage a child had not been born to 37 percent of the couples married in this decade. The interval between marriage and first child declined sharply during the next decade but gradually increased to an eighteenth-century peak interval of 14 months by mid-century. The interval then declined to below 12 months after 1780 and, indeed, fell to ten months in the decade 1791–1800.

From an examination of Table II–5 and Figure II–1 it is obvious that three interrelated things were occurring. The bride's mean age at marriage was decreasing to about 23 years while at the same time the mean

[18] Since only the date of marriage and the date of birth of the first child was needed for Figure II–1, the time period could be lengthened from 120 to 150 years and families who could not be completely reconstituted could still be used here.

39

number of children she could expect to bear also decreased. Concurrently the median interval between marriage and birth of a first child declined to ten months in the last decade of the eighteenth century. One is led to speculate that if a young woman marries at a younger age, has her first child earlier, and yet bears fewer children than her grandmother, she and her husband must be making some rudimentary effort to practice birth control. While acknowledging that birth control was known and practiced among the upper classes throughout the eighteenth century in France, Louis Henry says that "in the rural population, the practice of birth control began probably before the Revolution in some areas, although we have so far little proof of this."[19] Evidence from Lourmarin tends to confirm Henry's speculation.[20] In view of the nature of the subject, and lacking any direct proof, it is probably impossible to "prove" that the Lourmarinois were practicing any sort of birth control before the Revolution. Edward Wrigley has thoughtfully explored the question of birth control, particularly *coitus interruptus*, in pre-industrial societies and feels that it may have been practiced in Colyton by the mid-seventeenth century.[21] It is not unreasonable to think that this technique was available to the Lourmarinois.

Table II–6 shows the birth of the first child in relation to the date of marriage of those marriages discussed in Figure II–1. Assuming that those first children born before the eighth month after marriage were conceived prior to the marriage ceremony, 18.4 percent of all children born in the 150-year period studied were so conceived. Actually many of those born in the eighth and ninth months after marriage must also have been conceived prior to marriage, so that this figure is conservative. The proportion of first children born before the eighth month from 1701–1800 was 16 percent.

---

[19] Louis Henry, "The Population in France in the Eighteenth Century," in *Population in History*, eds. David V. Glass and D. E. Eversley (London, 1965). p. 456.

[20] Dupaquier, in summing up current research on the subject, says that on the question of "the voluntary restriction of births [in eighteenth-century France], it seems to have been practiced here and there" but one can make no generalizations about this phenomenon, "at least in the countryside." J. Dupaquier, "Sur la population française au XVIIᵉ et au XVIIIᵉ siècle," *Revue Historique*, CCXXXIX (January–June, 1968), 78–79.

[21] Edward A. Wrigley, "Family Limitation in Pre-Industrial England," *Economic History Review*, 2d Ser., XIX (April, 1966), 100–105. For a general discussion of birth control in France see Emmanuel Leroy-Ladurie, "From Waterloo to Colyton," *Times Literary Supplement*, September 8, 1966, pp. 791–92.

TABLE II–6. BIRTH OF FIRST CHILD IN LOURMARIN BY DECADE, 1681–1830

Percent in Each Category by Decade	1681 to 1690	1691 to 1700	1701 to 1710	1711 to 1720	1721 to 1730	1731 to 1740	1741 to 1750	1751 to 1760	1761 to 1770	1771 to 1780	1781 to 1790	1791 to 1800	1801 to 1810	1811 to 1820	1821 to 1830	1681 to 1830
Prior to 6 months from date of marriage	14.9	13.1	22.2	6.1	4.2	3.7	7.4	5.8	7.4	15.8	16.4	24.1	16.9	12.7	22.2	12.6
During 6th and 7th months of marriage	8.5	4.3	11.1	4.1	6.3	9.3	0	2.3	5.9	5.2	2.7	10.3	4.2	7.6	9.5	5.8
During 8th and 9th months of marriage	14.9	17.4	18.5	12.2	35.4	25.9	11.1	25.6	13.2	24.6	30.1	19.0	19.7	17.7	22.2	20.8
During 10th and 11th months of marriage	19.2	6.5	7.4	38.8	6.3	7.4	16.7	10.5	14.7	7.0	15.1	10.3	16.9	16.5	12.7	13.9
During 2nd year of marriage	34.0	21.7	33.3	22.4	37.5	31.5	51.9	32.6	38.2	35.1	20.5	24.1	28.2	29.1	22.2	30.6
During 3rd or subsequent years of marriage	8.5	37.0	7.4	16.3	10.4	22.2	13.0	23.3	20.6	12.3	15.1	12.1	14.1	16.5	11.1	16.3
Total number of births observed in each decade	47	46	27	49	48	54	54	86	68	57	73	58	71	79	63	880

SOURCE: A.M., R.P. Cath., R.P. Prot., Etat-Civil, 1681–1830.

The proportion rose toward the end of the century and at least 34.4 percent of all births in the last decade of the eighteenth century were conceived before marriage.[22] The figure for the first three decades of the nineteenth century decreased to a still high 24.5 percent, or 44.2 percent if those born in the eighth and ninth months are added. The figure for pre-marital conception in the eighteenth century is high when compared to three percent at Crulai, the village first studied by Louis Henry, although Henry admits that other villages had rates of pre-marital conception as high as 30 percent.[23] Pierre Goubert has found few pre-marital conceptions in the Beauvais.[24]

But even in rural areas with relatively high rates of pre-marital conception, Henry says that not many illegitimate births occurred.[25] Table II–7 illustrates the illegitimacy rate in Lourmarin.

TABLE II–7. ILLEGITIMATE BIRTHS IN LOURMARIN, 1696–1815

Years	Births		
	Total	Illegitimate	%
1696–1725	1,212	26	2.1
1726–1755	1,447	38	2.6
1756–1785	1,748	23	1.3
1786–1815	1,611	40	2.5
	6,018	127	2.1

SOURCE: *A.M.*, *R.P. Cath.*, *R.P. Prot.*, *Etat-Civil*, 1696–1815.

The above figures for the period from 1696 to 1815 tend to confirm Henry's judgment. Compared to urban areas, particularly Paris, in the eighteenth century, the figure for Lourmarin, which averages about two percent, must definitely be considered low, although the rate of illegitimacy in the Beauvais for the period 1656–1735 was less than one percent.[26] It

[22] This figure is for those first children born before the end of the seventh month of marriage. If those born during the eighth and ninth months are added, the figure jumps to 53.4 percent. See Table II–6.

[23] Henry, "Population in France," p. 450. He reports nine percent at St. Agnan, 15 percent at Ingunville and 30 percent at Sottesville-les-Rouen although the latter was not a rural village but rather a suburb of Rouen.

[24] Goubert, *Beauvais*, p. 69.

[25] Henry, "Population in France," p. 450.

[26] Goubert, *Beauvais*, p. 31.

is, of course, possible that some country girls who became pregnant went to Paris or other larger cities, but, as Henry says, this is further evidence of rural disapproval of illegitimacy.[27] These figures may indicate that little social stigma was attached to pre-marital conception in Lourmarin, or at least much less than was attached to illegitimacy. Illegitimate children were usually listed in the parish register as "natural" rather than "legitimate and natural." The father was simply entered as "*O O O.*" Occasionally when the mother of an illegitimate child married she and the groom declared the child to be theirs. The process of "legitimatizing" the child and thereby giving him the true father's last name became part of the marriage ceremony.

After a thorough examination of Lourmarin's parish registers, one is struck by the large numbers of infants and children who died young. Occasionally as many as 15 or 20 children died within a few weeks, most often in August and September. Deaths of the elderly were bunched in the winter.[28] Infant mortality was by no means confined to a particular season, however, and like death at all ages, it occurred throughout the year. An examination of Lourmarin's parish registers indicates that there were times when the number of burials increased so dramatically that one must suspect strongly the presence of an epidemic. However, from what is known about the years of crisis in Lourmarin, the plague of 1720, or the years of poor harvest, there seems to be little connection between Lourmarin's years of high mortality and these crisis years.[29] Table II–8 shows infant and child mortality in Lourmarin from 1681 to 1830.

Entries were usually made chronologically in the register and most recorded deaths of those over five or six years of age were made in this manner; however, there were great variations in the way in which children's deaths were recorded depending, it appears, on nothing more than

[27] Henry, "Population in France," p. 451. Henry notes our relative lack of information about Paris, although we do know that 31 percent of the babies baptized in Paris from 1770 to 1789 were foundlings, most of whom were illegitimate children of Paris serving women.

[28] Goubert finds this same pattern of infant mortality in late summer and adult mortality in the winter. See *Beauvais*, pp. 69–70.

[29] For a discussion of this question see J. Meuvret, "Demographic Crisis in France from the Sixteenth to the Eighteenth Century," in *Population in History*, eds. Glass and Eversley, pp. 507–22.

TABLE II–8. INFANT AND CHILD MORTALITY IN LOURMARIN, 1681–1830

Decades	Live Births	Deaths Under 1 Year	Infant Mortality Rate	Deaths Ages 1-6	Child (ages 1-6) Mortality Rate	Total Deaths (0-6 yrs)	Infant and Child Deaths As % of Live Births	As % of All Deaths
1681–1690	462	55	119	85	184	140	30.3	34.2
1691–1700	389	58	149	93	239	151	38.8	37.8
1701–1710	335	34	101	58	173	92	27.4	38.4
1711–1720	467	50	107	54	116	104	22.3	38.5
1721–1730	466	65	139	112	240	177	37.9	45.1
1731–1740	460	75	164	91	198	166	36.2	43.4
1741–1750	499	102	204	92	184	194	38.8	50.4
1751–1760	542	92	170	98	181	190	35.1	45.8
1761–1770	616	58	94	38	61	96	15.5	35.6
1771–1780	593	39	66	36	61	75	12.7	31.0
1781–1790	556	70	126	77	138	147	26.4	35.0
1791–1800	533	80	150	97	182	177	33.2	41.0
1801–1810	523	82	157	119	228	201	38.5	45.3
1811–1820	536	76	142	129	241	205	38.3	44.7
1821–1830	496	96	194	103	208	199	40.2	45.0
	7,473	1,032	146	1,282	181	2,314	31.0	41.3

SOURCE: A.M., R.P. Cath., R.P. Prot., Etat-Civil, 1681–1830.

the whim of the priest or minister.[30] In many years before 1792 it was the practice to record all infant deaths and some children's deaths in the margin opposite the respective birth entry rather than to make a separate death entry.[31] But it was not unusual for this procedure to be followed in recording some deaths of the young while separate entries were made for others. No pattern emerges and thus two sources must be utilized in counting the deaths before 1792. It seems very probable that this haphazard system resulted in many deaths not being recorded at all which, combined with the general underregistration of deaths, means that the infant and child mortality rates in Table II–8 almost certainly are too low. Thus the figure for the infant-child deaths compared to live births should be more than 31 percent. On the other hand, since underregistration of deaths probably was true of all age groups, one may estimate that 41.3 percent of all deaths were those of infants and children under six. The low infant and child death rate as well as the decline in all deaths from 1761 to 1770 is particularly suspect since Lourmarin experienced at least three very severe winters and extensive crop damage from flooding during these years.[32]

To an American or a Frenchman of the mid-twentieth century an infant mortality rate of almost 150 per thousand seems appalling. But this figure compares favorably with a rate of 216.1 in Sweden from 1761 to 1770.[33] The English village of Colyton had a rate of 138 in the first half of the seventeenth century.[34] Compared to present-day underdeveloped, rural, and predominantly agricultural countries, Lourmarin's infant mortality rate of 146 from 1681 to 1830 is about the same as India's (139), Pakistan's

---

[30] For a discussion of the deficiencies of parish registers and royal attempts to remedy them, see E. Maugis, "L'enquête du parlement sur la tenue des registres paroissiaux d'état civil dans les vingt dernières années de l'ancien régime," *Revue historique de droit français et étranger*, I (1922), 637–49.

[31] With the beginning of the *état-civil* in 1792, all deaths were recorded separately from births.

[32] Kenneth Lockridge experienced this same sort of haphazard recording of deaths in Dedham, Massachusetts. See his suggestive article, "The Population of Dedham, Massachusetts, 1636–1736," *Economic History Review*, 2d Ser., XIX (May, 1966), 318–44. See also a review article by Philip J. Greven, Jr., "Historical Demography and Colonial America," *William and Mary Quarterly*, 3d Ser., XXIV (July, 1967), 438–54.

[33] Thomas McKeown and R. G. Brown, "Medical Evidence Related to English Population Changes in the Eighteenth Century," in *Population in History*, eds. Glass and Eversley, p. 303.

[34] Wrigley, "Family Limitation in Pre-Industrial England," p. 99.

(146.2), and Ghana's (156), lower than the Brazzaville Congo's (180), and considerably higher than Venezuela's (50.0).[35] The infant mortality rate of advanced, industrialized countries is generally between 20 and 35—U.S.S.R. 32, Japan 25.8, France 25.5, United States 25.3.[36]

When the scattered studies made by demographers of the *ancien régime* are examined, Lourmarin's infant and child mortality figures do not seem excessively high.[37] It is obvious from Table II–8 that Lourmarin made absolutely no progress in reducing infant and child mortality during the 150-year period studied. Although other studies have shown a lower figure, Pierre Goubert has said that about one-quarter of the children born in the last third of the seventeenth century died before their first birthday, but Lourmarin's figure, at least from 1680 to 1700, was considerably lower.[38] René Baehrel has found that the eighteenth-century infant mortality rate in Provence varied from village to village but that the rate was often around 200 or just below.[39] The villages of Thézels and St. Sernin in Bas-Quercy had a rate of 191 from 1747 to 1792.[40] Goubert also states that evidence for mortality for ages one to 20 is less reliable but, on the average, that 50 percent of all children failed to reach their twentieth birthday.[41] If the deaths from ages seven through 20 are added to those deaths occurring from birth through age six, Lourmarin's figure is also about 50 percent.

Louis Henry believes that because there were no general famines, plagues, or bad years in France as a whole after 1750, mortality rates were considerably lower in the last 40 years of the *ancien régime* than during the first half of the century.[42] In the two periods just discussed, 1700–50

[35] The rate for India is for the years 1951–61; all other countries are 1961–64.

[36] United Nations Statistical Office, Department of Economic and Social Affairs, *Demographic Yearbook, 1966* (New York, 1967), pp. 280–95.

[37] Because of the extreme variation from one region to another and even within the same province, it is difficult to arrive at meaningful rates of infant mortality for eighteenth-century France. For a summary of current studies on infant mortality see Dupaquier, "Sur la population française," pp. 62–66.

[38] Pierre Goubert, "Recent Theories and Research in French Population between 1500 and 1700," in *Population in History*, eds. Glass and Eversley, p. 468. See also Goubert, *Beauvais*, pp. 39–41.

[39] Baehrel, *Une croissance*, pp. 263–67.

[40] Pierre Valmary, *Familles paysannes au XVIIIe siècle en Bas-Quercy* (Paris. 1965), pp. 141–47.

[41] Goubert, "Recent Theories and Research," p. 468.

[42] Henry, "Population in France," pp. 447–48.

and 1751–90, Lourmarin's infant mortality rate decreased from 146 to 112, although there is no evidence that there were fewer bad years after 1750 than before. On the other hand, the infant mortality rate from 1791 to 1830 again increased to 160.[43]

Any conclusions drawn from the tables, figures, and percentages in this chapter must be done with caution and a reminder that the data upon which the tables are based are not precise. The available information enables us to arrive at several general conclusions about Lourmarin's population. Table II–1a,b demonstrates the insular nature of marriages within the community, since 84.7 percent of all marriage partners in the years 1681–1830 were from the immediate vicinity. A relationship between a bride's age at marriage and the number of children born to her is shown in Table II–5. Although age at marriage decreased over the 120-year period studied, the mean number of children born also decreased—from 4.6 children in the first three decades to 3.9 in the final three—a development which strongly suggests that a conscious effort, probably the use of *coitus interruptus,* was being made to reduce family size. In addition, the number of families having more than four children also declined. The eighteenth century in Lourmarin witnessed a decline in the infant mortality rate up to 1790, but the trend was reversed from 1791 to 1830.

After examining the demographic data for one parish, one may more easily understand the problems involved in arriving at even approximate population figures for France as a whole, especially for the early eighteenth century. Louis Henry has collected much data, including contemporary estimates, and has calculated that the population of France grew from 21–22 million to 29 million between 1700 and 1800, an increase of 32 to 38 percent.[44] Although estimating Lourmarin's population in 1789 at 1,500 would seem to be relatively accurate, it is impossible to be as precise for the earlier period. The only firm figure we have is the number of abjurations in 1685. If we assume that the village had a Catholic population of 20 percent, a reasonable although by no means certain assumption, we can

---

[43] For reasons already discussed, the primary reason for the drop in the rate from 1750 to 1790 must be strongly suspected as being caused by underregistration of deaths, while the jump after 1791 was probably affected by improved registration in the *état-civil.*

[44] Henry, "Population in France," p. 455.

place Lourmarin's population at about 1,200, which gives us an increase of 25 percent from 1685 to 1789.[45] It is, of course, difficult to compare Lourmarin's growth with the national figure quoted above, because Lourmarin's projection includes the disastrous decade of the 1690's, when we know that its population declined, while the figure for France begins in 1700. Lourmarin's rate of population growth in the eighteenth century thus may have been slightly lower than that of the rest of France, due to a decrease in family size. This population growth had slowed down by 1800 and had begun to decrease by the second quarter of the nineteenth century. The further significance of some of the above figures and developments will become apparent in the chapters that follow.

[45] Arnaud has estimated that there were only 20 Catholic families (about 80 persons) in Lourmarin in 1661. If we project a Catholic population of 100 in 1685, it would mean that Lourmarin's population in 1685 was 1,000. Figuring Lourmarin's population in 1789 as 1,500, this would be an increase of 36 percent. From a study of the parish registers and council minutes, however, I feel that Lourmarin's Catholic population in 1685 was closer to 20 percent and that Lourmarin's rate of growth from 1685 to 1789 was probably less than 30 percent. E. Arnaud, *Histoire des protestants de Provence du Comtat Venaissan et de la principauté d'Orange* (2 vols.; Toulouse, 1884), I, 401.

III

VILLAGE GOVERNMENT

T HE POLITICAL SOPHISTICATION of Lourmarin, a village whose population was never much more than 1,500, was surprising. The community's political base was relatively broad and many decisions affecting the village were made by its inhabitants. Indeed, one of the themes of this chapter will be the degree of political participation at the village level. Lourmarin does not fit the stereotype of a sleepy provincial village, inhabited by a few rural *bourgeois* and large *fermiers*, the majority of whose inhabitants had little land, less education, and no influence upon decisions made for them by priest and seigneur. Instead, the political structure of Lourmarin was quite complex; for example, in the village there were 22 elected officials plus the treasurer, school teachers, midwife, and several other persons who performed essential functions. Since the influence of the Catholic church was weak and the villagers rarely saw their seigneur, most Lourmarinois were politically conscious and zealously guarded their rights of local self-government, tempered by the paternalism of the village notables.[1] Although there were differences among the villagers based on religious as well as social, economic, and familial divisions, the villagers tried, if not always successfully, to present a united front and oppose interference from any outside authority.

[1] See Chapter VI for a discussion of the seigneur, who never resided permanently in his chateau after 1680.

This chapter will examine the governmental structure of the village by enumerating the various political offices in Lourmarin, followed by a discussion of those village employees who provided various services to the community. If, as will be described, the political organization of the village was complex, so too was the process by which decisions were made. Furthermore, the range of subjects which occupied the village leaders was wide. Because of the religious composition of the village, religious issues occupied the council periodically from 1680 to 1750, after which their importance declined. The council was particularly active in times of crisis, such as the plague in 1720–22, and during the period of the French Revolution, when the village turned for leadership to its more wealthy citizens, who also provided financial aid to ward off starvation. A real concern for the villagers' welfare, combined with genuine apprehension that the indigent class might resort to violence, led the notables to aid the village in times of economic crisis. But except in times of crisis, the village council's attention was devoted to less momentous topics—building a new fountain, repairing a secondary road, or considering the schoolmaster's request for a raise in salary to meet "increased living costs." All other topics, however, were subordinated to the council's concern with fiscal matters and how best to levy and collect enough taxes to meet expenses.

Although the Lourmarinois usually tried to avoid all but the most essential contact with provincial and royal officials, they occasionally welcomed royal intervention, especially when they found themselves unable to cope with local problems. In discussing how Lourmarin was governed and how decisions were made, one must keep in mind that the two primary goals of the village leaders were to keep the local tax levy to a minimum and to protect the interests of the village against all threats from the outside.

Community affairs in Lourmarin were centered in the town hall (*maison de ville* or *hôtel de ville*). Even more than the church or the chateau, the town hall was the focal point of a spirited and sometimes quarrelsome community. The Lourmarinois were vitally interested in maintaining an efficient municipal government and neither the organizational structure of their local government nor the duties of its individual members changed appreciably between 1680 and 1789.

The villagers zealously guarded the local perquisites guaranteed by the Provençal constitution, the first of which was the right to elect their own municipal officials, who were the very lifeblood of the village.[2] Almost all important decisions affecting the community originated with the village council and, since the seigneur seldom visited Lourmarin, they were often able to influence him to adopt their point of view regarding the management of community affairs and problems. And although the community leaders were required to report the results of the annual election to their seigneur shortly after January 1, there is no evidence that the seigneur ever exercised a veto over the choices made by the community.

In 1648 the Parlement in Aix, in order to standardize municipal governments throughout Provence, sent a royal official to Lourmarin. He called a meeting of all heads of families (*pères de famille*) and, after obtaining information and advice from them, transmitted their views to the Parlement. The Parlement at Aix then issued *reglements*, or rules for the community, which governed the political organization of Lourmarin until the Revolution.[3] Municipal government was guided by two consuls who were elected annually. According to the *reglements*, both consuls were to own real property with a minimum capital value of at least 300 livres. The more important of the two was the mayor, sometimes designated as "mayor/first consul," while the other was called simply "second consul." During the 40 years from 1750 to 1789, when identification by profession is more accurate than for the earlier period, 22 different men served as mayor. Of these, 21 can be positively identified as *bourgeois*: the twenty-second, Jacques Roman, was listed as a *négociant*.[4]

With the exception of Roman, these men were all large property owners, paid a proportionally large amount of taxes, and were from families which had been prominent in Lourmarin since at least the seventeenth century.

[2] Masson, *Les temps modernes*, p. 149.

[3] Jacques P. Anastay, "L'administration des communes au XVIIe siècle: Lourmarin," *Provincia*, VII (1927), 97. Anastay, descendant of one of the several Anastay families of the eighteenth century, described the political organization of his native village. These regulations, except for the religious provisions, were similar to those governing other Provençal villages. See also Masson, *Les temps modernes*, pp. 149–63 for a complete discussion of this question.

[4] The question of identification of the *bourgeoisie* was discussed in Chapter I. Identification of the *bourgeois* was made from the 1770 and 1791 tax records or from their identification as such during the time they were mayor. It is possible that, both here and throughout this study, the meaning of *bourgeois* was not well defined and occasionally was used as a title of honor and respect for gentlemen farmers who, nevertheless, may have worked part of their land themselves.

51

The average value of real property owned by these 22 was 5,353 livres, and the median property value of the first consuls was 3,578 livres. Of the 21 *bourgeois*, two were also listed in the 1770 *cadastre* as *écuyer* and, until the Revolution, they used "de" before their last names. Despite this title, however, they were listed on the tax rolls and continued to pay taxes like everyone else.

One of these *écuyers* was Pierre Henri Joseph de Girard; the other was Dominique de Savornin, whose ancestors had moved to Lourmarin from the neighboring village of Lauris about 1600. Savornin had married Anne Girard, Pierre Henri Joseph's aunt, in 1731. Their marriage contract, which identified Savornin as *bourgeois,* provided a dowry of 3,374 livres— a sizable amount for a village community, but by no means rare since early the next year Antoine Ailhaud, another prominent *bourgeois*, provided a dowry of 5,000 livres for his daughter's marriage to Jacques Murat, a Marseilles merchant.[5] Excluding the seigneur, Savornin was the sixth largest landowner with property valued at 5,446 livres, compared to 13,864 livres for Girard. A genealogy prepared in 1894 and preserved in the Musée Calvet in Avignon traces the Savornin family back to 1287 and claims that the family was entitled to use *écuyer* at the time they moved to Lourmarin.[6] This may be true, but the "de" was never used in official documents until the second half of the eighteenth century. The Savornins, one of the most influential Protestant families in the seventeenth century, had, along with most other Protestant families, renounced their "heresy" in 1685. Their name reappears, however, in the Protestant parish register in the 1750's.

Elected in 1813, Dominique Daniel de Savornin served as mayor of Lourmarin for several years. His wife, pretentiously named Marie-Anne-Antoinette-Josephine-Honorine by her *bourgeois* father, Antoine-Louis Corgier, gave birth to a son, Dominique-Antoine-Alphonse de Savornin, in 1813. Little more is known of this son except that a marginal entry was made in 1859 in the *état-civil* opposite his birth entry stating that a decision of the Civil Tribunal of Apt had removed the "de" from his name.[7] Henceforth Dominique-Antoine-Alphonse, then 46, was to be called simply

---

[5] *A.Not.*, Jacquier, June 5, 1731; February 17, 1732.
[6] *M.C.*, 4548, fo. 106, *Généalogie de la famille de Savornin de Lauris.*
[7] *A.M., État-Civil*, December 15, 1813.

"Savornin." At least the Savornin name is memorialized by the main street which passes in front of the mayor's office—Rue Savornin.

The position of second consul was much different from that of mayor, and the men who were elected to this office came from among the craftsmen of the community, not from the *bourgeoisie*. In the 40-year period 1750–89, during which 22 different men were elected second consul, none owned real property valued at more than 1,200 livres and only two had land holdings exceeding 500 livres in value. No one who served as second consul was among the 30 largest taxpayers at the time of the Revolution. The average value of real property owned by the 18 of these 22 who can be traced was 361 livres, a very modest capital sum indeed. The median property valuation was 325 livres. Of these 18 only ten (56 percent) had more than the 300 livres' property valuation supposedly required for second consuls.[8]

Eighteen of those who can be identified by profession were artisans who, as a group, owned less property than the non-artisans who were elected second consul. For instance, the small house of Bernard Guillemet, master

TABLE III–1. PROFESSION OF SECOND CONSUL, 1750–89

Profession	Number
Carpenter	4
Tailor	3
Baker	3
Shoemaker	2
Dyer	1
Hatmaker	1
Stockingmaker	1
Mason	1
Wheelwright	1
Blacksmith	1
Innkeeper	1
Négociant	1
Travailleur	1
	21
Unidentified	1
Total	22

SOURCE: *A.M.*, *D.M.*, 1750–89, *Cadastre*, 1770, *Cont. Fon.*, 1791.

[8] See Table III–1. See also Table I–3 for the composition and income of the artisan class in Lourmarin in 1791.

tailor, also used as his workshop, was evaluated at only 25 livres. Since the *cadastre* evaluated only real property and did not include such items as specialized tools and equipment, the average value of the second consuls' property appears lower than it actually was. But the divergence between first and second consul is much too great to be bridged by an economic explanation alone. The second consuls represented a class of Lourmarinois obviously inferior, both economically and socially, to the mayor and other leading citizens serving on the municipal council. Most of the second consuls were either newcomers to the community or were born into Lourmarin families which had been craftsmen for generations. Owning little land, they were more mobile and tended to move from one village to another with relative ease, thus explaining why the second consuls are more difficult to trace. A high rate of mobility was not typical of either the larger landowners, who supplied the mayors, or the small peasant farmers, since both of these groups were tied to their land. But despite their lack of roots in the community, the artisans were socially superior to the large class of *travailleurs* and day-laborers. The superior social position of the artisans was also due to their economic importance in the village. And although the job of second consul was not a full-time position it was time-consuming, and the artisans, who spent most of their time in the village proper, were in a better position to be *au courant* about village problems.

From an examination of the council minutes it would appear that the second consul's inferior social and economic position was reflected in his political functions. For example, he was usually entrusted with overseeing those community expenditures amounting to only a few livres, while the responsibility for major matters, particularly those involving large expenditures or a visit to Aix, was usually entrusted to the mayor. The conclusion that social, economic, and political differences separated the two consuls is reinforced by noting that during the 110 years for which records are available, no individual ever served as both mayor and second consul. This indicates a tacit if not official recognition of different qualifications for the two consuls which therefore altered the intent of the original 1648 edict.

The two consuls were to serve one year only. At the end of their terms each consul chose his successor, subject to a seldom-used council veto, and the retiring mayor and second consul then became councillors for the next three years. Before the three-year council term expired, occasionally a councillor was re-elected.[9]

The mayor and second consul presided over a council of 12.[10] Deliberations of December 14, 1681, mention 13 councillors "according to the rules of this community."[11] It appears that the 12 elected members were joined by the priest, who was automatically a member, for a total of 13 councillors. After the first quarter of the eighteenth century, however, the priest was not mentioned as being a member of the council and no longer attended council meetings.[12] The property qualification for councillors was the same as that for mayor and second consul—300 livres—and each councillor served three years. Four councillors were retired annually, with two of the four vacancies being filled by the retiring mayor and second consul while the other two new councillors were elected by majority vote of the council. Entries in the council minutes indicate that the retiring consuls exercised considerable influence in the choice of the other two new councillors. A retiring councillor could not be re-elected to the council for two years, although in the interim he might be elected consul. Evidently the Lourmarinois hoped that under this system no one individual or clique would hold office long enough to abuse their power and that the important communal offices would be rotated among the village notables.

Lourmarin's local government may perhaps be best described as a rather broad-minded oligarchy. Although many artisans served as second consuls and some of the more wealthy *ménagers* as officers, the political life of Lourmarin was strongly influenced, if not actually controlled, by the *bourgeoisie,* since by the practice of co-option the members of a relatively few

[9] There is no evidence of "electioneering" for any of the village offices. No one ever "ran" for an office; rather, the current consuls and councilors merely announced their choice of a man to succeed them. These decisions were probably reached at an informal caucus over a glass of *eau de vie* and objections to the nomination were rarely voiced in the council meeting.

[10] Anastay, "Lourmarin," p. 98; *A.M., D.M.,* 1680 to 1790, *passim.*

[11] *A.M., D.M.,* December 14, 1681.

[12] *Curé* Girard, who died in 1729, had been Lourmarin's priest since the 1680's and had led the village through the turbulent years after the revocation of the Edict of Nantes. By not applying the letter of the law against the new converts he helped mend a badly split village. Generally popular among all the villagers, in 1718 Girard had donated 800 livres, the interest on which was to be used for poor relief. *A.M., D.M.,* January 1, 1718. After his death no Catholic priest was able to command the affection, not to say the loyalty, of the Protestant majority.

families rotated the various community offices among themselves. It was only on specific issues, discussed at a General Council, and not on the election of officers or the general running of the village, that the populace at large was given a voice. It is important to point out, however, that the initiative for the calling of a General Council usually came from this oligarchy, whose members we might term "enlightened" because they did not exercise power exclusively along narrow class lines.

In general, this system prevailed until the French Revolution, although there were many variations. The number of councillors elected each year varied from two to six since a councillor was often replaced before the end of his three-year term because of illness, death, resignation, removal from the community, or because he had accepted another local office. The rules also decreed that fathers and sons, fathers-in-law and sons-in-law, uncles and nephews, and first cousins could not hold local offices at the same time so that if a relative was also elected, a councillor might be replaced before his term expired. Occasionally a councillor did not retire at the conclusion of his three-year term. An extreme example was Jean Franc, *bourgeois*, who served as councillor for 26 consecutive years, from 1731 to 1756.

It appears that the religious question often divided the village leaders, at least well into the eighteenth century. Seemingly protected by the Edict of Nantes, Lourmarin was predominantly Protestant in the seventeenth century, and prior to 1685 the rules of the community decreed that six Catholics and six Protestants were to serve on the council, although no mention was made of religious requirements for the consuls.[13]

All Protestants, including the second consul, were removed from local offices in August, 1680, only to be readmitted January 1, 1681.[14] Orders from officials of the king in Provence declared that all Protestants were to be permanently excluded from holding positions in local government in September, 1683, more than two years before the revocation of the Edict of Nantes. Naturally the Protestants complained bitterly that the village's constitution was being violated.[15] After 1685 the same individuals clashed, this time as "old Catholics" and "new converts." Most of the Protestants

---

[13] See *A.M.*, *D.M.*, January 1, 1682, for a discussion of the religious composition of the council.

[14] *Ibid.*, August 25, 1680, January 1, 1681.

[15] *Ibid.*, September 12, 1683.

"abjured the heresy of Calvin" after October, 1685, without enthusiastically embracing Catholicism.[16] To the Catholic community these "newly-converted Catholics" were as dangerous as former Protestants. On January 1, 1715, after much prodding, the Intendant spelled out the intentions of the Act of Revocation promulgated by Louis XIV in 1685.[17] Not only did the king want and expect abjuration, but he required that the newly-converted attend mass and receive instruction in the "mysteries of our Holy Religion."[18] Only when the latter requirement had been met were the former Protestants to be allowed to hold office on a basis of equality with the old Catholics.

After 1715 there was less discussion of the religious issue, at least within the council, but as we shall see in Chapter VII, religious problems still plagued Lourmarin, especially on those occasions when royal officials tried to stamp out Protestantism by force. The new converts often did not perform their "Catholic duties," but apparently the only penalty imposed within the village itself was denial of burial in consecrated ground, that is, the Catholic cemetery. Except for enforcing this penalty, the priest, the seigneur, and the few important Catholic families such as the Girards did not intervene. Religious differences were definitely receding as the villagers realized the necessity for uniting against increased royal tax pressure and the continuing demands of the seigneur and the *dîme*. By 1750 Lourmarin had again become what it was in the seventeenth century, a predominantly Protestant village controlled by the Protestant majority. Although the Protestant church was not rebuilt until 1816, the Protestants had their own minister and after 1747 began once again to keep a parish register. The entries in this register clearly show that a large percentage of the more important families were Protestant. Table III–2 clearly shows that, at least after 1750, the Protestants controlled the village government.[19] The predominance of Protestant mayors after 1750 underscores this fact. Because

---

[16] *A.Not.*, Chastroux and Pacot, October 21, 1685 to February 23, 1686, *passim.*
[17] *A.M., D.M.*, January 1, 1715.
[18] *Ibid.*
[19] See Table III–2. Since Protestantism was not officially recognized until 1788, it must be emphasized that the percentage of Protestants in each category in Table III–2 may be too low. In each of the categories there were several individuals whose religion could not be positively determined. A positive identification was, however, made for those listed in the Protestant column.

of the absence of a Protestant parish register from 1685 to 1747 it is impossible to make any comparison with the period before 1750. However, the Protestant mayors and other officials after 1750 were usually from the same families as those who served before 1750. With few exceptions, the important Lourmarin families at the time of the Revolution were Protestant.

TABLE III–2. PROTESTANT OFFICERS OF LOURMARIN

Office	Total No.	Protestants	
		No.	%
Mayor/first consul, 1750–1789	22	18	81.8
Second consul, 1750–1789	22	7	31.8
All officers, 1765–1774	42	29	69.0

SOURCE: *A.M., R.P. Cath., R.P. Prot.*, 1750–89.

In addition to the two consuls and the 12 councillors the community elected eight other officials. The secretary (*greffier*) kept the official minutes of the municipal council meetings on stamped paper and, along with the local tax book (*cadastre*), the municipal deliberations filled the most important record book in the community. The secretary was responsible for listing the names of those who attended each meeting and he recorded the subjects discussed and the decisions made. He also transcribed orders from the Intendant, who often required that they be entered in the deliberations to make them a part of the official record. The secretary, along with the consuls, was the only elected official who could spend the village's money, although his expenditures were usually minor.

The quality of the extant minutes depended almost entirely on the intelligence and dedication of the secretary. The position was usually held by a *bourgeois,* occasionally by the schoolmaster, never by the *curé*.[20] It is impossible to tell what rules, if any, governed the secretary's tenure. In 1715 the village decided that the secretary would serve only one year and could not be re-elected for three years; this decision was immediately ig-

---

[20] The position often remained in the same family. For instance, in the eighteenth century up to 1789 the position of secretary was held by a member of the Ailhaud family, prominent *bourgeois* in Lourmarin, for 34 years. In the last 40 years before the Revolution a member of the Bernard family served as secretary for 13 years.

nored.[21] Occasionally a secretary served for five or ten consecutive years, but at other times he was replaced annually. When the mayor retired he either chose a new secretary or asked that the former one be "reconfirmed in his post." The final decision, however, rested with the council.

Three auditors (*auditeurs des comptes*), whose primary task was to audit the records of the community treasurer and report their findings to the council, were elected annually. Because of the importance attached to this job, the 1648 rules said that at least one must be "Catholique, Apostolique, et Romain."[22] In 1682 the Protestants complained that the system had worked up until that time but now there were only two auditors, both of whom were Catholic.[23] Although the rules called for three auditors, only two were elected annually until 1760. During this 80-year period (1680–1760) it was usual, although not mandatory, for one of the auditors to be either the *curé* or the *viguier*, the seigneur's officer. After a dispute in 1760 over the audit, caused in large part by the *curé*, the community, as required by the rules, elected three auditors instead of the usual two and the *curé* never again filled this post.[24] Henceforth three auditors were elected each year.

Two police officials (*intendants de police*), sometimes known as weighers (*pezateurs*), were elected annually. The police supervised all weights and measures used in the community and were empowered to inspect scales used in trade and to mark those they judged to give a correct weight with "LOUR" as an indication to the villagers of the scales' accuracy. Usually the police were changed each year.

There were also two estimators (*estimateurs*) elected annually. One estimator was to be a Catholic and one a Protestant, but for some time after 1680 they both were Catholics. Often the consuls from the previous year filled this office and thus acted as both councillor and estimator the year after their consulate. The 1648 rules state only that the estimators were to adjudicate "disputes" among inhabitants.[25] In other Provençal

---

[21] *A.M., D.M.*, January 1, 1716, and *passim.*
[22] Anastay, "Lourmarin," p. 99.
[23] *A.M., D.M.*, January 1, 1682.
[24] *A.M., D.M.*, 1760, *passim.* See Chapter VII for a discussion of this incident.
[25] Anastay praised adjudication by the estimators as a "very wise measure" which insured "prompt and fair justice," possibly because it avoided the time and expense connected with the established judicial system. Anastay, "Lourmarin," p. 99.

villages they estimated property values, evaluated property damages caused by animals, inventoried the belongings of the deceased, and fixed fines for those persons violating local police regulations.[26]

In its annual budget the council always allocated funds to pay certain of the municipal officials. The two consuls and the secretary each received salaries of nine livres per annum while the auditors, weighers, and estimators each received three livres in compensation. The 12 councillors served without pay. The community thus paid a total of 48 livres in salaries to its municipal officers, a sum hardly munificent enough to attract to public office men interested only in monetary compensation. The love of political office, no matter how insignificant, was evidently not confined to the big cities. Of course the attraction of status was probably strengthened in Lourmarin by the desire of the wealthier villagers to maintain control in order to protect their material interests. Men do not necessarily expect payment for looking after their own. The consuls and secretary were also allowed 200 livres to pay for miscellaneous, minor expenses for which they were responsible.

TABLE III–3. MUNICIPAL OFFICERS IN LOURMARIN IN THREE
SELECTED TEN-YEAR PERIODS

Years	No.	Estimated Adult Males in Lourmarin	Adult Males as Officers %
1685–1694	64	256	25
1725–1734	46	283	16
1765–1774	42	311	14

SOURCE: *A.M., D.M.*, 1685–94, 1725–34, 1765–74.

Table III–3 indicates the rather broad base of political participation in Lourmarin, although the poorer elements in the population were excluded because of the required property qualification. Although it may be a mere coincidence, it would appear that while the population was increasing in the eighteenth century, the selection of municipal officers was becoming

[26] For example, at Charleval, one of only two villages founded in Provence in the eighteenth century, the estimators were "to assist the consul in his administrative duties," possibly explaining the frequency with which consuls became estimators. Pierre Theus, *La fondation d'un village de Provence au XVIIIᵉ siècle: Charleval— 1741* (Aix-en-Provence, 1960), p. 205.

more restrictive. The percentage of adult males who served as municipal officers declined from 26 percent to 14 percent from the first to the third periods. It should be emphasized that the number of municipal offices remained the same.

At the regular council meeting held either the day after Christmas or on January 1 the council would "proceed to the election of the new government."[27] The *viguier* was always present to represent the seigneur. After invoking the blessings of God, the secretary began the election process by saying:

By the mayor and consuls here present it is stated that a year has passed since they had the honor of being elected to the office which they have fulfilled to the best of their ability. They pray the council to accept their apologies if they have been found lacking in any particular, having served with only the best interests of the community at heart. They therefore request that the council proceed to the election of the new government as is the custom.

With this formality completed, the council then elected those local officials mentioned above. The council, whose responsibility it was to choose the new officials, usually accepted the consuls' choice of successor. However, they had the right, which they occasionally exercised, to reject the men nominated by the consuls and either named the new consul themselves or required that a new name be submitted for their approval. On January 1 all of the newly elected officials appeared at the council meeting and took an oath to fulfill the duties of the office to which they had been elected.

This regular council (*conseil ordinaire*) conducted most of the business of the community. Present at regular council meetings would be the *viguier*, the two consuls, the secretary, and the 12 councillors (13 if the priest was included). Other persons might attend upon council invitation, especially if the council was dealing with matters which directly concerned them. Absenteeism was a chronic problem. The 1648 rules provided for a three-livre fine to be levied on councillors who missed a meeting without a valid excuse, but often council meetings had to be adjourned without decisions

[27] There were years when, due to royal orders or local circumstances, the annual elections were not held, but the usual, and legal, practice was for elections to be held each year.

being reached because the requisite quorum was not present.[28] Moral coercion did not improve attendance, so finally in 1763 Lourmarin persuaded the Parlement in Aix to increase the fine for absence at a council meeting to 12 livres because "of the sad state of the village."[29]

For other than routine matters, such as an increase in taxation, a Special Council meeting (*conseil extraordinaire*) was called which included, in addition to the regular council members, the ten individuals in Lourmarin who paid the most taxes.[30] Occasionally a General Council—a meeting of all family heads—was convoked to discuss important questions concerning the entire village. The General Council seems to have been an eighteenth-century addition and, since it required the approval of Parlement, was not often called.[31] Council meetings were called by ringing the town bell and by the public crier (*valet de ville*), who announced the meeting publicly. When a Special Council meeting was to be held, the ten highest taxpayers were notified by written invitations (*billets*).[32]

In addition to the regular meetings held annually to elect and swear in new officers, the council always met every May 1 to consider the expenditures and revenues for the current year and to levy a tax sufficient to cover the difference. Other council meetings were held periodically, the number and frequency being determined by the needs of the community. Usually the mayor called the meeting, but the *viguier*, as the seigneur's representative, might also take the initiative. The two consuls presented an agenda of matters to be discussed and the council debated each proposition in turn. If the council decided that action should be taken, it was they who provided the money and authorization necessary to implement their decision. The number of meetings held in a calendar year varied greatly; an aver-

---

[28] Anastay, "Lourmarin," p. 100; *A.M., D.M., passim.*

[29] *A.M., D.M.,* June 14, 1763.

[30] Anastay, "Lourmarin," p. 100; *A.M., D.M., passim.* Normally the regular council already included one or more of the ten.

[31] *A.M., D.M.,* April 2, 1786. For example, 176 heads of family were recorded as attending the General Council meeting of March 29, 1789, to discuss Lourmarin's *cahier* and elect delegates to the Estates General. They therefore represented about one-half of Lourmarin's population. It is probable that many of the poorer inhabitants, unused to direct participation in the local government, saw no reason to attend. It is also possible that some of those who did attend sat quietly on the back benches at the village church and, unable to sign their names in the minutes, were simply not recorded as having been present. *A.M., D.M.,* March 29, 1789.

[32] *A.M., D.M.,* February 16, 1725, and *passim.*

age was one or two council meetings per month. There tended to be few meetings in the summer and relatively more in the autumn, especially after the harvest had been gathered. In general, whenever there occurred any unusual event—plague, poor harvest, severe weather, presence of armies, or financial crisis—which adversely affected the village, the council met quite often. Whenever the number of meetings increased dramatically, the subjects most likely to be discussed were how to provide relief measures for the poor, the group most severely affected by a catastrophe, either natural or caused by man.

After a detailed examination of council minutes from 1680 to 1830, it may be said that there was no such thing as a "normal" or "average" meeting. It might be interesting to examine one council meeting without pretending that it is in any way typical as to the subjects considered or the decisions made. The meeting chosen for discussion occurred April 14, 1789, shortly before the Estates General was to assemble in Paris. It was a Special Council meeting, which meant that in addition to the regular council members, the town crier was instructed to inform the ten largest landholders in the village of the date and time of the meeting. The mayor had attempted to convoke the council on April 12, but so many members pleaded that they were occupied with other business that a quorum did not appear.[33] As a result, Jean Paul Corgier, the mayor and richest man in Lourmarin after Girard, became angry and let it be known that stiff fines would be levied unless the meeting were held on the fourteenth as scheduled.

At 1:00 P.M. on April 14 the members of the Special Council began filing into the meeting room in the town hall and seated themselves around a large rectangular table covered with green baize. The room was damp and chilly and even though the shutters were open the room was still rather dark. Mayor Corgier sat at the head of the table flanked by the second consul and the *viguier*. The councillors occupied the other chairs around the table and, since this was a Special Council meeting, the additional members sat against the wall on straight-back chairs. After the usual opening formalities recording those present and acknowledging the presence of the seigneur's *viguier*, Mayor Corgier reported that he, along

[33] *Ibid.*, April 12, 1789.

with Sieurs Antoine André Bernard and Antoine Abraham Goulin, both *bourgeois*, had attended the Assembly of the Third Estate in Aix for 11 days beginning with an 8:00 A.M. session on April 1 convoked in the Cathedral. They had presented Lourmarin's *cahier* to the assembled delegates and had assisted in drafting a general *cahier* for the Third Estate and electing deputies to the Estates General. They asked to be reimbursed for lodging and travel expenses amounting to 128 livres. The council, which had authorized the trip, quickly agreed to pay their expenses.

As the second order of business, Mayor Corgier presented a petition from four bakers who complained that since the suppression of the local grain tax the previous month they still had about 30 bushels of wheat on which they had already paid the tax.[34] In routine manner the council, as a matter of equity, approved the payment of 13 livres to the four.

Goulin then reported that he had been to Aix where, as instructed, he had spent 21 livres to purchase two scales. The council, suspecting that some scales being used to sell commodities, especially grain, to the public were inaccurate, ordered Goulin and Pierre Henri Bernard, Antoine André's brother, to travel throughout the parish and check all scales used in public transactions. The intendants of police and the consuls were to accompany them. If the scales were accurate they were to be so marked; otherwise, they were to be confiscated.

The secretary, Antoine Ailhaud, *bourgeois*, read two letters from the Intendant, informing the council of the king's concern about the scarcity of grain in Provence. In order to alleviate the situation, Louis XVI had ordered that six grain storehouses be set up in Provence; the nearest to Lourmarin was in Aix. Lourmarin was to decide how much grain it would need to carry it through the summer and then submit its request with the understanding that the grain would be allotted on the basis of demonstrated need and that the village must replace the grain borrowed one month after their harvest was completed. After a lengthy and heated discussion, the council decided to ask for 125 bushels which "we need immediately," with the notation that the village would certainly need more before harvest time. Lourmarin's council noted that when the time came to repay the grain borrowed, the village would then be forced to buy more.

[34] This tax will be discussed in Chapter IV.

They therefore decided to sell the king's grain to the "indigent classes," although at a price considerably below the market price. The council voted to provide the difference from current village revenue. Sieur André Aguitton was to transport the grain from Aix, Sieur Barthelemy Fayet was to supervise its delivery to the poor, and two other *bourgeois* were charged with collecting the price fixed by the council and depositing the money in the village treasury.

Mayor Corgier relayed another letter from Aix to the council in which the king requested a report of "losses suffered by each community since last December, either from the harshness of the winter or from popular emotions." A committee was appointed to draft an answer. The council reported that Lourmarin's losses came from the "almost total mortality of the olive trees," the loss of income from the village *fermes* and the purchase of grain during the winter to feed the poor, but that there were no losses from "popular uprisings."[35] Although the times were a bit more urgent, this meeting was not different from Lourmarin's council meetings from 1680 onward, and demonstrated that important decisions were made and appropriate action taken by the *bourgeoisie*.

In addition to these elected officials of Lourmarin, the village employed a number of persons to perform specific functions. One of the most important of these municipal employees was the treasurer, who had the overall responsibility for collecting all taxes. The treasurer was not an elective office but rather the community awarded it annually to the man who made the best offer. Individuals interested in serving as treasurer were encouraged to submit bids on three consecutive Sundays, usually in early spring. As bids were received they were officially recorded in the book in which the council minutes were kept and the lowest bidder became treasurer. Before 1760 bids were based on the number of sous and deniers the treasurer would retain of each *écu* he collected.[36] In the 80-year period prior to 1760, the highest bid was three sous, six deniers per *écu*, or a return of 5.83 percent to the treasurer, while the lowest bid was nine

[35] *Fermes* were concessions leased by the village to *fermiers* for various services. They are discussed more fully in Chapter IV.

[36] The *écu* is equal to three livres.

deniers, or 1.25 percent.[37] Both of these extremes were unusual; the normal return to the treasurer was between three and four percent.

In 1760 the council lengthened the treasurer's term to three years and substituted a straight money payment for the percentage of tax collections the treasurer had formerly received, although continuing the practice of having competitive bids. The treasurer's salary ranged from 300 to 550 livres with the average payment being 450 livres. In order to encourage the villagers to pay their taxes promptly, the treasurer was authorized to collect an additional one sou for each livre (5 percent) of tax delinquent on November 1. The treasurer's accounts were examined annually by the auditors.

Expenses associated with the treasury, such as the charge for registering the contract between the treasurer and Lourmarin in Aix, were paid by the village, and they also allocated a small expense account to the treasurer to cover trips made to deposit the money he collected in the district treasury at Apt.

In Provence, taxes owed to the royal, provincial, and district (*viguerie*) governments were levied on the community as a whole; it was the treasurer's responsibility to collect from individuals, whose rate of payment was based on the amount of real property they owned. Since the treasurer was expected to pay Lourmarin's levy in installments which came due at periodic intervals, it was not unusual for him to advance his own money, interest free, pending completion of his collections. On the assumption that money to repay the advances made by the treasurer was more readily available in the summer, in 1757 the village moved the beginning date of the treasurer's contract to July.[38] Because the office of treasurer required capital combined with business sense, the position was always held by an important and wealthy member of the community.[39]

A village school, financed by the community, existed in 1680 when this study begins, and the schoolmaster and schoolmistress, usually husband and wife, were important village employees. Decisions on hiring, subjects to be taught, and the amount of compensation to be paid were made by the

---

[37] *A.M., D.M.*, January 20, 1726, March 23, 1742.

[38] *Ibid.*, January 23, 1757.

[39] Like the position of secretary, the treasurer was often a member of the Ailhaud, Bernard, or other influential *bourgeois* family.

council with the advice of the priest. Final approval came from the Arch-bishop of Aix, but this seems to have merely been a formality. The major emphasis of the school was clearly secular and not religious, and the quality of education offered to their children was of great concern to the inhabitants of Lourmarin.

In the field of education the Lourmarinois demonstrated their pragmatic approach to local finances. The teachers were paid a salary by the village, the schoolmaster usually receiving twice as much as the mistress. If the council decided that a budget cut was necessary and consequently that the teachers' salaries should be reduced, the village's contribution was supple-mented by a small tuition charge which each student was required to pay. Presumably the tuition paid by the students was sufficient to provide the difference between the teachers' former and present salaries. If, then, all other village expenditures remained the same, the annual payment for edu-cation, and thus the tax rate, would decrease slightly while an extra burden would fall on the pupils' parents. But the council also recognized that although the tuition charge was modest, there would be families who could not afford to send their children. The council therefore included in the teachers' contract the provision that a certain number of "poor boys" or "poor children" were to be taught free of charge.[40] Determination of these children was to be made by the consuls in consultation with the priest. Although the specific number of children so educated is not usually given, it appears that most teachers were required to educate at least ten in this manner.[41] This does not mean, of course, that all village children attended school.

The teachers were required to instruct any of the village children who appeared at school in "reading, writing, and ciphering," although there is no indication that attendance was compulsory.[42] Priests often taught school in Provence, but there is no evidence that any religious instruction was offered in Lourmarin's public school and no churchman ever served as schoolmaster.[43] A prospective teacher was always examined by the council

---

[40] *A.M., D.M., passim.* This practice was followed, with some variations, in most Provençal villages. Masson, *Les temps modernes*, p. 670.

[41] *A.M., D.M.*, September 26, 1717, June 23, 1726, June 8, 1727, and *passim*.

[42] *Ibid.*, February 22, 1728, and *passim*.

[43] *Ibid., passim*; Masson, *Les temps modernes*, p. 668.

to determine his competence to teach the various secular subjects. Reputation and experience served as the main criteria for appointment.

In addition to the village children, the teachers were permitted to teach "foreign" pupils—those students living outside the parish—and they were also allowed to accept a small number of "pensionnaires" who lived at the school. Since classes were held in a house rented by the community for this purpose, the boarding pupils probably lived in the extra rooms along with the teachers. In 1717 the maximum number of boarding pupils was set at 12 and seems to have remained constant throughout the century.[44] Since the students who boarded at the school made an additional payment to the teachers, obviously they were interested in having as many pupils as possible "live in." The council, fearing this would cause a decline in the quality of education, was equally determined to enforce its limit of 12 and on at least two occasions teachers were relieved of their duties for violating this rule. In 1722 the consuls and priest demanded that the council replace the schoolmaster, since "he cannot give proper attention to the children of this place because of the great number of boarding pupils which he has."[45] Two prominent citizens complained in 1764 that Monsieur and Madame Richier had been remiss in their teaching duties, either through indifference or design, and consequently "the boys and girls do not want to return [to school]."[46] Since these teachers had been the subject of earlier complaints, the council decided that they were showing "favoritism to the foreign boarding pupils, which is contrary to the public good and to the rules for good order."[47] Such a situation was deplorable, the council went on, since the function of the school was "to instill in its students the love of virtue, which is the greatest good."[48]

In 1759 the council decided that "in imitation of many communities of Provence" the village should hire an additional teacher to instruct their children in Latin.[49] In typically frugal fashion, the council decided to reduce the salaries of the present teachers and to increase the tuition fees charged the students. The new Latin teacher was paid 120 livres, 95 less

[44] *A.M., D.M.*, September 26, 1717.
[45] *Ibid.*, September 12, 1722.
[46] *Ibid.*, April 1, 1764.
[47] *Ibid.*, September 6, 1761, April 1, 1764.
[48] *Ibid.*, April 1, 1764.
[49] *Ibid.*, June 24, 1759.

than he had requested, but the council agreed to supplement his income by allowing him to charge one livre per student each month "for the principles of Latin."[50] Ten Latin students during one year would have added 90 livres to his income.

From 1772 until the Revolution Sieur Brieugne and his wife were the teachers in Lourmarin, having come from a similar post in a nearby, but smaller, village. Schoolmaster Brieugne received an annual salary of 150 livres and his wife 75, a rather generous sum since many villages in Provence paid only 100 livres or less.[51] The community also paid 30 livres for the rental of a schoolhouse so that the village's annual expenditure for education amounted to 255 livres.

The boys were divided into three classes and the tuition they paid ranged from six sous per month for the younger boys in the third class to 12 sous for the older ones in the first class. At Auriol, a village slightly larger than Lourmarin, the tuition was 10, 15, and 20 sous per month.[52] The girls were taught in two classes and paid at the rate of six and four sous per month.[53] No figures are available on the total number of students, but if there were five students in each class, their tuition payments would have amounted to slightly more than 83 livres, based on a nine-month school year, thereby increasing the teachers' income by more than one-third. An increase of two students in each class would have increased the Brieugnes' income by more than one-half.

It may be assumed that in years when the village paid the entire salary of the teachers and instituted no tuition charges for local children, there were more children attending school. The tuition fees were certainly within the range of the *bourgeois* and most *ménagers* and artisans, but they would have been prohibitive for a poor peasant. Even were the school "free" to all local children, it is very possible that the poorer peasants, barely able to earn enough to feed their families, would not have been able to spare a son or daughter since young children were needed to work in the fields. But probably the greatest barrier to the education of the poor was that the poor themselves could see no practical advantage in learning to sign their

[50] *Ibid.*, October 21, 1759.
[51] *Ibid.*, March 29, 1772; Masson, *Les temps modernes*, pp. 669–70.
[52] *A.M., D.M.*, March 29, 1772; Masson, *Les temps modernes*, p. 670.
[53] *A.M., D.M.*, March 29, 1772, and *passim*.

names or being able to read Racine: the introduction of Latin into the school curriculum could hardly have impressed the poor peasant.

The little information available about literacy in Lourmarin was obtained from the notarial minutes and the parish registers. There were, however, two occasions, in 1685 and in 1788, when large numbers of men and women came before either the notary or the priest and were given an opportunity to sign a document. In 1685 the Protestants appeared to abjure and to assume the duties of the Catholic church, then in 1788 Protestants were allowed to legitimize their marriages and their children by simply appearing before the priest and swearing that such events had occurred.[54] From these documents one can determine the numbers of both sexes who could sign their names. Although Catholics would not be included in either list, these two documents do provide a look at all of the Protestants in the village, from the wealthy *bourgeois* to the poor *travailleur*. As the table below demonstrates, there was an increase over the century in the percentages of each sex who could sign their names, but the increase was not very dramatic.

TABLE III–4. LOURMARINOIS WHO COULD SIGN THEIR NAMES, 1685 AND 1788

	Number		Could Sign		Percent	
	1685	1788	1685	1788	1685	1788
Men	275	237	109	101	39.6	42.6
Women	303	241	21	27	6.9	11.2

SOURCE: *A.Not.*, Chastroux and Pacot, October 21, 1685, to February 23, 1686, *passim;* *R.P. Cath.*, April 1, 1788 to February 10, 1789, *passim.*

Among the multitude of transactions with which the notary was concerned was the drafting of marriage contracts and testaments. Not everyone, of course, was required to have either, but a surprisingly large number did. For example, in the decade from 1751 to 1760, there were marriage contracts for more than 60 percent of the marriages performed in Lourmarin. Since both partners to the contract were required to sign if they were able, one may examine these documents to determine if the number of

[54] *A.Not.*, Chastroux and Pacot, October 21, 1685 to February 23, 1686, *passim;* *R.P.Cath.*, April 1, 1788 to February 10, 1789, *passim.*

those able to sign increased during the eighteenth century.[55] Similar information about literacy can also be derived from the testaments, but because testaments often were not drawn up until a person was old or near death, one is often unable to determine whether a missing signature is due to the fact that the executor was illiterate or the fact that his illness prevented it.

TABLE III–5. LITERACY IN LOURMARIN, FROM MARRIAGE CONTRACTS, 1721–90

Decade	No. Examined	Groom Could Sign		Bride Could Sign	
		No.	%	No.	%
1721–1730	70	28	40	14	20
1731–1740	65	30	46	12	18
1741–1750	76	45	59	15	20
1751–1760	79	39	49	15	19
1761–1770	40	18	45	9	23
1771–1780	47	24	51	13	28
1781–1790	67	34	51	16	24
	444	218	49	94	21

SOURCE: *A.Not.*, Jacquier, Ailhaud, Rey, Borrelly, 1721–90, *passim*.

Literacy measured by the ability to sign is higher in the marriage contracts than that evidenced by the Protestants examined in Table III–4, but this is probably a reflection of the fact that the better educated Lourmarinois were more likely to spend the livres necessary to have a marriage contract drawn up. Pierre Valmary, using parish registers, has examined the signatures by bride and groom in 360 marriage ceremonies in the small rural villages of Thézels and St. Sernin from 1700 to 1792. Only seven percent of the men and 1.7 percent of the women could sign.[56] Even when one makes allowance for the fact that he examined marriage ceremonies rather than marriage contracts, Lourmarin's rates are considerably higher. The percentage of those able to sign increased after the decade of the 1720's; from about 1740 to the Revolution slightly more than one-half of the men could sign. The same general increase is evident for the women, with about one-quarter able to sign in the period from 1760 to the Revo-

[55] The notarial books analyzed were chosen at random and no attempt was made to examine all of the contracts in each decade. Thus the total number of contracts for each decade listed in Table III–5 was fewer than the total number of marriage contracts for that decade.

[56] Valmary, *Familles paysannes*, pp. 39–40.

lution, as opposed to just under one-fifth earlier. Although the increase was slow, the number of men and women who could sign their names was increasing.

In 1791 Master Brieugne and his wife were involuntarily retired, ostensibly because of old age, after the council received a petition signed by 29 "active citizens" who demanded their replacement. Brieugne was replaced by Pierre Ginoux, member of an old Lourmarin family, who was a surveyor and mathematician.[57] This event is also noteworthy because it marked the first time that a local man or women was appointed teacher although there is no ready explanation for the apparent lack of local talent to fill the position prior to Ginoux's appointment. It is possible, of course, that this exclusion was intentional because the council felt that an outsider, even though no more qualified, would command greater respect than a villager.

Although they were constantly concerned with reducing community expenditures, the Lourmarinois demonstrated a real interest in the education of their children and did a tolerably good job of providing an adequate and relatively egalitarian system of public education, at least for those who could afford the modest tuition charge and who were interested in education in the first place. But the time had not yet arrived for them to believe in "universal education." Except for the provision for free tuition extended to a few poor children, no attention was given to those who could not, or would not, avail themselves of Lourmarin's educational system.

The village allocated money annually for the employment of a rural constable (*garde terre* or *garde champêtre*). Lourmarin always employed at least one rural constable, usually a local man who owned little or no land of his own—the constable was never a *bourgeois*, artisan, or sizable landholder. Octave Festy has observed the low social status of the *garde champêtre* throughout France in the eighteenth century. Because of the time-consuming nature of the work, the small farmer could not afford to spare the time from his fields. Even if the *travailleur* had only a few acres, he enjoyed more security than the position of constable provided.[58] The position was for 12 months and each year the council either reconfirmed the constable or appointed a new one. In either instance open bidding

---

[57] *A.M., D.M.*, July 21, October 1, 1791.
[58] Octave Festy, *Les délits ruraux et leur répression sous la Révolution et le consulat* (Paris, 1956), pp. 115–25.

occurred on at least three consecutive Sundays, with the man who offered to take the job for the lowest salary, assuming he was qualified otherwise, being appointed.

The constable was the only full-time employee of the village engaged in law enforcement. His salary depended, of course, on the number of applicants bidding for the position but the figure was usually around 200 livres per year, paid on a monthly basis. His primary function was to guard all of the territory within the parish. He was to pay especial attention to the grape vines and the olive, fig, and mulberry trees, but in more general terms he was also to oversee the "orchards, meadows, and enclosed land."

The constable was awarded one half of all fines collected from law-breakers (the other half went to the seigneur) and he also received for his diligence three livres from the proprietors of land damaged by sheep and six livres from each shepherd he reported who did not have the required number of bells, fixed by law at one bell for each ten sheep. The erring shepherd also had to pay an additional six livres to the community. Most of the fines collected in this manner were allocated by the council for poor relief.[59] The constable had a full-time job which, if he were diligent, was potentially lucrative. To insure the constable's undivided attention to his job, in 1711 the council stipulated in the lease that he devote all of his attention to his office and instituted a ten-livre fine if he should be found working at any other job.[60]

In addition to the constable, special guards were hired to protect the vines as the grapes matured and were harvested during a period which began September 1 and usually lasted about 40 days. These temporary guards received seven sous per day and were required to remain day and night in the particular area of the parish to which they were assigned.[61] For unexplained reasons, no special guards for the vines were hired after 1719, and one can only assume that this seasonal function was taken over by the regular constables. Or it is possible that the constable himself was allowed to name temporary deputies whose appointment did not have to be approved by the council.

[59] *A.M.*, *D.M.*, September 16, 1788, and *passim*.
[60] *Ibid.*, July 26, 1711.
[61] *Ibid.*, September 5, 1717, August 4, 1718, and *passim*.

73

Since the primary reason for employing special guards in the fall was to safeguard the ripening grapes, the council appointed a four-member committee which went into the vineyards, judged the degree of ripeness, and fixed a date for beginning the harvest. For example, on October 1, 1786, the committee reported to the council that

. . . the grapes are not quite ready. It would be better to leave them a few days longer and then we would be assured of having good wine. This would be in the best interests of everyone and would preserve the good reputation that our wines have acquired over the years. The date is therefore set for next Thursday, October 5.[62]

In 1714 a fine of 50 livres, a considerable sum, was levied against those individuals who disregarded the council's date.[63] Since wine was one of Lourmarin's major exports, these precautions are understandable. Only in years of very poor harvest, such as 1764, were "foreign grapes" allowed in Lourmarin.[64]

The town crier (*valet de ville*) was chosen by the council and his appointment had to be approved by the seigneur. Like the constable, the town crier was usually a local man with little or no land.[65] Whereas the constable's office was an active and demanding one, the *valet*'s position seems to have been more honorific and the council usually selected an older man. His most important duty was to announce "in all the cross-roads" the meetings of the council and the times when bids would be accepted for the various leases. He also read publicly all royal and provincial decrees pertaining to Lourmarin. The town crier's pay increased slowly from 12 to 34 livres during the century before the Revolution. In addition to his rather nominal salary, the council also paid traveling expenses for trips he made for the community to neighboring villages and also provided the town crier with an entirely new uniform, complete from hat to shoes, every three years. In 1778 his new outfit cost 102 livres, an amount which also included

[62] *Ibid.*, October 1, 1786.
[63] *Ibid.*, September 30, 1714.
[64] *Ibid.*, September 23, 1764.
[65] *Ibid.*, April 2, 1725.

a new trumpet.[66] It is easy to imagine that the glory of such a resplendent uniform helped to compensate for his meager income.[67]

An equally low-paid, but functionally much more important village employee, was the midwife (*sage femme* or *mère sage*). Her annual remuneration was increased from nine to 15 livres during the century. In addition, each new mother was expected to pay the midwife a small sum depending on her means and conscience. Since there was no doctor in Lourmarin during much of the eighteenth century, the midwife assisted at all village births. There is no indication of what training or experience was necessary for this position, but one can surmise that the qualifications were not very high. One explanation for the poor quality of midwives in France was the low wages paid them and a frequent request in the *cahiers* of 1789 was that their pay be increased.[68] The midwife worked very closely with the priest, who appears to have had a voice in her appointment, since except for his parents, the midwife and priest were usually the first to see a new baby. An examination of the parish registers clearly shows that the midwife often baptized a new-born infant, especially one who was born prematurely, had serious birth defects, or obviously might not survive being carried to the church for baptism. Although she might have lacked experience initially, the midwife actively promoted the welfare of the village mothers and earned their respect.

Lourmarin also employed a keeper of the clock tower, who was usually a tool-maker (*maréchal à forge*). In return for an annual salary of 12 to 30 livres, he was expected to keep the clock tower in working order and to ring the bell when requested by the council. The bell was also to be rung at regular intervals during the day; in 1793 the council complained that this was not being done and was thus a great inconvenience to the "silk spinners and other workers who have fixed hours" and who depended upon it.[69]

Lourmarin retained an agent at Aix from 1748 to 1762 to provide liaison

---

[66] *Ibid.*, January 28, 1778.

[67] While visiting the town hall of the neighboring village of Lauris in February, 1968, I saw the uniformed town crier, complete with battery-powered megaphone, announcing a forthcoming council meeting.

[68] Marcel Marion, *Dictionnaire des institutions de la France aux XVIIe et XVIIIe siècles* (Paris, 1923), p. 497.

[69] Lourmarin evidently experienced the same problems in its new industries as was experienced by other pre-industrial societies. Learning to live by the clock was never easy. *A.M., D.M.*, July 7, 1793.

with the Intendant. For 30 livres per year the agent was expected to protect and defend the interests of the village. He seems to have been particularly helpful in obtaining funds to reimburse Lourmarin for expenses incurred during the War of the Austrian Succession, but by 1762 the village concluded that it could dispense with such an expensive service.[70] From this time onward Lourmarin kept no agent in Aix, sending instead its own "notables" to plead directly with royal or provincial officials.

In addition to the above-mentioned village employees who provided essential services to the community and who were paid on an annual basis, Lourmarin occasionally hired lawyers and artisans for specific purposes on a temporary basis. But the treasurer and the schoolteachers, who filled positions requiring special training and large amounts of time, along with the constable, received most of the money Lourmarin spent on local services. The village leaders were willing to spend moderate amounts of money to obtain capable persons for these positions, but they were not averse to economizing whenever possible, as in the case of the Latin teacher.

This chapter has pointed out that the municipal officers and other employees were numerous and the political superstructure of the village complex. The subjects with which the municipal council dealt, the decisions they made, and the means used to implement these decisions were also complex. The two subjects which consumed most of the council's time, however, were fiscal questions and the measures taken to provide for the poor, with all their ramifications.[71] There is no easy way to categorize the myriad of other subjects dealt with by the council, except possibly to mention those concerned primarily with the village itself and those in which the village had to contend with some outside authority, usually of royal origin.

The council underwrote all expenses for the various *Te Deums* and celebrations held in Lourmarin. It is difficult to generalize about the *fêtes* except to say that they occurred on joyful occasions, such as military victories or the birth of a royal heir, or on days when village celebrations were traditional. The community participated in an especially joyous *Te Deum* in 1723 when they gave belated thanks for the lifting of the dreaded plague.[72] The political adaptability shown by the village leaders reflected the obvious

[70] *A.M., D.M.,* May 2, 1762.
[71] These two subjects will be discussed fully in Chapters IV and V.
[72] *A.M., D.M.,* March 25, 1723. See also Chapter V.

fact that many of these celebrations took place under orders. For example, in April, 1791, a *Te Deum* was sung for the restoration of Louis XVI's health while in January, 1793, the village celebrated the death of "Louis Capet."[73]

The council also supervised an annual fair held in Lourmarin on November 30, the feast of St. Andrew, since "time immemorial."[74] Throughout the eighteenth century the council tried to obtain authorization to hold another fair and also to establish a weekly market day. In February, 1791, the National Assembly granted Lourmarin two annual fair days—August 4 and All Saints' Day, November 1—and a regular market day, Thursday. Perhaps the urging of the local "Club of the Friends of the Constitution" influenced the National Assembly's decision. This was a happy occasion for Lourmarin, one of the unexpected benefits of the Revolution, and some of the inhabitants began designing posters and making plans to publicize the new fair dates.[75]

The delivery of mail to and from Lourmarin was done by outside contractors and did not adequately meet the needs of the community. In 1784 the villagers complained that their letters were being carried to Cadenet, the nearest village to the south, by a young boy who either lost the letters along the way or allowed them to be stolen.[76] In 1788 the council awarded a contract to Joseph Julien, a stocking-maker from Lourmarin, who agreed to deliver mail to the post office in Cadenet for 24 livres per year together with a charge of one sou per letter. Those who subscribed to a newspaper or journal were also required by this contract to pay the postman three livres per year.[77] Although no precise figures are available, we can assume that, since this provision was inserted in the contract, some persons in the village received journals from Marseilles, Aix, and Avignon regularly. Although one cannot ascertain what effect these journals (or books, for that matter) had in the village, the fact remains that the Lourmarinois were exposed to outside ideas.

The range of other local problems with which the council was forced to deal was almost limitless and included everything from taking precautions

[73] *Ibid.*, April 10, 1791, January 28, 1793.
[74] *Ibid.*, December 10, 1713, and *passim*.
[75] *Ibid.*, January 21, February 13, 1791.
[76] *Ibid.*, June 11, 1784.
[77] *Ibid.*, July 13, 1788.

against wolves, brigands, and epidemics to providing, cheerfully it would seem, free food and lodging in 1778 for two royal engineers who were drafting a detailed map of France.[78] Most of these local problems were handled efficiently and conscientiously, and strict attention to the best interests of the community was usually placed above all other considerations.

The council, naturally, was equally concerned with the fiscal, judicial, and administrative bodies outside of Lourmarin with which it was forced to deal. Lourmarin, relatively isolated, had very little real contact with royal authority except when taxes came due or when a *travailleur* sent his son to serve in the king's army.

Lourmarin was involved with the royal militia in two very important ways: first, because the village furnished needed recruits and second, because the community was required to help provide materiel for any contingents of the king's army stationed in Provence. Each year the community was required to furnish one, two, or occasionally three, militiamen. For a few years after 1685 recruits were to be from "the best of the old Catholics" but this requirement was ignored in the eighteenth century.[79] As soon as the Intendant notified the consuls about the number of militiamen to be recruited, they appointed a committee of notables to draw up a list containing the "name, age, profession, and height of all young men of the parish between 18 and 40 years of age who were eligible for army service."[80] A separate list of married men, domestics, and boys aged 18 to 20 was also made. The eligibles gathered on a Sunday afternoon and watched while their names were placed in a hat and the second consul pulled out the number required.[81] The unfortunate new recruit was outfitted by the community, given a token payment as a sort of "enlistment bonus," and was delivered, usually protesting, to the nearest army commander.[82] Even should the village accomplish the successful delivery of the new militiaman, it often happened that the recruit escaped almost immediately and returned home. The village either had to find and return the deserter to his unit or, perhaps more difficult, find a replacement. Although the names of the more

[78] *Ibid.*, May 10, 1778, and *passim*.
[79] *Ibid.*, July 9, 1692, and *passim*.
[80] *Ibid.*, January 10, 1743, and *passim*.
[81] *Ibid.*, March 5, 1719.
[82] *Ibid.*, *passim*; Marion, *Dictionnaire*, p. 378; Masson, *Les temps modernes*, p. 221.

wealthy Lourmarinois did appear on the lists of those eligible to be drafted, by various stratagems the well-to-do entirely avoided conscription in the eighteenth century, although some did serve as officers.[83]

Lourmarin was responsible for furnishing uniforms to its militiamen while they were on active duty, paying recruiting bonuses, and exempting the soldiers from the *capitation* during the entire six-year term of service; no wonder the community felt this was a heavy financial drain on their resources. Upon discharge the soldier returned to the village and showed his separation papers to the consuls, who in turn officially registered his six years of service in the municipal deliberations and granted, as required by the Intendant, two additional years of exemption from the *capitation*.[84] It is therefore not surprising that the council habitually complained that Lourmarin's levy was too heavy.

A less consistently pressing problem, but one which disrupted the village much more when it occurred, was the requirement that all royal troops be fed and housed during times of war. Although theoretically the village was to be reimbursed for all expenses incurred in connection with the troops, often years passed before all the claims were settled. For example, two regiments were quartered in Lourmarin in the winter of 1708–9 during the War of the Spanish Succession and the village was required to furnish 19 sous per day for each soldier.[85] This was almost twice as much as a day laborer made at that time. During the 150 days while the troops were stationed in Lourmarin, the village was forced to borrow 3,500 livres at five percent interest. Before securing this loan from creditors in Aix, the village asked for and received the permission of the Intendant.[86] Moreover, the troops returned to winter quarters in Lourmarin in 1712–13.

Expenses incurred during the fighting of the War of the Austrian Succession in 1744–47,[87] when the Austrians advanced into Provence, were

---

[83] For example, see the list of those eligible for 1733. This list of 66 persons, like other such lists, included the names of the most wealthy. *A.M., D.M.*, February 22, 1733.

[84] *Ibid.*, April 25, 1753, and *passim*.

[85] *Ibid.*, December 9, 1708.

[86] *Ibid.*, December 16, 1708.

[87] For this phase of the fighting see Pierre Grillon, "L'invasion et la libération de la Provence en 1746–1747," *Provence Historique*, XII (October–December, 1962), 334–62.

still the object of discussion well into the 1760's.[88] The most direct and momentous effect of the war on Lourmarin occurred between 1744 and 1747 when several detachments were quartered in the village. Because of the actual fighting in Provence, Lourmarin had to provide men for emergency service—eight men in March, 1744, alone—plus large quantities of grain, vegetables, straw, hay, and several mules.[89] In 1757, while reviewing Lourmarin's expenditures during this period, the council discovered that the total expenditure in goods and services amounted to the staggering sum of 123,332 livres, or about 16 times the amount collected annually for all secular taxes.[90] Although some of the money came from communal revenues or loans, most of it was owed to individuals. Much time, energy, and money for attorneys' fees were expended before Lourmarin's claims were finally satisfied in the 1760's.

There are numerous examples of royal orders and instructions being transmitted to the village through the Intendant. More often than not these requests were for various types of information about the community and show the crown's rather broad interest in its villages. In 1723 alone, Lourmarin received three separate requests for reports on the quantity and quality of wood cut in the village since 1719, information about monasteries (there were none in Lourmarin) and details concerning the harvest, including requests for inventories of all kinds of grain, hay, and vegetables.[91]

The crown's interest in improving agriculture in France was demonstrated in 1778 when the Intendant announced that Louis XVI had approved a plan to establish a Society of Agriculture in Provence. A number of important persons, including Seigneur Bruny, who was very interested in agricultural improvements, sponsored this association.[92] However, it was not active and, prior to the Revolution, had no effect on agricultural conditions and practices in Lourmarin.

Occasionally the council appealed to the royal officials when they were in need of more stringent measures to deal with purely community matters. The consuls followed this procedure in 1783 when Pierre Eyssavel, wheel-

---

[88] *A.M., D.M.*, 1744–65, *passim*.
[89] *Ibid.*, March 15, July 29, 1744, July 4, 1745, and *passim*.
[90] *Ibid.*, April 3, 1757.
[91] *Ibid.*, January 13, August 29, October 27, 1723.
[92] *A.D., Bouches-du-Rhône*, C 93, fo. 253, April 18, 1778.

wright, built some sort of undescribed structure which obstructed the right-of-way of the "great road" from Cadenet to Apt, the major royal road through Lourmarin. After trying unsuccessfully to have the obstacle removed, the consuls informed the royal Procurers in Aix that they had decided "to put this business in your hands since you have more efficacious means than we do to have your orders respected and to maintain the good conduct that you want to establish."[93] This appeal to superior authority is an indication of the growing impact of the royal presence in Lourmarin.

One can see from this discussion of Lourmarin's political organization that many people had a role in making the village function properly. There was no one "strong man" or narrow clique which made all the decisions. For the *ancien régime* the degree of political participation in Lourmarin is about as great as could be expected and was considerably more than occurred in some parts of France. On the other hand it was normal that the "better people" excluded the lower classes from this political structure for the very real reason that they did not have the necessary ability or interest to govern themselves. As evidenced by the dubious reception given the works of Rousseau by most of the *philosophes,* even eighteenth-century liberals did not want everyone to participate in government. For the Lourmarinois, education had not become the avenue to political democracy it would become for later generations. The truth is that the notables in Lourmarin probably did as good a job, if not better, in protecting the interests of the lower classes than they could have done for themselves. As will be demonstrated in a later chapter, much of the council's time was devoted to finding ways of relieving the misery of the poor. It is a tribute to many hard-working, dedicated men to say that the village administration, with its complex structure, worked reasonably well and was not altogether to blame if by the time of the Revolution many of the village's problems remained unsolved. The leaders' sensitivity to local problems, their concern for the welfare of the entire village, and their willingness to tolerate religious differences, in exchange for a united front and a local *esprit de corps,* are not to be disparaged. Paternalistic and oligarchial, though not narrowly so, the village government was reasonably efficient and responsive to the needs of the local population.

[93] *Ibid.,* C 1177, October 18, 1783.

IV

VILLAGE FINANCES

THE MANAGEMENT OF Lourmarin's finances was the responsibility of the village council, but it exercised a varying degree of control over the several taxes which left the village. The council had the least control over the seigneurial dues and monopolies and, except for occasional complaints that the seigneur's ovens or mills were functioning improperly, this subject was seldom mentioned in the council minutes.[1] The council played a secondary role in the collection of the church *dîme*, governed by a 1615 agreement between the village and the church, and the royal *capitation*, neither of which was included in Lourmarin's yearly budget.

All other taxes—royal, provincial, and district—were listed together in Lourmarin's annual budget as "expenditures," a category that also included all money actually spent in the village, most of which was allocated to pay the salaries of those village officials and employees discussed in Chapter III. Although always treated separately in the annual budget, these two types of expenditures were combined for purposes of collection. The money needed could be obtained from only two general sources—current village revenue or a local tax levy. Current revenue was derived almost exclusively from the rents of the local *fermes* and seldom totalled more than one-quarter of the amount necessary. Thus the village was forced to levy a tax, based on the *cadastre*, in order to make up the difference.

[1] The various seigneurial dues will be discussed in Chapter VI.

The type of fiscal management practiced by the local officials of Lourmarin is the primary theme of this chapter. Most taxes were levied by the royal government on the community as a whole rather than on individuals, and the council then apportioned the total required among the inhabitants. This chapter will discuss the various taxes paid by the Lourmarinois and, where possible, the services their taxes were supposed to provide. This chapter will also examine the community *fermes*, some of which were designed to obtain revenue, others to provide a service in addition to income, while a third group yielded no income but were regulated by the council in order to insure that the villagers received an important service at a reasonable price. An examination of the council's role in the administration of the *fermes* and other economic matters provides information about the development of a type of local mercantilism comparable to the political paternalism described in the last chapter. The economic functions of the village council were reflected in its regulatory role as protector of individual villagers against high price and/or poor quality merchandise. The Revolution at Lourmarin, however, discredited this mercantilism in favor of *laissez-faire,* which may have benefited local "sellers" but placed the average Lourmarin consumer at the mercy of the market.

Lastly, this chapter will treat the process whereby Lourmarin calculated its annual tax rate in order to pay the various taxes assessed on the village as well as community expenditures. It will stress the complexity of the financial issues, the relatively large numbers of persons involved in making fiscal decisions, and the competence and care of the village officials in carrying out their fiscal responsibilities.

The council played a minor role in administering the *dîme* by selecting one villager to aid in collection from among three candidates nominated by the *fermier* of the church tithe-collector. The tithe-collector (*decimateur*) was a stranger to the village, usually resided at Avignon, and was responsible for several villages. The villagers never had any contact with him, but rather paid the *dîme* to the *fermier* and the local citizen chosen by the council. The *fermier* himself was always an important Lourmarin *bourgeois,* usually Catholic. A member of the Girard family often held this position during the period after 1680. The exaction of the *dîme* was based on a contract executed in 1615 between Lourmarin and the tithe-collector, which stated that the *dîme* would be equal to the value of five percent of all wheat, grapes, hemp, and sheep.[2] An agreement was reached in 1731, however, whereby the *fermier* collected 1,000 livres annually, 200 from the seigneur's land and 800 from that of the village, rather than five percent of the enumerated goods.[3] Since the *dîme* was collected in coin rather than in grain, the tithe-collector was unable to benefit from the eighteenth-century rise in the price of grain. It is also obvious that, since the 1,000 livres figure remained constant in the years before the Revolution when prices were increasing, the relative burden of the *dîme* had declined since the 1731 contract.

It is worth mentioning here that the tithe-collector to whom the *dîme* was paid was responsible for paying the salaries of the *curé* and the vicar. The *fermier* also had to provide six *charges* (about 30 bushels) of grain annually for the poor.[4] Thus, in terms of social services, the villagers could reap some benefits from their payments to the church, whereas the much larger payments to the seigneur were considered by the villagers as a total loss.

The *capitation* was a personal tax on all Frenchmen, who were divided into 22 economic classes so that the wealthier paid more. Beginning in 1695, the king agreed that the *capitation* was to be levied on Provence as a whole. The provincial officials then divided this personal tax among the districts, which in turn allocated a specific amount to each individual community.[5] Lourmarin was notified of its annual *capitation* assessment by the Intendant in Aix and the amount of the levy was announced at a council meeting, usually in December. It then became the responsibility of the municipal council to levy a tax on the heads of families (*chefs de famille*) sufficient to pay the community's assessment. The treasurer did not collect the *capitation*; instead, the mayor and second consul, assisted by two notables chosen on a rotating basis by the council, were responsible for gathering the money. The four tax collectors deposited their receipts with the treasurer, who in turn made two payments, one in February and the other

---

[2] *A.D., Bouches-du-Rhône*, C 139-3928, April 15, 1731. The 1615 contract has not survived, but its terms were repeated in this 1731 agreement.

[3] *Ibid.*

[4] This form of relief for the poor will be discussed more fully in Chapter V.

[5] Masson, *Provence*, pp. 181–83; Masson, *Les temps modernes*, p. 628.

in August, to the district capital in Apt. For his trouble the treasurer was allowed to retain 1.67 percent of the amount collected.[6] There is no evidence that the other four collectors received any compensation. The fact that a considerable amount of coin was transported overland with no reports of thefts or even attempted thefts must indicate that there was little danger of brigands and that the countryside, contrary to the usual picture of rural France, was fairly peaceful, at least in Provence.

Despite an increase in population, the *capitation* did not increase over the course of the century: Lourmarin paid 1,628 livres in 1718, 1,650 livres in 1782, and never more than 1,200 livres per year between 1783 and 1789.[7] However, significant variations, which seem to bear some relation to Lourmarin's ability to pay, did occur during the eighteenth century. For example, during the plague years of 1720–22 the *capitation* dropped from 1,227 livres in 1720 to 517 livres in 1721. The village's share was further reduced to 257 livres in 1722. The plague was contained by the fall of 1722, and when the assessment for 1723 was announced, Lourmarin's assessment had been increased to 780 livres.[8]

The council was permitted to exempt those persons in the community whom they felt were unable to pay the *capitation*. A thorough examination of the individual's economic condition was made before an exemption was granted. For example, in 1715 a feud erupted between the council and the Intendant as to whether the widow of Pompée Monge, who had been one of the few Catholic leaders in 1685, should pay a *capitation* assessment of 30 sous.[9] In spite of a "certificate of poverty" signed by Messire Raphael Girard, the Catholic priest, the council insisted that the Widow Monge was able to pay, but the Intendant upheld the certificate of poverty, overruled the village leaders, and declared that she was exempt from the *capitation*.[10]

Once a year all of Lourmarin's finances were considered at a council meeting, usually convoked on May 1, when the council reviewed the vil-

[6] *A.D.*, *Bouches-du-Rhône*, C 354, "Capitation," 1745; *A.M.*, *D.M.*, *passim*.
[7] *A.M.*, *D.M.*, December 27, 1717, January 27, 1782, and *passim*.
[8] *Ibid.*, July 7, 1721, February 1, November 29, 1722.
[9] *Ibid.*, March 24, 1715.
[10] *Ibid.*, December 8, 1715.

lage's expenditures and revenue for the present year and levied a tax to make up the deficit which always existed.[11]

Lourmarin was assessed for royal, provincial, and district taxes on the basis of the number of taxable units (*feux*) for which the community was charged.[12] In 1731 an increase in the number of *feux* from four and one-half to six brought an indignant protest from the Lourmarinois.[13] A General Council meeting was called to review the history of Lourmarin's *affouagement*, the process whereby the number of *feux* was set for each community, and found that the village had been charged for one and one-half *feux* in 1479, three in 1665, and four and one-half in 1698.[14] If figures later in the century are taken at face value, it would appear their complaint was justified. Using the figure of 55,000 livres as the approximate value of a *feu*, four and one-half *feux* would have meant the actual value of real property in Lourmarin was 247,500 livres whereas at six *feux* it would have been 330,000 livres. The actual value of real property in the 1770 *cadastre*, 249,250 livres, would indicate Lourmarin's *affouagement* should have been four and one-half *feux*.[15] The Lourmarinois further argued, using both historical and contemporary examples, that compared to neighboring villages, Lourmarin was being taxed too heavily.[16] Reviewing their responsibility to pay the *dîme* and the seigneurial charges, the municipal council concluded that an increase to six *feux* would ruin the village's economy.[17] Despite such dire predictions and the fact that the *affouagement* was not reduced, Lourmarin was able to meet its financial responsibilities.

[11] As was mentioned earlier, the *capitation, dîme,* and seigneurial dues were not included in this accounting since these were calculated and collected separately.

[12] *Feu* in its more usual fiscal connotation means "household," but was also used in Provence as a relative estimate of the population and wealth of each community compared to the wealth of the province as a whole. It was therefore used as a coefficient in calculating the annual tax. The value of a *feu* represented an ever-increasing amount but by the end of the eighteenth century it was set at 55,000 livres. Marion, *Dictionnaire*, p. 466; Masson, *Les temps modernes*, p. 545.

[13] Fearing an increase was imminent, the community in 1728 had appealed to their seigneur, without success, to aid their cause. *A.M., D.M.*, October 17, 1728.

[14] *A.D., Bouches-du-Rhône*, C 139-3927, April 15, 1731.

[15] Although this would make it appear that Lourmarin had a legitimate complaint, it must be emphasized that the 1770 figure was almost certainly undervalued. See Chapter I.

[16] The validity of this argument cannot be judged, but almost every Provençal community used this argument sometime in the eighteenth century.

[17] *A.D., Bouches-du-Rhône*, C 139-3927, 3928, April 15, 1731.

One can assume that at least part of the council's cry of woe in 1731 was the natural desire to keep the number of *feux*, and therefore their tax, to a minimum, although they knew that the village could afford the additional levy if necessary.

Once the amount of royal, provincial, district, and local charges to be paid by Lourmarin was allocated, the total village tax was apportioned on the basis of the *cadastre*, which contained an evaluation of all real property in the village. The council referred to the *cadastre* frequently in the eighteenth century. It was consulted when they levied taxes, checked property qualifications for elections, or convoked a Special Council. Until a new *cadastre* was finally drafted in 1770 at the enormous expense of 2,400 livres paid to expert surveyors, Lourmarin had to rely on its outdated 1640 tax roll despite repeated urgings of the council and a 1715 royal edict that new *cadastres* were to be drafted.[18] The main reason for the long delay in drawing up a new *cadastre* was that many influential persons probably benefited from the outdated evaluation and obviously saw little reason to urge a change. The reason usually given in the official village minutes, however, was the high cost. The new *cadastre* was finally drafted by two surveyors who were aided by village notables. The two-volume 1770 *cadastre* has survived and measures 30 inches by 18 inches, bound in heavy leather with metal decorations.[19] Obviously the community was very proud of its splendid new volumes which were much more accurate and provided a more solid basis for fair tax collection than had the old tax roll.[20] The 1770 *cadastre* was used until after the Revolution, when a new tax roll was made.

It would be difficult to overestimate the importance of the *cadastre's* central position to any discussion of the village's fiscal activities. Rarely did a year pass without one or several persons appearing before the council to plead for a reduction in their evaluation. The village estimators investigated all such requests and reported their findings to the council for a final determination of the case. When the new *cadastre* was finally completed in 1770, elaborate safeguards were set up to insure that every individual, no

---

[18] *A.M., D.M.,* July 1, 1724, contains a copy of the royal edict of July 9, 1715.

[19] To the best of my knowledge there were no accompanying maps, or if there were, they have not survived.

[20] *A.M., Cadastre,* 1770.

matter how poor, would have an opportunity to review his entry and to appeal his evaluation if he so desired. For 60 days after the surveyors had deposited the *cadastre* with the consuls, the secretary was ordered to make himself available daily so that every Lourmarinois could review his entry.[21] At the end of the 60-day period the *cadastre*, with corrections, was accepted as official.

Although many village notables were reluctant to have a new *cadastre* drafted, either because of the expense or because they feared their own property evaluation would be increased, an examination of the completed *cadastre* points to the thorough and honest job of the surveyors hired by the village. It would be unrealistic to expect the wealthy villagers to agree to a completely impartial evaluation. The truth probably is that once the council decided to draw up a new tax roll, the numerous notables who assisted the experts acted as a check on their colleagues who might attempt to lower their assessment. By this sort of mutual suspicion the notables prevented shifting a disproportionate share of the taxes onto the shoulders of the peasants.

In order to understand how an individual's tax was determined, we will first examine the community's total expenditures, then its sources of revenue, and finally the manner in which the annual tax levy was computed in order to reconcile the difference between Lourmarin's expenditures and its income. With some exceptions, Lourmarin's annual accounts from 1716 to the Revolution are available. The budget for 1775 is exceptionally complete and, although it contains a few unusual items, may serve as a typical example.[22] It is interesting to note that the two categories of taxes, those paid to the king, district, and province on the one hand and local charges on the other, were always listed as "expenditures." During most of the eighteenth century about three-fourths of the total collected left the village while the remaining quarter had to cover all local services.[23] No wonder the villagers viewed these taxes as money lost to "outsiders" from which they received little benefit.

[21] *A.M., D.M.,* June 11, 1770.
[22] *A.D., Bouches-du-Rhône,* C 1765, "Impositions," April 30, 1775.
[23] See also Bancol, *Monographies communales,* pp. 89–94, for a similar, although less complete, budget for the nearby village of Lacoste for 1785.

TABLE IV–1. EXPENDITURES FOR 1775

Charges for King, Province, and District	Livres	Sous	Deniers
For the current imposition for the charge for King and Province at the rate of 772 livres per *feu* and for six *feux* for which this community is charged	4,632	0	0
For the levy of the two *vingtièmes* and 4 additional sous per livre for the first *vingtième* according to the disposition made by the Procurers	1,150	17	0
Taillon, fouage, subside at the rate of 38 livres 19 sous 4 deniers per *feu*	236	16	0
Payment of the tax of the *lates* and *inquants*	14	15	6
Payment for the upkeep of illegitimate children	170	10	0
For the maintenance of the second-class roads of Provence	150	0	0
Special imposition of the district	156	0	0
Arrears owed to the treasurer of the district	459	0	0
	6,969	18	6

Charges for the Community			
For *demi-lods* paid to M. le Baron by M. Cavallier, mayor	600	0	0
For the salary of the treasurer	455	0	0
For the salary of the schoolmaster and mistress	255	0	0
For the salary of the constable	250	0	0
For the expenses of the mayor, consuls, and secretary	200	0	0
For the poor	40	0	0
For the town crier	34	0	0
For management of the clock tower	30	0	0
For the candles for the festival of Corpus Christi Day	21	0	0
For the salary of the mayor, consuls, and secretary	27	0	0
For the midwife	15	0	0
For the salary of the auditors of accounts	9	0	0
For the salary of the police officers	6	0	0
For unforeseen expenses, at least	204	0	0
	2,146	0	0
Total Village Charges	9,115	18	6

SOURCE: *A.D., Bouches-du-Rhône*, C 1765; *Impositions*, April 30, 1775.

More than one half of the total collected went to pay the royal and provincial taxes, which in 1775 were assessed at 772 livres per *feu*. The assessment per *feu* increased almost continuously during the eighteenth century. In the period 1724–36 Lourmarin paid 600 livres per *feu*, then the rate dipped to a low of 510 livres in 1738 before starting a long, steady climb to a high of 917 and 910 livres per *feu* in 1787 and 1788 respectively. After the disastrous winter of 1788–89 the rate was cut to 771 livres, 8 sous per *feu*.[24] The royal tax consistently accounted for one half of all expenditures; in 1787 it accounted for more than 60 percent. Since this item loomed so large in the budget, any significant change in Lourmarin's assessment materially affected the community. Thus the decrease in the provincial tax from 1788 to 1789 amounted to a savings of 834 livres for the village on this one item alone.

There were three other groups of royal taxes paid in Lourmarin, all supplementary to the primary royal tax above. By far the most burdensome was the charge of the *vingtième*, begun in 1749. A second *vingtième* was added in 1773, and was later increased by levying an additional 20 percent of the first *vingtième*, or four sous per livre. Thus in 1775 it amounted to approximately one-quarter of the primary royal tax. A third *vingtième* was added in 1783, and until the Revolution Lourmarin's levy was 1,551 livres. This meant that while Lourmarin had paid 5,783 livres for the regular royal tax and the *vingtième* in 1775, they were paying 7,009 livres in 1788—an increase of 21 percent in 13 years.[25]

A second set of supplementary taxes, the *taillon*, *fouage*, and *subside*, which were collected together, were of medieval origin, and were based on the established tax rate multiplied by the number of *feux*. The established rate did not vary appreciably after 1724, although the amount Lourmarin had to pay increased 58 livres in 1731 when the village's number of *feux* was increased from four and one-half to six.[26]

A third supplement to the royal taxes were the *lates* and *inquants*, also of medieval origin, a relatively insignificant item in the budget because they were never assessed at more than 18 livres. Other royal taxes such as the *dixième* had been imposed earlier in the century but were withdrawn later. Royal taxes thus accounted for 6,034 livres or 66.2 percent of the entire budget for 1775. Despite the increase in the *vingtième*, these taxes continued to account for about two-thirds of Lourmarin's annual spending until the entire tax system was restructured at the time of the Revolution.

[24] *A.M.*, *D.M.*, May 13, 1787, May 4, 1788, May 24, 1789, and *passim*.
[25] *Ibid.*, May 4, 1788, and *passim*.
[26] *Ibid.*, August 13, 1724, and *passim*.

The district tax was also levied on the number of *feu*.[27] The assessment was five livres per *feu* in 1724, 26 livres per *feu* in 1775, and 54 livres per *feu* in 1788 and 1789. The assessment in these last two years, when Lourmarin paid 324 livres to the district, was by far the highest district levy, with the single notable exception of 1745 when, because of the large number of troops quartered in the district during the War of the Austrian Succession, the levy was increased to 1,225 livres.[28] The 1745 increase in district taxes, combined with a rise in royal assessments, caused Lourmarin's tax burden to reach 7,841 livres, an increase of 27 percent over the previous year.[29] The per capita assessment was about 26 livres per family. This additional tax burden, aggravated by a slight drop in revenue from the village *fermes* and the enormous extraordinary expenditures for food, blankets, mules, and other materiel for the royal army, was a heavy financial burden on the community. Lourmarin was still paying arrears to the district in 1751.[30] Therefore the arrears payment which occurred in the 1775 budget was not a regular annual payment, but neither was it unique. It is noteworthy that although Lourmarin occasionally was indebted to individuals, such as to its own notables or the seigneur, or owed back taxes, it always managed to pay. In most of the budgets examined its taxes were used only for current expenses. Lourmarin incurred no long-standing indebtedness in the eighteenth century.

Once the tax money had left the parish, the village council considered that it was irretrievably lost. Except for the periodic celebrations of France's military or naval victories, there is no indication that the Lourmarinois felt a sense of participation in the glorious achievements of the French crown which their money had helped bring about. The council was so occupied with local affairs and with keeping taxes as low as possible that there was no incentive to develop a more cosmopolitan outlook, although individual councillors were certainly aware of events outside the village and even outside the province.

---

[27] The districts (*vigueries* in Provence), were the intermediate administrative unit between the local government and the province. After 1760 there were 22 districts in Provence; Lourmarin was in the *viguerie* of Apt. See Masson, *Provence*, pp. 175–79.

[28] *A.M., D.M.*, May 16, 1745.

[29] *Ibid.*, May 14, 1744, May 16, 1745.

[30] *Ibid.*, January 17, 1751.

Two tax payments, for the support of Lourmarin's illegitimate children and for the maintenance of its second-class roads, although they represented only four percent of the village budget, provided specific services to the community. Until 1773 no separate entry was made for the support of Lourmarin's illegitimate children, but from 1773 until the Revolution the payment amounted to between 170 and 180 livres.[31] Since Lourmarin sent illegitimate children and foundlings to the Hospital of St. Jacques in Aix throughout the century, one may assume that prior to 1773 money for their care was included in the general provincial assessments.

One hundred fifty livres were allotted for the upkeep of the second-class roads in the territory of Lourmarin. Assessments for these roads, primarily the streets within the village proper, were in addition to occasional local payments for the main road from Aix to Apt and the many service roads which criss-crossed the parish. Although secondary roads in the parish were under the jurisdiction of the municipal council, Lourmarin occasionally appealed to Aix for financial aid when serious damage to the roads occurred.[32]

Despite the regular village allotment, there was little in the way of preventive maintenance; instead, the council acted to repair the roads only when they threatened to become impassable. For example, in 1724 each proprietor was given one month to repair all roads running through, or adjacent to, his property. If the owner did not take the initiative, the consuls threatened to hire the necessary labor and charge him. When a major repaving was done in 1758, the council announced that the community would pay the workmen but that each proprietor must provide his own paving material, usually crushed rock. Of course the council paid for repairs to streets in front of the community's property, such as the shelter house for the poor.[33]

The council applauded a 1765 provincial project to build a bridge over the Durance River, "an insurmountable barrier" between "the two parts of Provence which depend so much on one another."[34] The proposed bridge would, of course, provide a more direct and faster means of trans-

---

[31] *Ibid.*, May 2, 1773.

[32] *A.D., Bouches-du-Rhône,* C 1177, March 2, 1773, May 29, 1776, August 22. 1780, *passim.*

[33] *A.M., D.M.,* April 2, 1724, and March 27, 1758.

[34] *Ibid.*, November 19, 1765.

porting Lourmarin's textiles to Aix and Marseilles, their principal markets, as well as bringing needed grain back from these two cities. It would also shorten the many necessary trips to Aix, the administrative center of Provence, required of the council, thereby decreasing the expense. In this instance community self-interest in obtaining better access to markets was combined with a growing awareness that Provence had aid to dispense.

The remaining expenditures were all relatively small and local in nature. A royal edict promulgated in August, 1716, during the Regency, decreed that after the "taxes for King and Province" were paid, local expenditures were to have priority.[35] Included under this heading were the salaries for the village officials—mayor, second consul, schoolteachers, midwife, public crier, and the keeper of the clock tower—plus a sum set aside for small, unexpected expenses. The salaries of the treasurer and the constable, which would certainly qualify as "local expenses," were excluded from this priority. However, by 1750 the council no longer made any distinction among the various local expenses and simply listed them all with no obvious priority.

The annual salaries for the schoolmaster and schoolmistress were set in 1716 at 100 livres and 60 livres respectively and were included in the local expenditures which were to be paid first.[36] However, because of the manner by which teachers were hired, it soon became obvious that the village would have to pay more than 160 livres to employ capable teachers and by 1724 the council added 50 livres "to augment" the teachers' salaries while retaining 160 livres as a base figure.[37] The salary of 255 livres in Table IV–1 —less than three percent of the annual budget—was an average expenditure for education after the middle of the century.

In 1716 the salary of the public crier was set at 11 livres, that of the midwife at nine livres, and that of the keeper of the clock tower at 18 livres.[38] Remuneration to these community employees increased in the eighteenth century, although hardly enough to make those who held these

35 *Ibid.*, September 13, 1716.
36 *Ibid.*
37 *Ibid.*, May 1, 1724.
38 *Ibid.*, September 13, 1716.

positions wealthy. While the midwife's annual salary only increased from nine to 15 livres, it may be assumed that her major source of income throughout the century came from the small payments made in cash or produce by grateful parents. The public crier's office was a sinecure usually reserved for an older man, and the combination of relatively light duties and the public esteem which accompanied him as he made his rounds in his splendid uniform helped keep his salary low. The supervisor of the village clock was always a local artisan who performed this duty to supplement his annual income.

The community provided the village church with candles for the celebration of the annual spring festival of Corpus Christi. The 40 livres for the poor, coming from the annual five percent return on the invested capital of the Girard legacy, had been paid regularly since its inception. Since the legacy's capital was doubled in 1786, the 1787 budget showed 80 livres to be used for the poor.[39]

The salaries received by the village officials were small, but they were about on a par with other villages in Provence.[40] In addition, the two consuls and the secretary, who conducted most of the village's business, were allowed 200 livres for various expenses associated with their offices, but all such expenditures had to be reported and approved by the council before the officers were reimbursed. There was also a separate account for "unforeseen" or "extraordinary expenses" varying between 150 and 300 livres annually to cover petty expenses such as minor repairs to one of the fountains or the clock. Even the most minor repairs, however, required an estimate before the work was done. When asked to approve a proposed repair, the council usually replied affirmatively, stipulating that the mason, carpenter, or other artisan make the repair "as economically as possible." It often seemed that the council, as evidenced in the case of the village clock, which was in a state of perpetual disrepair, was more concerned with pinching livres than with having the repair made correctly and permanently. They often talked as if they expected both economy and quality, but in case of a conflict, they usually chose economy.

[39] *Ibid.*, May 13, 1787.
[40] For comparative figures see Baehrel, *Une croissance*, p. 308; Masson, *Les temps modernes*, pp. 667–71.

Because of the demand for these offices, the salaries of the constable and treasurer varied from year to year. Since the constable could augment his salary by a share of the fines collected from those whom he apprehended, his total income depended on his diligence. In addition to the treasurer's salary, expenses associated with the treasury including the cost of registering his contract in Aix and reimbursement for the treasurer's regular trips to Apt were paid by the community. The *demi-lods* in the budget were paid by the council to the seigneur for property owned by the community.

Although it was not levied in 1775, mention should be made of the *capage*, a local tax peculiar to Provence which, like the *capitation*, was a direct tax on individuals and was progressive in nature so that the wealthy paid at a higher rate than the poor.[41] Imposition of the *capage* required the approval of the *Cour des Comptes* in Aix, which stipulted that it could be collected for a specific period of time only, e.g., three years. Thus it was not an annual item in the budget. The *capage* was levied to provide income for specific extraordinary local expenses—repairs to local fountains, the clock, or the roads—or to supplement the salaries of village employees, such as the schoolmaster.[42] The individual levy seldom amounted to more than two livres annually. As with the *capitation*, the council had the authority to exempt those it felt were too poor to pay the *capage*. The seigneur and his employees also did not have to pay this tax: at least twice in the eighteenth century the council had to refund the *capage* paid by officials of the seigneur—once to the seigneur's miller and once to the seigneur's *viguier*.[43]

The only source of village income came from the *fermes*. The village *fermes* were concessions perhaps best described as exclusive rights to provide goods or services to the villagers at community-regulated prices, leased to the highest bidder by the municipal government.[44] It must be emphasized

[41] For a discussion of the *capage* in Provence see Jean Cornée, *Les débuts de la Révolution aux Baux-en-Provence, 1788–1792* (Aix-en-Provence, 1957), p. 80.

[42] *A.M., D.M.,* January 27, 1709, June 12, 1729, *passim*; Marion, *Dictionnaire*, p. 69.

[43] *A.M., D.M.,* March 16, 1749, July 11, 1762.

[44] For a discussion of communal *fermes* in Provence see Baehrel, *Une croissance,* pp. 316–18.

that at least some of these *fermes* were much more than revenue-producing instruments and demonstrate mercantilistic and paternalistic policies employed by the village fathers not only to provide certain services to the villagers, but also to protect them as consumers.

The communal *fermes* existing in the century preceding the Revolution retained the monopolistic character that they had had in the Middle Ages, but as in other Provençal villages, ownership had been transferred by the seigneur to the community in exchange for a "seigneurial payment."[45] Since the income from leasing the *fermes* was vital to Lourmarin's financial equilibrium, the council was not always averse to permitting an increase in the price charged by the *fermier,* thereby making the lease more attractive to prospective bidders. If village revenue from the *ferme* leases then increased, and if expenditures remained constant, the council would be able to lower taxes, always a popular move. This tax reduction was, of course, chimerical, since the charge an individual paid for a service, such as the cost of having his bread baked, would be increased. It is possible that some villagers preferred this indirect form of taxation, paid daily or weekly, much like our modern sales tax, to an increased tax levy on May 1.

In 1780 the *Cour des Comptes* at Aix, anxious that all villages in Provence manage their *fermes* in a businesslike manner, and "in order to prevent cabals and monopolies," promulgated rules to be followed by the communities in awarding their *fermes.*[46] The town crier notified the villagers in advance when a particular *ferme* was to be let. Interested bidders were invited to submit offers on three consecutive Sundays, usually in the presence of one of the consuls and the secretary, who recorded the bid. Within 24 hours after making a bid, the prospective *fermier* was required to appear before the council with another person, often a relative, who posted bond as his guarantee (*caution*).[47] Bids were not restricted only to inhabitants of Lourmarin, but when a "foreigner" presented an offer for a *ferme*, a Lourmarin notable often acted as his *caution*. Public bidding

---

[45] *Ibid.*, p. 316.

[46] *A.M., D.M.*, June 20, 1780. Copy of *Arrêt* of the *Cour des Comptes*. It would appear that Lourmarin was already observing these rules and entered the *arrêt* in the book of deliberations simply as a formality.

[47] This agreement between "principal" and "caution" was then registered as an *obligation* in the minutes of the local notary and thus became part of the public record. *A.Not., passim.*

ceased on the third Sunday and the council examined the bids, usually awarding the *ferme* to the highest bidder with the provision that it would not become final for eight days. During the eight-day period other bids, usually more favorable in terms of revenue to the community, were often received. The best offer was announced on the eighth day (Monday) and a special candle used only at this time was lit. Other bids might be made until the "extinction of the candle," when bidding was closed and the new lease was drawn up.[48] All the leases were executed by a notary so that there would be no misunderstanding on the part of either the community or the *fermier*. An examination of the individual *fermes* will demonstrate the variety of services provided to the inhabitants of Lourmarin and also show how the council tried to act in the general interests of its citizens.

Two of the *fermes*, the lease of the bakery (*boulangerie*) and the tax levied on grain to be made into bread and sold in the inns of Lourmarin (*piquet de la farine*), were closely related and never were let in the same year. The *ferme* of the bakery, already in existence in 1680, was ended in 1727, while the grain tax was not begun until 1714. During the 14-year period when both existed, only one was imposed in any single year so that bread never bore both charges.

The baker's lease was for three years and required him to bake bread and sell it in a public store. The price of bread was in conformance with the tariff of Aix, which meant that in 1709 a two-pound loaf of bread cost two sous.[49] The terms of the lease stipulated that inns, taverns, and other public eating establishments, the largest consumers of bread, were forbidden to make their own and had to purchase it from the *fermier*. In exchange for this monopoly the *fermier* paid rent quarterly to the community.[50]

The tax on grain, paid before the wheat or rye was ground into flour, was more lucrative for the community than the *ferme* of the bakery and the grain tax *fermier*, instead of providing a service as did the baker, acted simply as a tax collector. Like the bakery, the grain *ferme* was let for three years and the *fermier* paid his rent to the community quarterly. Since this

[48] *A.M., D.M.*, June 20, 1780. Copy of *Arrêt*.
[49] *Ibid.*, May 20, June 29, 1709. This would have taken about 25 percent of the wages of a day laborer in 1709.
[50] Leases for the *boulangerie. A.Not.*, Chastroux, July 21, 1684; *A.M., D.M.,* July 27, 1711, and *passim*.

ferme brought considerably more money into the village treasury than did the bakery, it was inevitable that it finally supplanted the latter.[51]

The bakers no longer had the exclusive right to bake bread in the village, but neither did they have to pay rent to the community for their position. On the other hand, the council still exercised supervision over the bakers and continued to correlate the price of bread in Lourmarin with the tariff of Aix. If the price of grain rose to a point where the baker pleaded to be allowed to raise the price of bread in order to stay in business, the council invariably asked that local notables sell their grain to the baker at a reduced price or, if this were not possible, a wealthy *bourgeois* such as Girard purchased grain himself at the market price and sold it to the baker at a lower price.[52] Either way the more wealthy Lourmarinois subsidized the baker in order to keep the price of bread down.

The ferme of the grain tax was instituted in 1714 when Jacques Corgier, surgeon, was granted this lease when he offered to pay 200 livres for the right to collect 20 sous per *charge* of wheat and 12 sous on each *charge* of rye to be made into bread for ultimate sale to the inns, taverns, etc.[53] The innkeepers, on whom the tax was levied, were required to pay Corgier when they took their grain to the seigneurial mill for conversion into flour. The fine for violation of the grain tax was 10 livres.[54]

After much debate the council decided in 1765 to revoke the grain *ferme* and to replace it with a "double piquet" thereby increasing the tax per *charge* to 40 sous for wheat and 24 sous for rye while the fine for violating the lease was raised to 20 livres.[55] Jacques Roman, master baker, paid 500 livres for the *ferme* in 1765, exactly twice as much as the rent in 1762; in 1768 the *fermier* paid 615 livres, a sizable increase in the

[51] For example, the 1723 *fermier* of the grain tax paid 144 livres for his lease, while the 1724 *fermier* of the bakery paid only 93 livres. *A.M., D.M.*, July 25, 1723, June 18, 1724.

[52] *Ibid.*, August 15, 1765, *passim.*

[53] A *charge* of grain was roughly equal to five bushels.

[54] Those most likely to be fined were the innkeepers, tavern operators, etc. who tried to evade the payment by putting their grain directly into the hands of the seigneur's miller. The *fermier* of the grain tax cou'd also, of course, be fined if he overcharged or otherwise cheated the villagers. *A.M., D.M.*, August 5, 27, 1714, and *passim*. See also *A.Not.*, Ailhaud, May 25, 1762.

[55] *A.M., D.M.*, May 5, June 2, 1765. *A.Not.*, Ailhaud, July 16, 1765.

community's revenue.[56] Of course the innkeepers now paid twice as much tax on the grain.

The disastrous winter of 1788–89, the council decided, had "prevented the poorest class of day workers from working and they are therefore unable to sustain themselves as are the more wealthy (*bien nés*) inhabitants of Lourmarin."[57] The community could best show its concern for their welfare by suppressing the *ferme* of the grain tax. A resolution to this effect was unanimously passed by the council six weeks before the Estates General met. A valid question which, unfortunately, is not answered in the council minutes is just how many day workers would have been eating in inns, etc. Unless the number were substantial, it is hard to see how this "concession" could have been of much practical help to the poor.[58]

Begun in 1715, another source of village income was directly related to the seigneur's *banalité* of the ovens in Lourmarin. The seigneur had the right to collect a baking tax (*droit de fournage*) and his *fermier* was responsible for baking the bread.[59] Each year the village let a *ferme* to the highest bidder for the right to supply the wood used to stoke the fires of the seigneur's ovens. He therefore was responsible for supplying the necessary quantity of wood, for which he charged six deniers per *panal* used.[60] The village *fermier* of the ovens, or *fournier*, also received "one loaf of bread for each one-half *charge* of grain that was converted into bread."[61]

A second oven was built in 1743 and the village now needed two men to provide the necessary wood and consequently gained an additional source of revenue.[62] The community's revenue did not increase dramatically because of the new oven in 1743, but by 1748 the income from the wood provided to two ovens had climbed to 648 livres compared with 384 livres

---

[56] *A.M., D.M.,* June 2, 1765, June 11, 1768.

[57] *Ibid.,* March 26, 1789.

[58] *Ibid.* Mayor Corgier evidently had the same doubts because the next day, March 27, 1789, he expressed similar reservations. *Ibid.,* March 27, 1789. See also Chapter VIII.

[59] See Chapter VI for a discussion of this *banalité.*

[60] *A.M., D.M.,* September 17, 1725, and *passim; A.Not.,* Ailhaud, September 28, 1761.

[61] *A.Not.,* Ailhaud, September 28, 1761, and *passim.* I can find no discussion of the relationship between the seigneur's *fermier* and the community *fournier,* but it must have been amicable because two separate taxes were collected at the ovens.

[62] *A.M., D.M.,* October 15, 1743.

in 1742 when only one oven existed.[63] The amount of rent paid to the community by the two *fermiers* for the right to stoke the oven fires and supply firewood increased slowly after 1748, reaching a peak of 725 livres in 1786.[64] The *ferme* of the ovens existed until 1791 when the *fermiers* complained that because the seigneurial rights associated with the ovens had been suppressed, people were using other ovens and thereby reducing their income.[65] The council responded by discharging the *fermiers* and nullifying their contract.[66] This action effectively eliminated the *ferme* of the wood for the seigneurial ovens.

A tax on the consumption of wine (*rêve du vin*) was one of the three *fermes* which provided the bulk of revenue to the community. Since the other two major *fermes* were taxes on the consumption of bread—a tax on grain and another on the use of the ovens—it is clear that two important items in the villagers' diet provided a sizable revenue. Although attempts were made to institute the wine tax earlier in the century, it was not firmly established until 1765 when the lease was sold for 350 livres.[67] Similar to the tax on grain, the wine *fermier* collected a tax on all wine consumed in the inns, taverns, and cabarets of the community at the rate of six deniers per *pot*.[68] Levied on wine at the time of delivery, it was therefore paid by the tavern keeper, who was then allowed to pass it along to his customers. Since this tax did not apply to wine consumed at home, two notables were appointed to determine how much of the wine delivered to the tavern could be consumed tax-free by the innkeeper and his family; all other wine sold in the tavern was subject to duty.

The *fermier's* profit was the difference between the rent he paid and the amount of tax money he collected. Because his lease was for three years, the *fermier* had to gamble that economic conditions would not be too unfavorable since hard times would adversely affect the consumption of wine in public houses. Collection of the wine tax was relatively uncompli-

---

[63] *Ibid.*, December 2, 1742, October 27, 1748.

[64] *Ibid.*, December 26, 1786, and *passim*.

[65] Prior to this time the monopoly was supposed to be absolute, and there is no evidence that it was not. However, because of the nature of the sources, it is entirely possible that there was some home-baking.

[66] *A.M., D.M.*, June 5, 1791.

[67] *Ibid.*, September 22, 1765.

[68] A *pot* is a liquid measurement equal to about one pint.

cated, since the risks and administrative responsibilities were incurred by the *fermier*, and it provided the community with a steady source of revenue until it was suppressed on March 28, 1789.[69]

Another important *ferme* to the average villager was the butcher shop (*boucherie*). Initially the monopoly on the sale of meat, excluding pork, in the village went to the person who made the highest bid, 240 livres in 1680.[70] The butcher then charged whatever price he wished for meat. Presumably in the interest of the consumers, the system of bidding was changed in 1693.[71] Those bidding on the *ferme* announced their price per pound for "mutton and other milk-fed meat less than one year old," and another, lower, price per pound for beef, ewe, and goat, which were considered less desirable.[72] The bidding followed the usual pattern and the lease was awarded to the person who agreed to furnish meat at the lowest price.[73]

Often two bidders offered to sell at the same price per pound and both refused to go any lower. Instead of decreasing further the price for meat, a bidder might offer to furnish a stipulated amount of meat, usually mutton, free to the poor of the community. It was not uncommon, especially in hard times, for the council to require as a condition of the lease that the butcher give meat free to the poor. Although records are incomplete, prior to 1750 at least 12 leases including free mutton for the poor were enacted; the largest amount provided was 300 pounds in 1718. After 1750 meat for the poor was seldom included in the butcher's lease and the price of all meat tended to rise. This may have reflected increased prosperity or higher costs for the *fermier*, but certainly did not indicate a decline in competition for the *ferme*.

---

[69] *A.M.*, *D.M.*, March 28, 1789. See also leases for the *rêve du vin*, *A.Not.*, Ailhaud, August 12, 1765; *A.D.*, *Bouches-du-Rhône*, B 3263, July 31, 1780.

[70] *A.M.*, *D.M.*, March 17, 1680.

[71] *Ibid.*, March 14, 1693.

[72] Leases for the *boucherie*. *A.M.*, *D.M.*, August 10, 1711, March 9, 1723. An examination of Appendix A as well as references throughout the council minutes indicate that the primary meats were lamb and mutton, although the cost was higher than for other meats. The lower price for beef must indicate that it was not appreciated in Lourmarin.

[73] Although no records for meat consumption are available, the amount of attention devoted to this *ferme* by the council and the lively bidding for the privilege of being the *fermier* indicate that, contrary to popular belief, the eating of meat, especially lamb and mutton, was fairly general.

Those persons authorized to receive meat free from the butcher were required to present chits signed by the consuls.[74] Once or twice a year the council reimbursed the butcher for the meat furnished to the poor in excess of the amount stipulated in his lease. He also had to provide the community with two or three young oxen at Easter. In addition, he was required to live in Lourmarin with his family and was not allowed to sublet his lease. He must "kill the animals with his door open" and it was absolutely mandatory that he use the scales provided for weighing all meat sold. Furthermore, he must give the same service "to the poor as to the rich" and "neither war nor plague," wrote the council in 1723, would relieve him of his responsibility.[75] The only exception to this egalitarian outlook was the requirement that the butcher sell meat to the seigneur at a price at least 50 percent lower than that paid by the Lourmarinois.[76] The council protected the *fermier's* monopoly by making it illegal for any other person in the village to sell meat although a person might slaughter animals for his own use. Fine for violation of this law was 30 livres. This system which provided the *fermier* with a lucrative monopoly, balanced by strict community control and a fixed selling price, met with general approval and was in the best interests of the village.[77]

The butcher sold all kinds of meat except fresh pork, upon which a separate tax was levied. Bids were taken on the *ferme* of fresh pork (*souquet des pourceaux*) and the person who offered the highest payment to the village received the lease. The retail price of pork was set by this lease but, unlike the procedure for the butcher shop after 1693, the price was not dependent upon the *fermier's* bid. However, the price of pork was consistently higher than the prices for meat sold by the butcher. Individuals were allowed to butcher pigs for their own use, but they were required to pay a predetermined sum to the *fermier* for this privilege. Failure to do so resulted in a five-livres fine for each offense plus confiscation of the pork.[78]

---

[74] *A.M., D.M.*, March 9, 1723, and *passim*.
[75] *Ibid.*, March 9, 1723.
[76] *A.D., Bouches-du-Rhône*, C 139-3928, April 15, 1731.
[77] Leases for the *boucherie. A.Not.*, Chastroux, March 28, 1686; *A.M., D.M.*, August 10, 1711, March 9, 1723.
[78] Leases for the *souquet des pourceaux. A.Not.*, Chastroux, June 27, 1684, November 4, 1686, Ailhaud, May 25, 1762, September 23, 1765; *A.M., D.M.*, November 13, 1713.

Like the tax on grain, the tax on fresh pork was suppressed in March, 1789.[79]

The council also received bids and selected a *fermier* who was placed in charge of Lourmarin's pig population. Since the pigs could not be allowed to run loose and because most men worked and thus were unable to care for their pigs themselves, the pig *fermier* provided an essential service.[80] The community thus arranged to have a needed service provided at a very minimal cost and with the further advantage that any risks were borne by the *fermier*.

The stucco-covered buildings of Provence, with their distinctive red-tile roofs, attest to the necessity of having standardized tiles readily available at a reasonable price. In the eighteenth century Lourmarin leased its tile works to the highest bidder, who agreed to make several different kinds of tiles of standard quality and measurement at mutually agreed upon prices.[81] Under the terms of his lease the *fermier* was required to furnish 200 tiles free of charge to the village for repairs to the parish church and the shelter house for the poor and he also gave 200 tiles as *cens* to the seigneur.[82] The term of the lease was for either three or six years and it was the rule, rather than the exception, for a *fermier* to serve several terms in succession.

The upkeep of the tile works was a community responsibility as was the acquisition of an adequate supply of good quality clay. Evidently the tile maker felt that the village was shirking its responsibility since he complained again and again about the poor condition of the tile works and its adjacent oven.[83] Perhaps the very moderate revenue from the tile works discouraged the village leaders from spending money to improve the physical plant. This lack of interest in the tile works is reflected in the lack of competitive bidding for the *ferme*.

The council established specifications for the different types of bricks and tiles made and also set the price per 100 for each kind. Tiles needed for roofing and for chimneys were more expensive than those used to line culverts. To insure uniformity of the tiles sold, the 1765 lease stated that the

[79] *A.M., D.M.,* March 28, 1789.

[80] *Ibid.,* February 7, 1723, and *passim; A.Not.,* Chastroux, January 20, 1684.

[81] Leases for the tile works. *A.Not.,* Ailhaud, March 4, 1765; *A.M., D.M.,* September 24, 1775, February 17, 1788.

[82] *A.M., D.M.,* October 16, 1739, and *passim.*

[83] *Ibid.*

tile maker could sell tiles to the villagers only in the presence of one of the consuls, who evidently acted as a quality control inspector.[84] The tile maker was moderately successful in supplying a needed commodity to the village, his primary function, but the revenue accruing to the community was small.

The numerous village transactions involving buying and selling on the basis of weight naturally necessitated an accurate means of measurement which was provided, in part, by the *fermier* of the public scales (*poids publiques*). Three community scales were operated on a fee basis by the *fermier*.[85] The three-year *ferme* of the public scales was begun in 1681 when the highest bidder offered nine livres, reached its apex in 1756 when 150 livres were offered, but had declined to 135 livres at the Revolution.[86] All persons in the village selling goods by weight had to use the public scales or risk paying three livres for each offense.[87] Charges for the use of the scales were moderate but quite comprehensive and these prices were fixed by the community. Prospective *fermiers* made their bids with the knowledge that the prices had been established. The successful bidder then entered into a contract with the community, at which time he acknowledged the prices.[88]

The *fermier* of the public scales was required to keep a register with exact information for each transaction including the day of the sale, complete names of both buyer and seller, product sold, and price received. The *fermier* then certified each entry and sent his register to the consuls for their verification.[89]

No other single subject, including the question of poor relief to be discussed in the next chapter, consumed as much of the council's time as the administration of the *fermes*. These *fermes*, of course, provided a revenue for the community, but since this revenue came almost exclusively from the Lourmarinois, it could have been obtained by simply raising regular taxes. The major function of the *fermes*, therefore, was to regulate, supervise, and set prices on various services provided the villagers so as not to place them at the mercy of a few entrepreneurs who, without competition and with the

[84] *A.Not.*, Ailhaud, March 4, 1765, and *passim*.
[85] *A.M.*, *D.M.*, July 18, 1716, and *passim*.
[86] *Ibid.*, October 29, 1681, December 19, 1756, October 22, 1786.
[87] *A.Not.*, Ailhaud, May 25, 1762, and *passim*.
[88] *Ibid*.
[89] *Ibid*.

consumers vulnerable to violent shifts in production, could have charged higher prices with no effective control over the quality of their services. In the 1775 budget (Table IV–1) the income from the *fermes* provided 2,036 livres, or slightly less than one-quarter of the amount needed to cover the village's expenditures. In other words, the annual income from the *fermes* was just about enough to meet local expenses without any direct taxes.

The difference between the total of Lourmarin's taxes and local expenses on the one hand, and the revenue from its *fermes* on the other, was 7,079 livres in 1775. The village *taille* was based on this figure.[90] The amount of an individual's *taille* was calculated by referring to the *cadastre*, which listed the evaluation of all real property in Lourmarin, and included a detailed entry for every property holder, whether he was domiciled in the community or not. A royal edict signed July 9, 1715, by Louis XIV set the value of one *livre cadastral* as equal to 1,000 livres of real property.[91] This was an attempt to abolish inequities in the administration of the royal tax by standardizing the value of a *livre cadastral* for all of Provence. Prior to this change, a *livre cadastral* in Lourmarin had been valued at 200 livres.[92] Provence, as a *pays d'état*, was assessed *en bloc* for royal taxes and they were then apportioned among the communities by the Provincial Estates. Standardization of the tax base was designed to make the tax burden more equitable throughout Provence.[93] Lourmarin's assessment in 1775 was levied on 253 *livres cadastral*, which meant that theoretically the value of the real property in Lourmarin was 253,000 livres, a figure that probably undervalued the true amount by as much as one quarter.[94] It then became the council's responsibility to levy a tax sufficient to cover Lourmarin's assess-

[90] In Provence the term *taille* was used to mean the total tax upon which the village levy was based and not, as in other parts of France, to denote a specific royal tax. See Table IV–2 which shows the local *taille* for 1730–45 and 1770–90. The dramatic rise in 1745 was caused by the War of the Austrian Succession. The high point in 1790 was occasioned as a result of the expenses brought about by the Revolution and the concurrent loss of revenue due to the suppression of some local *fermes*.

[91] *A.M., D.M.,* June 18, 1724. Copy of "Declaration du Roi" of July 9, 1715.

[92] As was discussed earlier most communities, when drafting new *cadastres*, continued to undervalue their property.

[93] For a discussion of this question see Cornée, *Baux-en-Provence*, p. 79.

[94] According to the 1770 *Cadastre*, itself probably undervalued, the total value of real property in Lourmarin was 249,250 livres.

ment. Therefore, in 1775 a tax of 28 livres for each *livre cadastral* of evaluation was imposed, that is, 28 livres for each 1,000 livres of capital value of real property, or 2.8 percent. This tax was not levied on personal property or on income. The actual amount of tax that an individual owning real property had to pay was determined by multiplying the number of *livres cadastral*, or fraction thereof, times 28. A tax rate of 2.8 percent was a heavy burden if the net return on arable land was a maximum of five percent.[95] In 1788, when Lourmarin had to raise 8,602 livres to pay its taxes, a tax of 34 livres per *livre cadastral* was levied, or 3.4 percent.[96]

Using the 1770 *cadastre* and the 2.8 percent levy in 1775, it is possible to determine the tax burden on individuals. Sieur Pierre Henri Joseph de Girard, Lourmarin's largest landholder after the seigneur, whose income could not have exceeded 2,700 livres, paid 388 livres, or about 14 percent of his income, in 1775. Barthelemy Reymond, *travailleur*, had an income that could not have exceeded 56 livres, but paid seven livres, about 13 percent of his income, on property valued at 249 livres.[97] The estimated village income for 1791, obtained by adding the revenue from real property in the 1791 *Contribution Foncière* to the estimated income from the textile industry in Appendix A, was about 63,000 livres. Lourmarin's payment of 8,602 livres for the 1788 *taille* represents a payment of about 14 percent of income in 1791.[98] This 14 percent figure, when compared to the payment of Girard and Reymond, underscores the fact that the *taille* was not progressive and undoubtedly Reymond had more difficulty paying than did Girard. Still, 14 percent is a long way from Taine's pessimistic conclusion about the effect of the burden of royal taxes on the rural population of the *ancien régime*, since Taine estimated the royal tax burden at over 50 percent of

[95] A. L. Lavoisier, *Oeuvres*, II (Paris, 1862), 816.

[96] *A.M.*, *D.M.*, May 4, 1788.

[97] Since the 1770 *Cadastre* did not record income, but only capital value of real property, the income quoted here comes from the 1791 *Contribution Foncière*. There are several uncertainties here—possible undervaluation in 1770, inaccuracies in revenue figures in 1791, increased income from the same land between 1775 and 1791—but it would appear that the tax bite in 1775 was slightly less than 15 percent.

[98] It must be emphasized that the figures upon which this computation is based come from different sources in different years and consequently the figure of 14 percent must be regarded as a rough approximation at best.

FIGURE IV-1. LOCAL TAILLE FOR LOURMARIN, 1730–45 AND 1770–90

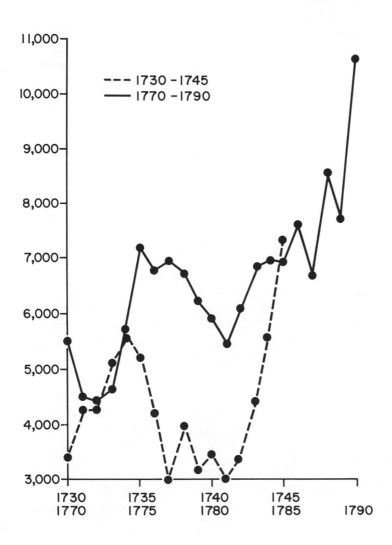

peasant income.[99] Recent historians have also emphasized how burdensome royal taxes were for the eighteenth-century peasant.[100]

It is not surprising that with so many different taxes, Lourmarin's council spent an inordinate amount of time devising ways to pay them. With the rather heavy payments to the seigneur, the church, and the king, as well as the many smaller expenses, it is to be wondered that there were no more complaints. Villagers may have grumbled over a glass of wine at the *Auberge du Cheval Blanc* or around their table at home, but very few complaints found their way into the municipal deliberations or other official documents. Perhaps this reflects the villagers' feeling that any attempts to effect fundamental changes were futile: it is certain that they never really challenged the principles of the *ancien régime*. On the other hand, much council time was spent evaluating villagers' requests to have their property valuation in the *cadastre* lowered.

The notables serving on the council were pragmatic, oriented toward the attainable. Accepting payments to the church and to the seigneur as a fact of life, they chose, probably wisely, to expend their energies in areas where they could hope to effect some change. Although they petitioned officials in Aix for a reduction in the village's royal assessment in vain, the council was more successful in its management of the *fermes*, a local matter which they could control in the interests of the inhabitants. If the council did not receive bids they liked, it was not unusual for them to "leave the *ferme* free" and hire someone to administer it in the name of the community.

Within the very real limitations imposed upon it, the council managed Lourmarin's economic affairs fairly well. It allocated its resources so as to provide certain services to all inhabitants of the village and showed a definite concern for the poor. If its accomplishments outside the village were small, and if its appeals were seldom heeded at Aix, it was more the fault of the system than of the municipal government.

[99] Hippolyte A. Taine, *The Ancient Régime*, trans. by John Durand (New York, 1888), pp. 412–13. Lourmarin's *capitation* for 1788 was 1,150 livres, which would increase the village's direct taxes to about 16 percent. *A.M., D.M.,* February 17, 1788. Even if indirect taxes are added in it is difficult to see how Lourmarin's royal tax burden could have been much over 20 percent.

[100] For example, Albert Soboul, *Précis d'histoire de la Révolution française* (Paris, 1962), p. 48, says that the direct taxes alone accounted for 28 percent in northeast France (Flanders) during the reign of Louis XVI. See also Ernest Labrousse, *Origines et aspects économiques et sociaux de la Révolution française. 1744–91*, I, "Les cours de Sorbonne" (Paris, 1946).

V

POOR RELIEF AND THE PLAGUE

I N ADDITION TO THE constant preoccupation with how best to manage the village's economy, the municipal government was also confronted with the perpetual problem of providing for Lourmarin's poor. The municipal deliberations give the distinct impression that Lourmarin's continuing commitment to its poor was caused primarily by humanitarian impulses, although self-interest also motivated the local *bourgeoisie,* which was determined to keep the poor pacified. Since neither Paris nor Aix provided a centralized, planned program for relief, the council relied on village resources to care for those Lourmarinois, particularly children and the elderly, who otherwise would not have survived.[1] Efforts to aid the poor were intensified in times of crop failure, severe weather, or the outbreak of contagious diseases, when the number of persons who needed relief naturally increased. In such times of particular hardship, it was necessary to supplement the council's resources by gifts or loans from the king, the seigneur, or the *bourgeoisie* of Lourmarin. Estimating that in a normal year 150 persons, or about ten percent of the population, received some type of

---

[1] For a discussion of the various sources of relief and their inadequacies in two northern French cities, see Olwen Hufton, *Bayeux in the Late Eighteenth Century: A Social Study* (London, 1967), pp. 81–112; Jeffry Kaplow, *Elbeuf during the Revolutionary Period: History and Social Structure* (Baltimore, 1964), pp. 100–101. See also Camille Bloch, *L'assistance et l'état en France à la veille de la Révolution (Généralités de Paris, Rouen, Alençon, Orléans, Chalons, Soissons, Amiens), 1764–1790* (Paris, 1908).

aid, it is necessary to examine the variety of ways by which Lourmarin provided relief to the poor.[2] To show how the village functioned in a crisis, this chapter will conclude with a discussion of the measures taken in 1720 against the outbreak of the plague in Provence.

Two more or less constant sources of poor relief were meat from the butcher and bread from the baker. We have seen how bidders for the butcher shop often offered to include in their leases a stipulated amount of meat that they agreed to provide free to the poor of the community. If the consuls authorized the butcher to provide more free meat than his lease required, he was reimbursed by the council. The baker's lease never required him to furnish free bread; however, he would give bread upon presentation of chits signed by a consul and later was reimbursed by the community. Times of crisis increased the demands for aid, of course, but there were always the "poor and sick" (*pauvres et pauvres malades*) who needed help in good times and bad. Consequently, the council often authorized aid to specific individuals, such as occurred in 1716 when approval was given for the "distribution of two loaves of bread per day to Etienne Pacot and his wife, both poor sick, because of their extreme poverty."[3]

Another regular and predictable source of relief for the poor was the six *charges* (30 bushels) of rye which a transaction of 1615 obligated the tithe-collector to donate to the village.[4] The *fermier* of the *dîme*, who was always a prominent Lourmarin citizen, gave his donation in rye and the community was responsible for "converting it into bread and distributing it to the poor at the door of the town hall" in the presence of the priest, the seigneur's agent, the consuls, and several other village notables.[5] Distribution occurred the weekend before Christmas, although in difficult times it could be given whenever the council deemed it necessary. Although the *fermier* received numerous requests for additional grain, he felt little obligation to the poor or to the community beyond furnishing the required six *charges* of grain. In fact, especially during the first half of the eighteenth century, the community was fortunate if the *fermier* furnished the six *charges*. Although six *charges* of rye did not satisfy the needs of the village

[2] On the general question of humanitarianism, see Shelby T. McCloy, *The Humanitarian Movement in Eighteenth Century France* (Lexington, Ky., 1957).

[3] *A.M., D.M.,* February 2, 1716.

[4] *A.D., Bouches-du-Rhône,* C 139-3927, 3928, April 15, 1731.

[5] *A.M., D.M.,* January 15, 1761, and *passim.*

poor, at least the grain did have the advantage of being distributed regularly and, insofar as Lourmarin had a plan for relief at all, they could count on this annual donation.

After 1718 Lourmarin also received income from the interest on 800 livres invested from a legacy established by Messire Raphael Girard, the village priest, who donated this sum to the poor of Lourmarin by "a pure and simple motive of charity."[6] Girard had been the vicar of a predominantly Protestant village during the difficult days after the Revocation of the Edict of Nantes and he seems to have been genuinely respected by all the villagers. Father Girard and his sister, who donated one-half of the capital, transferred 800 livres in promissory notes to the community, stipulating that the village was to use the interest, computed at five percent or 40 livres annually, "to aid the poor and ill." Distribution was to be made by the priest and the consuls.[7]

The capital of the Girard legacy was doubled in 1784 by a gift of 800 livres from Sieur Pierre Henri Joseph de Girard and Marie Anne, his unmarried sister.[8] These Girards were members of a prominent Catholic family but were not directly related to the former priest. Interest paid on the additional capital was to be distributed to the poor in exactly the same manner as the earlier bequest.

Marie Anne de Girard's share of 400 livres was left to the Girard Foundation in her will.[9] Four hundred livres was a very large sum to be included in a will, and its application to the Girard legacy was unusual, but the principle of leaving a part, however small, of one's earthly treasures to the poor was a long-established practice in Lourmarin. The most common bequest was in the form of either grain or money, and was usually distributed to the needy at the door of the deceased's house or at the town hall the Easter or Christmas after death.[10] Whether this was done because of a

---

[6] *Ibid.*, January 1, June 12, 1718.

[7] *Ibid.*

[8] *Ibid.*, November 21, 1784.

[9] *A.Not.*, Borrelly, July 5, 1784.

[10] For example, from 1741 to 1750 *notaire* Jacquier registered 94 wills, 60 percent of which made provision for payment of money or grain to the poor. *A.Not.*, Jacquier, 1741 to 1750, *passim*. From 1781 to 1785 an average of 12 wills were registered annually with the notary. Of these an average of two-thirds, or eight, provided money or grain for the poor. *A.Not.*, Borrelly, 1781 to 1785, *passim*.

genuine interest in the poor or as a last act of penance or as a combination of the two, legacies to the poor were extremely important supplements to the regular sources of relief funds. It must be emphasized, however, that this type of poor relief, although representing a considerable amount of grain and cash, was very irregular and could not form the basis of any systematic relief plan.

A less common bequest was made by Suzanne Tasquier, who designated the "poor of this place" as her universal heirs at her death in 1712. She left the poor 95 livres in cash and a small piece of land in a neighboring village which subsequently was sold.[11] The money realized from the sale of her land was combined with the 95 livres in cash and part of the sum was used to repair the village shelter house for the indigents. The remaining capital was invested and each year the community received an interest payment of three livres, 15 sous, which was used to carry out the terms of her will.[12]

The only charitable institution in Lourmarin, other than the church itself, was the shelter house for poor wayfarers (*maison des pauvres passants*). This small building was purchased in 1711 with a donation of 180 livres and the *fermier* of the seigneurial dues was instructed not to collect *lods* on the transfer.[13] Other donations, the Tasquier legacy, and tile from the tile maker were used to maintain this house, which also served as an infirmary for the poor.[14]

In times of particular hardship aid came from various other sources— royal aid through the Intendant, aid from Provence, aid from the seigneur. While much of this aid was earmarked for distribution to the indigent classes, in years such as 1709 and 1766 when there were very severe winters, monetary relief was given to the village as a whole. Poor harvests in 1712 forced the officials of Provence to buy foreign grain and distribute it to the villagers "in order to try to avoid famine and to combat the high prices which accompany the shortage of grain."[15] In their request for aid the consuls stated that Lourmarin needed at least 300 *charges* of grain in order to

---

[11] *A.Not.*, Chastroux, August 14, 1712.
[12] *A.M.*, *D.M.*, January 15, 1713, and *passim*.
[13] *Ibid.*, May 7, 1711.
[14] *Ibid.*, November 20, 1776, and *passim*.
[15] *Ibid.*, September 4, 1712.

avoid hardship in the village.[16] After a summer flood in 1726 washed away much of the spring planting, royal aid amounting to 700 livres was granted to the village.[17] A snow in 1728 was so heavy that it "has prevented the poor from working and consequently they cannot even earn enough to buy bread for their pressing needs and now they find themselves reduced to charity."[18] Immediate aid was forthcoming from the consuls and vicar and eventually the community received a gift of 250 livres from its seigneur with the promise of more if that amount should prove insufficient.[19]

From 1766 until his death in 1774 Louis XV, acting through his Intendant, was very generous to Provence and to Lourmarin in particular. The crown's annual donation varied from 500 to 900 livres, distribution being supervised by a committee of village notables.[20] In 1766 the consuls notified the Procurer in Aix that 37,424 of the 41,338 olive trees planted in the parish had been killed by the severe cold of the preceding winter.[21] The loss of 90 percent of the village's olive trees was a hard blow since the village depended upon the income from the sale of olive oil to help buy grain. Lourmarin produced only about one half of the wheat required to feed the villagers each year.[22] Soon new olive trees were planted and after a period of time began to produce once more, but disaster again struck in the winter of 1788–89.[23]

When times were hardest the priest and some of the well-to-do *bourgeois* came forward with offers of money or grain. For instance, in 1763–64 a poor harvest pushed the price of wheat up dramatically. Since the scarcity of grain had increased the price, the bakers threatened to raise the price of bread above the set tariff, arguing that they were losing money because of the inflated price they had to pay for grain. Pierre Henri de Girard offered to sell 130 *charges* of the grain stored in his granaries at the "former price in order to supply the needs of the community."[24] In addition to these and

---

[16] *Ibid.*
[17] *Ibid.*, June 23, 26, July 13, 1726.
[18] *Ibid.*, February 13, 1728.
[19] *Ibid.*, August 1, 1728.
[20] *Ibid.*, 1766 to 1774, *passim*.
[21] *A.D., Bouches-du-Rhône*, C 1177, September 15, 1766.
[22] See Appendix A, *État* of the Community, 1790.
[23] *A.D., Bouches-du-Rhône*, C 1177, May 30, 1789. See Chapter VIII for a discussion of the effects of this loss in the early days of the Revolution.
[24] *A.M., D.M.*, May 1, 1764.

other documented cases of aid from individuals, one can imagine many, many more instances of the villagers rallying to concerted action in times of crisis.[25]

Illegitimate children, foundlings, or indigent adults who became ill while away from Lourmarin utilized the facilities of hospitals in other communities at Lourmarin's expense. There was no real hospital in Lourmarin, nor are there any extant hospital records for the majority of Lourmarinois who did not use public funds. The care to be provided by the hospital at Aix or in neighboring communities was a constant source of friction, as was the question of who was to pay the bill.

Not wishing to incur the cost of hospital care, the council was loathe to admit any responsibility to contribute toward the care of indigents away from home. The council often argued, sometimes with justification, that persons claiming Lourmarin as their residence had, in actuality, never lived there. In 1771 the Hospital of St. Jacques in Aix demanded reimbursement for treating two ill men who said they were residents of Lourmarin.[26] The council refused to pay, arguing that one of the men had worked in the village only a few months while the other had lived in Lourmarin "only as a domestic." Furthermore, neither had been born in Lourmarin. Adjudication of this question continued through the winter with the council producing "expert" witnesses, including the priest, who testified that neither man was a resident of Lourmarin. The council lost its case, however, and in April, 1772, the community was forced to pay the hospital 68 livres.[27]

Although many examples are available, two unusual and unique cases involving public expenditures will be examined. Obviously both were *causes célèbres* in the village and tell more about the village and its attitudes than about the administration of poor relief. Nevertheless, they will give two concrete examples of how the council acted to resolve such problems.

It was reported to the council in May, 1759, that Rose Barthelemy was pregnant "the work of Joseph Grimand of Menèrbe," a village 50 miles

[25] Jeffry Kaplow has also found that, in the years just preceding the Revolution, certain wealthy inhabitants at Elbeuf rallied to the support of the poor of that city. Kaplow, *Elbeuf*, p. 101.

[26] *A.M., D.M.*, October 8, 1771.

[27] *Ibid.*, October 8, 1771 to April 15, 1772, *passim*.

northwest of Lourmarin.[28] Rose was sent to Avignon where she spent part of the summer consulting lawyers at community expense. The mayor, requesting funds for legal and medical expenses, said that "the honor of this poor girl must be restored."[29] When a baby was born in October to a still unwed Rose Barthelemy, the priest and Daniel Savornin, a wealthy *bourgeois*, together with a lawyer from Avignon, arranged a confrontation with the accused boy and his father "to make them give satisfaction to this poor girl as well as to repay the community [for its expenses]."[30] In December the mayor was able to announce with satisfaction that Grimand and Rose were now married.[31] There is no indication, however, that Lourmarin ever recovered its expenses.

Since illegitimacy and pre-marital conception were not foreign to Lourmarin, it is difficult to explain the keen community interest in Rose Barthelemy, the daughter of a relatively unimportant family. It is evident that the keen interest in this case was more than simply a fear that the village would have to bear the expenses of the baby's care. The answer may lie in the fact that Grimand was a "foreigner" who had brought dishonor on the entire village by his refusal to marry Rose, as well as a general disapproval of illegitimacy. From the tone of the proceedings in this instance, as well as in similar cases, it is obvious that the girl was not harshly stigmatized. The blame for pregnancy rested primarily upon the man.

The second example involved the only recorded homicide in Lourmarin, which was committed by Jean Barraud, 25-year old son of Jean Barraud, apothecary and respected member of the community. Jean was convicted of killing Anne Aguitton, 50, wife of André Anezin, "in his madness" on February 17, 1757, and was committed to the insane asylum in Aix.[32] Lourmarin was ordered to pay 250 livres per year for his care.[33] One would have to assume that the insane asylum's security system was a bit lax, since Barraud escaped in July, 1757, July, 1759, September, 1759, June, 1761, November, 1761, and January, 1764.[34] He was finally recaptured in March,

---

[28] *Ibid.*, May 20, 1759.
[29] *Ibid.*, July 29, 1759.
[30] *Ibid.*, October 21, 1759.
[31] *Ibid.*, December 26, 1759. The marriage had actually taken place on November 24, 1759. *A.M., R.P.Cath.*, November 24, 1759.
[32] *A.M., D.M.*, July 29, 1759, and *passim*.
[33] *Ibid.*
[34] *Ibid.*, 1757 to 1764, *passim*.

1764, and was condemned to be imprisoned and enchained for life in the insane asylum.[35] However, he managed to escpae twice again before his death in prison in August, 1769.

Barraud represented a considerable financial drain on the community, compounded by the added cost of apprehending him.[36] In 1759, after escaping from the asylum, he appeared in Lourmarin still dragging his chains and brandishing a gun and knife as he threatened to kill anyone who approached him.[37] The community had to pay four constables from a neighboring village to apprehend him. Barraud was periodically detained in the seigneurial prison, but this proved costly and nerve-racking because he broke all of the serving utensils and furniture in his cell. A mason had to be called in August, 1761, to clean up the debris in the prison and to repair the plaster Barraud had destroyed in his "great fury."[38] One can imagine that the news of Barraud's death was received in October, 1769, with a sense of relief. When informed of Barraud's death in Aix, the council minutes recorded simply: "The council approves the death of the said Barraud."[39] It is noteworthy, given what we know about the frugality of the council, that they never attempted to repudiate the community's debts to St. Jacques in Aix for Barraud's care.

The last great outbreak of plague in France began at Marseilles in the summer of 1720. The crisis lasted in Lourmarin until 1722, a two-year period whose dramatic events were not matched until the Revolution. An examination of the measures taken to insure the village's safety will show how the municipal council acted to arrive at decisions, sometimes painful, and to care for the poor, while trying to alleviate the terrible tensions produced by sealing off Lourmarin from the rest of France.

France had suffered before from the devastation of the plague. As the major southern port through which ships passed bound to and from North Africa and the Middle East, Marseilles had experienced the horrors of the

[35] *Ibid.*, March 4, 1764.
[36] As early as 1757, the council had proposed that the tax on wine be reinstituted and that the proceeds be used to support Barraud. *Ibid.*, April 3. 1757.
[37] *Ibid.*, July 29, September 1, 1759.
[38] *Ibid.*, August 16, 1761.
[39] *Ibid.*, October 1, 1769.

plague several times before and had instituted safeguards to prevent a recurrence. All ships were to be inspected, their cargoes quarantined on an island in the port, and any suspect goods confiscated. When the *Grand St. Antoine*, carrying goods from Syria, entered the port of Marseilles it was sent to this island. The ship's captain, Chabaud, submitted his cargo to the health commissioners and also reported the fact that seven sailors had died en route to Marseilles. The inspectors decided, however, that they had died from poor nutrition or inadequate hygiene and not from the plague.[40] There is clear evidence that several local officials had a financial interest in the cargo of the *Grand St. Antoine* and, wishing to avoid delays, conspired to unload contraband lengths of cloth without going through the customary procedures.[41] Unfortunately for the buyers, the merchandise was contaminated and in late June, 1720, the plague appeared and began to spread rapidly.[42]

Men died horrible deaths in the streets of Marseilles or in their rooms unattended.[43] Doctors, priests, and administrators made an heroic, albeit unsuccessful, attempt to contain the disease. Finally on August 1 a blockade of Marseilles was ordered.[44] A make-shift wall was built around the city and no one was allowed to enter or leave. Royal troops were stationed throughout southern France, particularly along the banks of rivers. The final result was that, unlike previous outbreaks, the 1720 epidemic was confined almost exclusively to Provence. The plague was especially severe in Marseilles, where perhaps 40,000 to 50,000, or about one half of the population, died, but Aix, Arles, and Toulon also lost between one-quarter and one half of their population, and most other Provençal communities felt its

[40] Jean-Noël Biraben, "Certain Demographic Characteristics of the Plague Epidemic in France, 1720–1722," *Daedalus,* XCVII (Spring, 1968), 536; Charles Mourre, "La peste de 1720 à Marseille et les intendants du bureau de santé," *Provence Historique,* XIV (April–June, 1963), 135–43.

[41] Biraben, "Demographic Characteristics of the Plague," p. 536; Mourre, "La peste de 1720," pp. 138–39.

[42] Biraben, "Demographic Characteristics of the Plague," pp. 536–40; Raoul Busquet, V. L. Bourrilly, and Maurice Agulhon, *Histoire de la Provence* (Paris, 1966), p. 78; Masson, *Les temps modernes,* pp. 117–19.

[43] The first death, on June 28, 1720, was that of a tailor who had bought the prohibited cloth. The plague spread rapidly and by early August beggars and convicts had to be conscripted to bury the dead. Of the 217 convicts conscripted in August to bury the dead, only 12 remained alive by September 1. Biraben, "Demographic Characteristics of the Plague," pp. 536–38.

[44] *Ibid.,* p. 539.

effects.[45] Abbé Expilly estimated that 170,000 persons, one-quarter of the population, died in Provence, although Paul Masson thinks that this figure is too high. A conservative estimate is that between one-sixth and one-fifth of the population of Provence died from the plague between 1720 and 1722.[46]

Lourmarin first learned of the trouble to the south in a letter sent to the village by Seigneur Bruny on August 4, 1720.[47] Bruny informed them that because the plague had appeared in Marseilles, the Parlement at Aix had forbidden all commerce with that city: the Lourmarinois were warned to stay away from Marseilles.

The council discussed the situation in Marseilles at a meeting of August 12 and reviewed the measures taken when the plague occurred at Toulon in 1664. The council established a Bureau of Health which operated independently of the regular council, although some *bourgeois* served on both concurrently. During the next 18 months the Bureau met each Tuesday, Thursday, and Saturday at noon to consider questions dealing specifically with the plague while the council continued to concern itself with other village business. The Bureau of Health kept its own minutes and named six Intendants of Health to assist the consuls, who served on both bodies.[48] The priest, Messire Girard, and the seigneur's agent were usually two of the Intendants. Because it was crucial that Lourmarin be protected from the plague, the Bureau of Health was granted extraordinary authority which it then exercised until the plague was contained in 1722. Most major decisions during the two-year period originated with the Bureau of Health rather than with the municipal government.[49]

The Bureau was responsible for issuing *billets de santé* authorizing travel outside Lourmarin. Since most other villages in Provence had similar regulations designed to prevent the plague from spreading, *billets* were necessary if one wanted to move from one place to another. In January, 1721,

[45] *Ibid.*, pp. 541–43; Baehrel, *Une croissance*, pp. 267–69.
[46] Masson, *Provence*, pp. 17–19; Masson, *Les temps modernes*, pp. 117–29.
[47] *A.M.*, *D.M.*, August 4, 1720.
[48] *Ibid.*, August 12, 1720, and *passim*. The minutes of the Bureau of Health and the village council were both kept in the same book from 1720 to 1722. For this reason footnote references to these two groups of minutes will both be listed simply as *D.M.*
[49] *Ibid.*, September 22, November 17, 1720, and *passim*.

the Bureau ordered 1,000 *billets* printed in Avignon reading "M.——, thanks to God has no suspicion of the plague nor any other contagious disease."[50] Jean Roman, dyer, was imprisoned for 40 days and was fined 25 livres for traveling to Bonnieux without a *billet*. Some Bureau members argued that he should not be fined but the fine was allowed to stand because Roman "could afford it" and the money "is to be used to help the poor and will serve as an example to others."[51]

In early September, 1720, the villagers began to repair existing gates, which had served no functional purpose for the past 50 years, and built others.[52] The gates were all erected by November 18 and the Bureau ordered that since Lourmarin, unlike several neighboring villages, was not walled, the doors of every house, apartment, and other structure facing the outside of the village were to be closed permanently while all windows would be boarded up.[53] Guards were stationed at the various gates in Lourmarin's temporary wall and were to admit only those who had *billets*. To further protect the village, admission of those persons with valid *billets* had to be authorized by the consuls. The village gates were closed from 5:00 P.M. to 6:00 A.M. and could be opened during these hours only upon authorization by the Captain of the Guard. There was a fine of 25 livres (distributed to the poor) for disturbing the guard at night.[54]

In mid-November a General Council authorized the establishment of a *Garde Bourgeoise* and appointed six Captains and six Lieutenants of the *Garde* to oversee the village militia which was on duty day and night.[55] One captain and one lieutenant were assigned to each of the six sections of the village and were to draw up a list of all families who lived in each section. Visiting each section daily, they were to check each family and if the guards discovered any new persons or any merchandise purchased elsewhere, they were to inform the Bureau. Should they see anyone ill or dead, they were to notify the Bureau so that a doctor could be called. Fearing that

---

[50] *Ibid.*, August 23, 1720, January 9, 16, July 3, 1721. The period of the plague was one of the very few times in the eighteenth century in which mention was made of the deity in any kind of official document. And even these scattered instances, always in a time of crisis, seem perfunctory.

[51] *Ibid.*, May 7, 1721.

[52] *Ibid.*, September 1, 1720.

[53] *Ibid.*, November 18, 1720.

[54] *Ibid.*, November 18, 27, 1720.

[55] *Ibid.*, November 17, 1720.

it might be difficult to obtain needed goods, the council made each of the six captains responsible for setting aside a two-month supply of "wood, oil, wine, salt, vinegar, and wheat" for his section. In addition to the lieutenants and captains, six *bourgeois* inspectors were also named to supervise each section.[56] Most of the guards served without pay except for a few from among the *travailleur* class who received ten sous per day. Serving on the *Garde Bourgeoise* was a volunteer duty and the guards' vigilance might be the difference between life and death.

Obviously the Bureau was suspicious of any illness in the village and many families were quarantined, usually for 40 days. In most cases a quarantined family was required to pay the cost of posting two guards at their home.[57] At a February 27, 1721, meeting the Bureau decided that each head of family should assume the responsibility for reporting any illness in his family to one of the consuls, who would then dispatch a doctor to investigate and quarantine the house if necessary. Once a house had been declared off-limits anyone who entered was fined 100 livres, to be used for poor relief.[58] Less than a month later Sieur Pierre Sambuc, surgeon, investigated the death of Pierre Goulin's widow and concluded that she died of "natural causes" and not the plague.[59] As a precautionary measure the Bureau ordered that Anne Mille and Martha Goulin, the dead woman's sister and daughter, be confined to their house for 40 days. After making sure that the two women had enough wine, cooking oil, and other supplies, they called in a mason who plastered up the front door and window facing the street to prevent contact with any of the villagers.[60]

The Marquis d'Argenson was sent to northern Provence in September, 1720, to command the king's brigade and organize a defensive line against the spread of the plague. On September 4, 1720, d'Argenson requested that Lourmarin dispatch "six men, armed and with sufficient powder and food" to guard the northern bank of the Durance.[61] They were ordered to shoot to kill any unauthorized person who attempted to cross the river. The Lourmarinois voted to pay their guards 20 sous per day and in order not

[56] *Ibid.*, November 30, 1720.
[57] For example, see *ibid.*, March 12, 27, 31, 1721.
[58] *Ibid.*, February 17, 1721.
[59] *Ibid.*, March 15, 1721.
[60] *Ibid.*
[61] *Ibid.*, September 8, 1720.

to interfere too much with the harvest, the six were replaced weekly. By January, 1721, a *cordon sanitaire* around Provence employed one-third of the infantry and one-fourth of the cavalry of the entire French army.[62]

The many demands the threatening plague made on human and monetary resources were indeed a heavy burden on the village and the municipal council justifiably complained that compared to Cadenet, which was walled, Lourmarin needed "a great number of men to guard the several gates and barricades that have been placed on all the approaches to this place."[63] Eleven more men were needed for militia service and the village was required to house a detachment of 65 royal troops in November, 1720.[64] By the end of the year the plague had struck the villages of Cucuron and Bonnieux, both within ten miles of Lourmarin, and more troops were needed to blockade them.[65] The financial burden on the village was further increased when, in addition to the regular annual district levy, the authorities at Apt demanded 800 livres to pay the troops manning a supplementary line to the north.[66]

Village regulations were tested on October 10, 1720, when Anne Sambuc, daughter of Pierre Sambuc, *bourgeois* and mayor in 1720, and wife of Sieur Jean Ailhaud, a doctor from Pertuis, a village southeast of Lourmarin, appeared at the village's gates accompanied by three sons, two daughters, and a wet-nurse and asked for permission to stay with her father. The Bureau of Health denied her request; instead the family was quarantined for 40 days in a small house on the road to Cadenet and was guarded day and night.[67] The 40 days ended November 20 and the guards reported to the council that "by the grace of God they are all healthy."[68] Anne Sambuc and her family were allowed to enter the village and went to live in Sambuc's comfortable town house. By applying the regulations to the daughter of the mayor, the Bureau notified the villagers that no one would be exempted from these stringent rules.

[62] Mourre, "La peste de 1720," p. 136.
[63] *A.M.*, *D.M.*, September 22, 1720.
[64] *Ibid.*, November 3, 1720; February 3, 1721.
[65] *Ibid.*, December 3, 25, 1720; January 1, 5, 1721.
[66] *Ibid.*, October 20, 23, 28; November 2, 1721; January 18, 1722.
[67] *Ibid.*, October 10, 1720.
[68] *Ibid.*, November 20, 1720.

It was essential that the villagers have enough to eat since they could die of starvation as well as from the plague, and as the winter became more severe, the Bureau pleaded with the villagers to help the poor. At least 76 persons appeared at the Bureau meeting on January 3, 1721, and each agreed to contribute sufficient wheat to feed two or three poor during the winter.[69] The council also took up a collection for the poor to which was added the fines collected from those violating the Bureau of Health's regulations.[70] Much of the money was spent for poor relief but 362 livres still remained in the fund in June, 1721, and the council decided that "since God in His infinite mercy has spared us and has allowed us to hope that He will continue to favor us if we throw ourselves on His divine protection," the money will be saved and used in the future to "succor the poor if God should again afflict us with the plague." If Lourmarin were spared, the money would be kept "in perpetuity" and used for poor relief.[71]

In October, 1720, the council decreed that inns and taverns could not serve food or drink after 9:00 at night during the week and might not serve at all on Sunday "during the time of the contagious plague." A fine of ten livres was to be levied against an offending innkeeper, and patrons found there after the curfew were fined three livres.[72] Throughout the entire period after 1680, there are only a few recorded incidents of physical violence in Lourmarin. The majority occurred between 1720 and 1722, indicating the tension which existed in the village. Shortly after ten o'clock on the evening of January 18, 1721, Jean Chauvin, mason, and Joseph Monge, assigned to the guard for that night, entered the inn of Jean Aguitton and found that he was still selling wine. When the guards attempted to close the tavern, Barthelemy Vien, Claude Danizot, and Augustin Richier, three somewhat inebriated *travailleurs*, attacked them with rocks and bottles. During the ensuing scuffle Vien allegedly told Chauvin that if he had a gun he would kill him.[73] The next day all of the principals appeared to testify before the Bureau of Health whose members, because of the forced confinement of the village, were understandably alarmed. But

[69] *Ibid.*, January 3, 1721.
[70] *Ibid.*
[71] *Ibid.*, June 25, 1721.
[72] *Ibid.*, October 2, 1720.
[73] *Ibid.*, January 19, 1721.

they decided not to press charges against the three after the offenders apologized and said that they had meant no harm.[74]

Tension was evident again in November when Jacques Vial, *bourgeois*, one of the Captains of the Guard, was attacked by François Caire, apprentice of Antoine Jean, master hatmaker. Caire was apprehended while stealing wood and threatened to hit Vial with his ax. Two guardsmen restrained Caire and arraigned him before the Bureau of Health. Holding Jean responsible for his apprentice's actions, the Bureau sentenced Jean to serve 20 days in the seigneurial prison and fined him 20 livres.[75]

Tension reached a peak in early 1721 because the villagers expected daily to learn that the plague was among them. At this inopportune moment Sieur Silvy, priest and resident of La Tour d'Aigues, arrived with an entourage at the gates of Lourmarin. Silvy introduced two old issues, religious and seigneurial, at a time when the village was fighting for its survival. Silvy handed the Captain of the Guard a letter from the seigneur requesting "the Council of Lourmarin to admit Monseigneur Silvy and his followers who have come to perform a baptism."[76] The Bureau, headed by Mayor Henri de Girard, an old Catholic, met hurriedly in the town hall while Silvy waited *outside* the gate. They decided "to plead very humbly with Monsieur le Baron de La Tour d'Aigues to be strongly persuaded of the submission and the profound respect that we have for him and to receive kindly, if it pleases him, our refusal to admit Sieur Silvy."[77] Supporting its decision, the Bureau said that the seigneur's letter asked admission for Silvy alone and furthermore that "the pretext of the baptism that Silvy will perform is a hoax since there is no infant in this parish to be baptised."[78]

At this point more must be said of Lourmarin's quiet and kindly *curé*, Messire Raphael Girard, who came to Lourmarin from Pertuis in the 1680's and immediately inherited the religious problems engendered by the Revocation of the Edict of Nantes. Messire Girard handled his difficult assign-

---

[74] *Ibid.*, February 15, 1721.

[75] *Ibid.*, November 28, 1721.

[76] *Ibid.*, February 18, 1721.

[77] Jean-Baptiste de Bruny, seigneur of Lourmarin, had purchased the neighboring village of La Tour d'Aigues shortly before he acquired Lourmarin. He began to use the title of baron attached to La Tour d'Aigues even before his son formally assumed it in 1742. See Chapter VI for a discussion of the Bruny family.

[78] *A.M., D.M.*, February 18, 1721.

ment well and earned the affection of all Lourmarinois, Protestant and Catholic alike.[79] Feeling that his primary goal was to restore the community spirit damaged when the government moved against the Protestant majority in the village, Girard did not attempt to enforce all of the restrictions against the Protestants and *nouveaux convertis* and he evidently chose to overlook the lack of religious zeal displayed by many of his parishioners. Although he encouraged the Catholic minority to support their church, evidently he did not actively proselytize among the Protestants, attempting to maintain a delicate balance between religious fervor on one hand and the best interests of the community on the other. This compromise was undisturbed prior to Lourmarin's purchase by Seigneur Bruny. But the newly ennobled seigneur, aware of the religious history of Lourmarin, decided to send Silvy to enforce Catholic observances, particularly the baptism of those suspected of Protestant leanings. It is not clear why he chose this worst of all possible times to send Silvy, who was certainly not a very diplomatic courier. Denied entrance by the municipal council, Silvy returned in a rage to La Tour d'Aigues and informed the Baron of the insufferable insubordination of his village.

Having persuaded Bruny that he should stand firm, Silvy reappeared at the gates on May 9. This time he obviously had no intention of suffering the indignity of standing outside the barricades and debating with the village elders. He pushed the guards aside, refused to show a *billet de santé*, and shouted that the Intendants of the Bureau of Health were "rabble."[80] Despite entreaties to lower his voice, his tirade continued as he marched down the main street until he was confronted by the *curé* and the *viguier*. Silvy, still "full of anger," shouted at the *curé* that "you will pay for this in heaven. You have not baptized as you should and I have come here to correct your deficiencies." Girard tried to calm him, but he continued his "slander and menacing gestures" which he punctuated by "swearing in the name of God" and threatening Girard. In the face of this threat the Bureau met and agreed to write to their seigneur that the scandalous actions of Silvy were a clear threat to local authority and "like cases cannot

---

[79] In his will Girard made several charitable bequests to the poor of Lourmarin and left his extensive library and *prie dieu* to M. Figuière, his assistant. *A.Not.*, Jacquier, February 28, 1729.

[80] *A.M., D.M.*, May 10, 1721.

be tolerated."[81] Although the village was predominantly Protestant, the municipal government rallied behind their priest to repel the Catholic representative sent by their seigneur.

As Lourmarin entered the winter still under seige all of the safeguards and precautions established in 1720 were continued. Since it was necessary to insure that the villagers did not eat contaminated meat, the already strict rules regulating the butcher were tightened. All villagers were required to sell their animals to the local butcher; under no circumstances were they permitted to sell meat to "foreigners."[82] Only the butcher was allowed to kill and sell meat, which first was inspected and certified safe by a local committee of experts appointed by the Bureau.[83] The Bureau demonstrated that it intended to enforce its regulations when it sentenced Jacques Etienne to one month in the seigneurial prison and fined him ten livres for slaughtering a sheep.[84]

In August, 1721, the Bureau of Health discovered that the local butcher, Jean Antoine Anezin, was selling mutton which had not been inspected. Instead of fining Anezin, the Bureau confiscated 13 of his sheep, sold them, and gave the proceeds to the poor.[85] Furious because his sheep had been seized, in November Anezin appeared at the home of inspector Jean Monbrion at two o'clock in the morning and demanded that Monbrion inspect a sheep he was preparing to slaughter. Not surprisingly, Monbrion refused his services "at such an indecent hour." Anezin slaughtered the sheep anyway and sold the meat to Pierre Tertian, proprietor of the *Auberge de la Croix d'Or*. The meat was contaminated and a three-sided argument between Anezin, Tertian, and Monbrion ensued because Tertian felt he had been tricked into buying unfit meat. The Bureau of Health reprimanded Anezin and sent all the details to d'Argenson.[86]

Most of Lourmarin's restrictive measures continued as late as June, 1722. The Bureau met regularly, reviewing its efforts to control the plague and making provision to keep a surgeon on permanent duty. At a meeting of June 12 it was reported that the preceding night three soldiers had appeared

---

[81] *Ibid.*
[82] *Ibid.*, January 25, 1721.
[83] *Ibid.*, February 14, 1721.
[84] *Ibid.*, March 29, 1721.
[85] *Ibid.*, August 8, 1721.
[86] *Ibid.*, November 15, 1721.

at the village gates without *billets de santé* and were immediately put in the seigneurial prison.[87] But this was the last time the prison was used during the plague, and by harvest time the village had almost returned to normal.

It would be impossible to calculate the expenses, psychological as well as economic, which the plague caused Lourmarin. The only total figures available, calculated in March, 1722, set Lourmarin's expenditures, primarily for supplying and paying the militia and its own guards, at just under 12,000 livres.[88] Many expenses, of courses, were not included in this figure; in January, 1721, alone the village spent 408 livres just to erect doors and walls.[89] It is clear that a substantial burden fell on the villagers and that the village's regular expenditures were at least doubled during these two years. But the cost to Lourmarin must also be measured in terms of the disruption of normal village life. Lourmarin was fortunate because the plague never actually struck the village, due in part to the tight security measures taken, but also to a great deal of luck since the plague did strike several nearby villages.[90] Emotions often ran high and the animosities which surfaced during the period of forced confinement brought violence to a peak and must have lingered for many years, but despite the continuing financial and emotional problems, the Lourmarinois breathed more easily as 1722 drew to an end.

The events surrounding Lourmarin's successful attempt to ward off the plague have demonstrated the vitality of the village. Fortunately Lourmarin was not called upon to meet another such emergency until the era of the French Revolution. Records of the plague years show how the village cared for its less fortunate inhabitants although no "grand design" emerges from the council minutes. Doggedly pragmatic, the village council, whether in an average year or during the trying months of 1720–21, managed to finance a program of poor relief which at least kept the indigent classes alive. We must not judge their actions by our own present-day standards.

---

[87] *Ibid.*, June 12, 1722.

[88] *A.D., Bouches-du-Rhône*, C 936, March 24, 1722.

[89] *A.M., D.M.*, July 13, 1721.

[90] Lourmarin fortunately was spared the tales of ghostly moaning said to come from the mass graves in Cucuron and other nearby villages. Jean-Baptiste Castel, *Histoire de Cucuron: Period de la peste de 1720 à 1730* (Cucuron, n.d.), p. 37.

The eighteenth century was the era of the Enlightenment with its preach-
ments about the dignity of each individual, but it was also a time when
poverty and famine were accepted as the common fate of the poorer classes.
Since the Lourmarinois lacked a centrally-directed program of "rehabilita-
tion," we can hardly condemn them for meeting each crisis as it occurred
and the village council's minutes evince a deep, consistent commitment, if
not to all of humanity, at least to the less fortunate of Lourmarin.

VI

THE SEIGNEUR

LOURMARIN'S MAGNIFICENT Renaissance chateau did not house a resident seigneur during the eighteenth century; instead of living in the village, the lord chose an agent to represent him and to manage and protect his seigneurial interests while he lived elsewhere. The history of the eighteenth century in Lourmarin would be much more exciting if serious conflicts and struggles had occurred between the seigneur and his village. The truth, however, is that there was no confrontation between the two which might have produced feelings of hatred or deep resentment before the Revolution, although it would be equally wrong to depict the relationship between seigneur and village as idyllically paternal-filial. The Lourmarinois might best be described as overtly respectful. Accepting the class structure of the eighteenth century, the village seldom challenged the lord's authority directly. Yet, as it did in its relations with *any* superior authority, the village stood ready to defend its rights, both collectively and individually. If any one word can capture Lourmarin's attitude toward its seigneur, the word would be "adaptability."

Although Lourmarin maintained a deferential air of formal respect and affection toward the seigneur up to the Revolution, disputes between the two parties increased after 1750 and official mention of the last seigneur became more rare after Jean-Baptiste Jérôme de Bruny succeeded his father in 1772. The degree of sincere affection that the village displayed toward François de Bruny, seigneur from 1723 to 1772, was not transferred to his son. It appears that M. le President, as Jean-Baptiste Jérôme was known after 1775, immersed himself in the political machinations of the Parlement in Aix where he was councillor. Except for ceremonial occasions, there were few contacts between the seigneur and his village. Does lessening contact mean diminished loyalty? Once the Revolution and the National Assembly had upset the accepted structure of the *ancien régime*, Lourmarin was quick to assert its new-found independence against its former seigneur.

The village's concept of its relationship to the seigneur is clarified by the multitude of entries in the council minutes. Other documents relating to the seigneurie are in the departmental archives at Marseilles and Avignon, as well as in the Musée Calvet at Avignon. The notarial archives in Lourmarin, which are quite complete, shed light on the kinds of leases entered into by the seigneur, but since he was not often at Lourmarin, many of the leases concerning the seigneur's property in the village were drafted elsewhere and unfortunately are not available.

Since the seigneur did not live in Lourmarin, he was represented by his agent (*viguier*). Often the *viguier* was a local notable, but even when he was an outsider, he was accepted more or less enthusiastically by the village leaders as one of their own. Of course he immediately became involved with all village business since he attended the meetings of the village council, but his main functions were to manage the affairs of the seigneur, to protect his interests, and to see that all of the seigneur's rights including payments in money or kind, were observed. An interesting note of continuity was that the major agent of the seigneurie remained the same during three transfers of the property, from the Duchesse de Les Diguières to the Duc de Villeroy and from the Duc to Jean-Baptiste de Bruny.[1]

Three members of the Bruny family held the seigneurie of Lourmarin from 1719 to the Revolution. As will be explained briefly below, the Brunys are an example of a *bourgeois* family that made its fortune in commerce, used this money to buy a seigneurie, and eventually moved into the local *parlement*. Pierre Bruny, the first important member of the family, was born in 1615 in Toulon and moved to Marseilles to engage in com-

---

[1] *A.M.*, *D.M.*, May 7, 1711, July 19, 1713, September 6, 1716, January 24, 1717, September 17, 1719.

merce around 1650.[2] One of his two surviving sons, Jean-Baptiste Bruny, born about 1661, inherited his father's wealth and became a *négociant,* banker, and manufacturer, established soap factories at Marseilles, and by the end of the seventeenth century was the richest man in Marseilles.[3]

FIGURE VI–1. THE JEAN-BAPTISTE DE BRUNY FAMILY IN THE EIGHTEENTH CENTURY

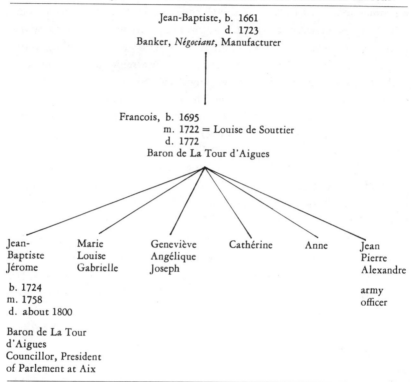

Jean-Baptiste, b. 1661
d. 1723
Banker, *Négociant,* Manufacturer

Francois, b. 1695
m. 1722 = Louise de Souttier
d. 1772
Baron de La Tour d'Aigues

| Jean-Baptiste Jérome | Marie Louise Gabrielle | Geneviève Angélique Joseph | Cathérine | Anne | Jean Pierre Alexandre |

b. 1724
m. 1758
d. about 1800

army
officer

Baron de La Tour
d'Aigues
Councillor, President
of Parlement at Aix

SOURCE: Joseph Didiée, "Notes bibliographiques," *Académie de Vaucluse,* XVII (1917), p. 227.

In 1697 Jean-Baptiste Bruny became a municipal officer (*échevin*) in Marseilles and shortly thereafter purchased La Tour d'Aigues, the first and most important seigneurie in his "valley." The purchase price of 900,000 livres included a chateau, built about 1500, one of whose towers dated from

[2] See Figure VI–1 for a genealogical chart of the Bruny family.
[3] Masson, *Provence,* pp. 340–41.

the eleventh century.[4] The beauty of this huge walled chateau is still evident today although it was sacked and burned by angry peasants during the Revolution and only vestiges of its former magnificence remain.[5] The Brunys' holdings in their "valley" were later expanded to include several other villages bounded on the north by the massive, forbidding Luberon Mountain and by the Durance River on the south.

The westernmost village in the Luberon valley, about 12 miles from La Tour d'Aigues, was Lourmarin. Bruny purchased the property of Lourmarin for 314,075 livres in August, 1719, from the Duc de Villeroy, who had inherited the seigneurie from his mother-in-law, the Duchesse de Les Diguières.[6] The document recording the sale described the buyer as "noble Jean-Baptiste Bruny, écuyer."[7] The Bruny family was still living in Marseilles in 1719 and it was not until 1742 that they finally abandoned commerce, bought an elegant town house in Aix, and assumed the title attached to the barony of La Tour d'Aigues.[8] Having built a strong economic and social base, the Brunys became active in Provençal politics in the second half of the eighteenth century and the last Baron before the Revolution was a councillor in the Parlement at Aix.[9]

The exactions made by Lourmarin's seigneurs were based on an agreement signed April 28, 1523, between Seigneuresse Dame Louise d'Agoult and the villagers which recognized the municipal organization of Lourmarin and spelled out the inhabitants' obligations vis-à-vis their seigneur.[10] This pact governed relations between the two parties until the Revolution.[11]

[4] *Ibid.*, p. 341; Joseph Didiée, "Notes bibliographiques," *Académie de Vaucluse,* XVII (1917), 227–29.

[5] Masson, *Provence,* p. 437.

[6] *M.C.*, 4580 fo. 124, August 4, 1719.

[7] *Ibid.*

[8] Didiée, "Notes," pp. 227–32. From an examination of records concerning the Brunys, however, it would appear that they began using the title of Baron de La Tour d'Aigues much earlier than 1742.

[9] Michel Vovelle has used the Brunys as an example, not uncommon in Provence, of a family that passed "not only from commoner to nobility, from commerce to the Parlement, but from Marseilles to Aix . . . and to the chateaus of the Luberon." Vovelle, "État présent des études de structure agraire en Provence," p. 80.

[10] *M.C.*, 4580, fo. 1, August 14, 1497; Mathieu Varille, *Lourmarin de Provence, capitale du Luberon* (Lyons, 1967), p. 16; *A.M., D.M., passim.*

[11] Fragments of this document were translated into French from the original Latin in the early eighteenth century and the council often referred to the agreement when defending the collective rights of the community. Unfortunately this document no longer exists.

Discussions of the seigneur's rights occurred throughout the eighteenth century in various documents, including the 1719 contract which recorded the sale of Lourmarin to Bruny. The best surviving description of the seigneurie of Lourmarin occurs in a copy of a 1739 report to the Intendant at Aix discussing the seigneur's rights with relation to the inhabitants of Lourmarin. The village council carefully entered a copy of the report in the council minutes.[12] Rather complete and useful enumerations of the seigneur's rights are also recorded in the minutes of November 10, 1704, and in an extract of a document sent to Aix in 1731 to protest a recently enacted increase in Lourmarin's tax levy.[13]

Attached to the seigneurie were three monopolies (*banalités*) governing the ovens, grain mills, and olive oil press. In Provence there was no tradition of attaching a monopoly to the seigneur's wine press although it could be, and usually was, used by the inhabitants.[14] During the eighteenth century all persons were required to bake their bread in the seigneur's ovens, grind their grain in his grist mills, and use his press to extract oil from their olives. The millers, who were the seigneur's employees, retained one-sixteenth of all grain brought to them for grinding into flour while the oven-keepers, as their charge for baking dough into bread (*droit de fournage*), were allowed one-fortieth of the bread.[15] These monopolies were routine in eighteenth-century France, and although the charges were higher in Lourmarin than the average for Provence, they were not the subject of any particular protest prior to the Revolution. Baehrel says that millers in Provence normally received between one-twentieth and one-fiftieth of the grain; the figure in the village of Charleval was one-twentieth.[16] Baehrel also says that the charge for using the seigneur's oven in three-quarters of the 36 villages he studied was one-twentieth or less.[17] The one-sixteenth charged by the miller in Lourmarin was rather high, although the charge for *fournage* was about average.

[12] *A.M., D.M.*, October 16, 1739.

[13] *Ibid.*, November 10, 1704; *A.D., Bouches-du-Rhône*, C 139-3927, April 15, 1731.

[14] Baehrel, *Une croissance*, p. 334.

[15] See Chapter III for a discussion of the relationship between the seigneur's oven-keeper and the village *fermier* who provided fire-wood and stoked the oven fires.

[16] Baehrel, *Une croissance*, pp. 333–35; Theus, *Charleval*, p. 118.

[17] Baehrel, *Une croissance*, pp. 333–35.

In return for the above payments to the seigneur the villager received a tangible service even if he might occasionally complain, as he did in 1704, that the oven-keeper was taking more than his share of bread.[18] The council, reviewing the transaction of 1523, complained that the miller was also overcharging the villagers by not furnishing the stipulated amount of flour after grinding. The *viguier* issued instructions that criminal action would be instituted against the miller if he were found guilty of cheating the inhabitants by giving them less flour by weight than required.[19] Complaints about the services provided by the oven-keeper were renewed in 1724 and the council succeeded in having him replaced.[20] There were other complaints during the century against specific abuses associated with these monopolies, but otherwise they seem to have been accepted as a fact of life and the villagers never challenged the seigneur's basic rights.

The inhabitants of Lourmarin were also required to give a part of each harvest to the seigneur as payment of the *tasque*, the Provençal equivalent of the *champart*. The charge in Lourmarin, one-eighth, was applied to all cereal grains, vegetables, grapes, olives, hemp, almonds, and other nuts produced in the seigneurie.[21] The figure of one-eighth was heavy. Baehrel has examined the payment of the *tasque* in Provence and has found other rates as low as one twenty-second. For example, the rate at Charleval was between one-tenth and one-fifteenth although rates in some villages were occasionally as high as one-sixth. The charge at Baux varied from one-eighth to one-fifteenth depending upon the commodity.[22]

A much less significant item in the seigneur's revenue, but an important recognition of his position, was the *cens*. Fixed charges in money or kind, the *cens* were set forth in the 1523 transaction. Since collection of the *cens* varied greatly from one place to another in Provence, it is impossible to make any generalizations.[23] According to Theus, the situation in Lourmarin, which had a multitude of different *cens*, was unusual because elsewhere the *cens* was usually applied to only one item, such as land or houses.[24] In con-

---

[18] *A.M., D.M.*, November 10, 1704.

[19] *Ibid.*

[20] *Ibid.*, May 21, 1724.

[21] *Ibid.*, October 16, 1739.

[22] Baehrel, *Une croissance*, pp. 336–38; Theus, *Charleval*, pp. 108–10; Cornée, *Baux-en-Provence*, pp. 105–6.

[23] Baehrel, *Une croissance*, pp. 335–36.

[24] Theus, *Charleval*, pp. 106–7.

trast to other taxes and dues, the charge for the *cens* was nominal in all of the villages in Provence, including Lourmarin.

In Lourmarin the *cens* charge was five deniers for each bushel of olives taken to the olive press for conversion into oil and eight deniers for each quart of wine extracted from grapes taken to the wine-press in the cellar (*cave*).[25] Various other *cens* payments based on the 1523 transaction depended on the amount of property held by an individual. For example, there was an annual payment of one denier for each *éyminé* of grain land and two deniers for each *éyminé* of orchard.[26] Reflecting the premium placed on it, the Lourmarinois paid a *cens* of five deniers for each *éyminé* of meadowland. These payments were certainly small and support the generally held view that by the eighteenth century the various *cens* payments were more of a nuisance and a reminder of the seigneur's authority than an actual burden on the peasant. At least compared to other obligations that the villagers had to pay, the *cens* payments were minor. The seigneur also had the right to collect *cens* on all buildings and enclosed property (*bien enclavé*) within the seigneurie. He was to receive two chickens (*poulets*) for each garden in Lourmarin and two young hens (*gelines*) for each house. In addition he received one young hen for each courtyard, stable, and auxiliary building. One must assume that in 1523 this tax was paid in kind, but by the eighteenth century (and possibly much earlier) the villagers were permitted to pay all *cens* in cash.

The seigneur had many other rights including the collection of *lods*, a mutation fee, on all land transactions in the seigneurie at the rate of one-sixth, a rate which would have discouraged most land exchange. Baehrel says that one-sixth was the upper limit of the *lods* charge and that the range was between one-sixth and one-twelfth with some communities paying even less.[27] Theus says one-twelfth was normal for Provence, while at Charleval the *lods* charge was one-tenth and at Baux one-eighth.[28] Marion agrees that in general *lods* were collected at one-twelfth throughout France and that

---

[25] These *cens* rates are estimates based on conversions of eighteenth-century Lourmarin measurements of uncertain accuracy. For additional information on the *cens,* see *A.M., D.M.,* November 10, 1704, and *passim.*

[26] One *éyminé* equals .15 acres; therefore, the tax on one acre of grain land would be six and one-half deniers.

[27] Baehrel, *Une croissance,* p. 338.

[28] Theus, *Charleval,* p. 110; Cornée, *Baux-en-Provence,* p. 107.

in no area did the seigneur receive *more* than one-sixth. He also says, however, that it had become the practice for the seigneur voluntarily to reduce this mutation fee in the eighteenth century.[29]

Among the myriad of other rights, there was an annual "personal levy" of two sous on each family head. Each person who owned two draft animals was required to plow one day in the seigneur's fields; in addition, he was required to furnish one *charge* of wood for each beast of burden he owned while those who had a cart filled it with wood and delivered it to the seigneur. The seigneur had the right of first refusal on all poultry, as well as beef, cow, and veal tongue before it could be sold, and the community butcher sold meat to the seigneur at two sous per pound less than the price established by his lease. Since the price of even the most desirable meat was seldom more than four sous per pound, it is obvious that the butcher was forced to sell it to the seigneur at a loss. Although no annual figures exist on the amount of meat the seigneur purchased, since he was seldom in Lourmarin, this probably was not a particularly heavy burden on the community butcher.

The southern slope of the Luberon Mountain formed the northern boundary of Lourmarin and belonged to the seigneur, "never having been cleared."[30] The inhabitants were allowed to use the mountain for pasturing and gleaning, but those caught by the constable cutting green wood or otherwise violating the seigneur's rights on the mountain were fined by the council. The seigneur received one half of the fine levied; the other half was allocated to the village poor.[31] Finally, the local *fermier* of the tile works was required to furnish 200 tiles as Lourmarin's *cens* on the "old tile works."

The *viguier* was entrusted with most of the seigneur's official business, such as overseeing the drafting of leases for the lord's land. Another agent of the seigneur, who usually did not live in Lourmarin, collected the various dues owed to the lord. Since leases for the rental of the seigneur's land were not always executed in Lourmarin while those leases which were signed in the village did not always cover the same pieces of seigneurial property, it is difficult to reconstruct any meaningful comparison of the

[29] Marion, *Dictionnaire*, pp. 338–39.
[30] *A.M., D.M.,* October 16, 1739.
[31] *A.D., Bouches-du-Rhône,* C 139-3928, April 15, 1731.

leases and their terms. However, there is enough information available to enable us to examine those rights and taxes which were "farmed" and also to look at that property "dependent upon the seigneurie."[32]

In 1764 Jean, André, and Pierre Gaudin, brothers, signed a lease (*bail à rente*) with the seigneur's agent in Lourmarin.[33] For an annual rent of 3,000 livres the Gaudins rented the exclusive use of the seigneur's ovens (*fours bannaux*) along with the right to collect the charge for baking (*droit de fournage*) from the villagers for six years. The *corvée* of one day per year paid by those with draft animals was to be applied to the seigneurie now being farmed by the Gaudins and they also received, for the term of the lease, "all the farmlands, meadows, and gardens" of the seigneurie. The Gaudin brothers were required to hire two competent oven-keepers (*fourniers*) who had to be approved by the seigneur. Within three months they evidently had found two oven-keepers agreeable to the seigneur because there are separate leases subletting to Jean Roman, baker, and Pierre Meynard, *travailleur*, the two ovens and the right to collect the seigneur's charge for baking. Roman and Meynard were to pay the seigneur annually 425 livres and 375 livres respectively for this right. Thus the seigneur received an additional 800 livres in income.[34]

The most complete lease in the notarial minutes was executed in January, 1789, by Bruny and Sieur Mathieu Colletin, *ménager*. Colletin rented for nine years the "farmland, meadow, orchard, and gardens" which belonged to the *domaine* of the chateau except for a small portion of meadowland nearest the chateau.[35] Colletin also received the use of the chateau, two storehouses, the small hayloft, the stables, and the fountains. Colletin agreed to pay 2,400 livres each of the nine years.[36] For the most part this is a classic eighteenth-century lease with the obligations of the lessee spelled out in detail. The lease would seem to assure the continued good maintenance of the property, but it did not encourage innovations or improvements.[37]

[32] For example, see *A.Not.*, Jacquier, August 11, 1764.
[33] *Ibid.*
[34] *Ibid.*, November 2, 1764.
[35] *A.Not.*, Borrelly, January 12, 1789.
[36] *Ibid.*
[37] See Appendix E for a copy of this lease.

By a separate lease signed the same day Colletin and a colleague rented the two seigneurial ovens and the right to collect the baking fee, agreeing to pay 1,800 livres annually for nine years.[38] The seigneur's income from the seigneurie and the *banalité* of the ovens thus increased from 3,800 to 4,200 livres between 1764 and 1789. The document which recorded the sale of Lourmarin to Bruny in 1719 included the information that the seigneurie had been leased in 1717 for five years for 2,650 livres per year, the lease to be continued after the sale. Assuming that this lease included the *banalités* of the ovens (since no separate figure is given), the seigneur's income from this source appreciated 58 percent in the 70 years prior to the Revolution.[39]

In 1765 the seigneur signed a three-year lease for rental of the olive press (*moulin seigneurial à huile*). The lessees were to pay 2,000 livres annually "after each harvest" and in addition were to provide the seigneur with two turkeys and four large capons; they were also required to plant 30 mulberry or almond trees to be provided by the seigneur.[40] There are no other leases concerning the olive press in the notarial records at Lourmarin and therefore one must assume they were drafted in Aix, La Tour d'Aigues, or some neighboring village. Other leases in the notarial minutes deal with small and scattered holdings rented by Bruny to individuals in Lourmarin. Unfortunately the rent was usually low, the pieces of land too diverse, and the entries too few to add any significant information about the seigneur's income.

Complete records of the seigneur's receipts from Lourmarin are available for 1746, 1747, and 1748.[41] Recorded at the end of each year by his agent, they reflect a detailed account, month by month and occasionally weekly, of the sale of goods received from Lourmarin as payment in kind of the *tasque* and other seigneurial dues. However, since these accounts record only that produce which was sold, there is no record of how much,

---

[38] *A.Not.*, Borrelly, January 12, 1789. An interesting exception was made for Sieur Pierre Paul Cavallier, the seigneur's legal representative (*procureur fondé*), who had drawn up the lease and who was also the *fermier* for the tithe-collector in 1789. During the term of the lease Cavallier's bread was to be baked free from the usual charge.

[39] *M.C.*, 4580, fo. 124, August 4, 1719.

[40] *A.Not.*, Jacquier, May 11, 1765.

[41] *M.C.*, 4580, fo. 56–113, 1746–49.

if any, was actually consumed by the seigneur and his family and, combined with the fact that no mention is made of the monetary income from the seigneur's leases in Lourmarin, means that the figure for total income from the village appears lower than it actually was.[42] I was unable to find comparable estate figures for earlier or later periods; thus, these figures do not indicate any long-range pattern of seigneurial income from Lourmarin. But since the estate books for each of the three years list income from the same sources, they are important in allowing us to learn the relative importance of various commodities to the seigneur's income and also in making a rough approximation of the seigneur's return from his 1719 investment.

TABLE VI–1. INCOME FROM THE SEIGNEURIE OF LOURMARIN[a]

	Livres				% of 3-Year Total[b]
Source	1746	1747	1748	3-Year Total	
Tasque (cereal grains)	3,383	5,058	2,589	11,030	27.5
Tasque (olive oil)	2,328	1,362	—	3,690	9.2
Lods	290	855	676	1,821	4.5
Cens	183	181	1,078	1,442	3.6
Cereal grains received in payment for grinding	2,871	3,251	3,139	9,261	23.1
Sale of Hay	2,037	2,044	69	4,150	10.4
Sale of Wine	1,993	1,616	1,440	5,049	12.6
Product of Dovecote	70	53	52	175	0.4
Miscellaneous (chickens, almonds, etc.)	2,329	619	530	3,478	8.7
	15,484	15,039	9,573	40,096	100.0

SOURCE: *M.C.*, 4580, Fo. 56–123, 1747–49.

[a] Figures throughout the table are rounded to nearest livre.

[b] Percent figures are rounded to nearest tenth of one percent.

The income from the *lods* and *cens*, the only items in Table VI–1 that the Lourmarinois paid in cash, represents only 8.1 percent of the total income. The charges on cereal grains, an absolute necessity in the peasant's diet, provided the seigneur with more than one half of his income. The charge for the *tasque* took one-eighth of the harvested grain while the fee

[42] The only lease that I can find for 1748 was a five-year lease to Jean Ginoux for the seigneurie at 2,200 livres annually, but it did not include the right to collect the baking tax (*fournage*). *A.Not.*, Jacquier, March 12, 1748.

for the use of the seigneurial mill took an additional one-sixteenth; together they amounted to 50.6 percent in this three-year period. It is likely that these two charges amounted to about one half of the total payment until the Revolution. The villagers often complained about the unpredictability of the olive harvest since the right weather conditions were essential for a successful yield. Poor weather may account for the variation and, in one year, the absence of income from the *tasque* on olive oil. The most logical explanation for the sharp drop in income from the sale of hay in 1748 is that the armies stationed in and around Lourmarin during the War of the Austrian Succession had left. The principal reason for the drop in income in the miscellaneous column in Table VI–1 was that the walnut crop was very good in 1746 and the oil was sold for 1,313 livres, but the crop declined in 1747 and 1748 and the seigneur elected to store the oil rather than sell it. Presumably this oil was sold at some later date and the income counted in the year it was sold.

An examination of the account books indicates that the sale of grain began in September when the harvest was completed and continued through the winter—the amount of grain being held back presumably depended on the storage facilities of the seigneur and his need for cash. Sixty percent of the seigneur's wheat from the 1746 harvest had been sold by October 18 of that year at 25 livres per *charge*, but the last six *charges*, sold in April, 1747, brought 44 livres each. The same is true for rye, of which there was about two and one-half times as much as wheat. The first sale in September, 1746, brought 19 livres per *charge* while the final sale in March, 1747, brought 31 livres.[43] The practice of holding one's grain as long as possible, which could be done only by those who did not need cash immediately, could increase one's income by as much as 80 percent. Unfortunately most peasants were in no position to do this and were usually forced to sell when the price was lowest.

The seigneur's average annual income, as reflected in the above table, was 13,365 livres.[44] Based on a capital expenditure of 314,075 livres in 1719, this figure represents an annual return of 4.3 percent. However, it would seem fair to assume that the seigneur realized enough other income to raise the average to at least 16,000 livres, thus providing a return of 5.1

[43] *M.C.*, 4580, fo. 56–113. 1747–49.
[44] *Ibid.*

percent. Because data covering an extended period of time is not available and because it is impossible to arrive at an exact figure even for the three years for which data exists, one cannot compute the seigneur's income with exactitude, although the available evidence indicates that the return was around five percent, a figure with which the seigneur certainly could not have found fault. The return of five percent was the current rate from government bonds. For two of the three years the account books show no expenditures on his property in Lourmarin at all; in 1747 Bruny spent 181 livres, only 1.4 percent of that year's income. There is other evidence that minor expenditures occurred periodically throughout the century, but the only evidence of a major expenditure was in 1739 when the seigneur paid two local masons 1,150 livres to rebuild the olive press.[45] Except when necessity dictated, the seigneur was not interested in making improvements in the village or on his own land.

Except for a brief period in the early sixteenth century, Lourmarin's seigneur did not reside in the village.[46] At the death of Monseigneur le Duc de Les Diguières in 1681 the seigneurie passed to his wife, who held it for 35 years.[47] This 35-year period witnessed the religious troubles of the 1680's, the long, disastrous wars of Louis XIV, and the economic crisis of 1709 brought about by a severe winter and spring. Upon the death of the Duchesse in 1716 Lourmarin passed to her son-in-law, the Duc de Villeroy, minister and councillor to the king during the Regency.[48] On January 1, 1718, Sieur Antoine Ailhaud, mayor of Lourmarin, journeyed to Aix where he pleaded with Lourmarin's *viguier* and *lieutenant de juge* to intercede with the Duc "to try and prevent the sale of this place."[49] Probably one reason the Lourmarinois wanted to prevent the sale was because their former seigneurs had made little attempt to enforce religious conformity and, in general, had allowed the villagers to govern themselves. They feared the reaction of a zealous new seigneur. Ailhaud's mission was unsuccessful and one may assume that M. le Duc was not overly concerned with his provincial seigneurie and even less concerned about whether the proposed sale of the village met with the approval of its inhabitants.

[45] *A.Not.*, Jacquier, April 6, 1739.
[46] Varille, *Lourmarin*, p. 16.
[47] *A.M.*, *D.M.*, May 18, 1681.
[48] *Ibid.*, February 23, 1716.
[49] *Ibid.*, January 1, 1718.

Informed by letter in August, 1719, of Lourmarin's sale in Paris to "Seigneur Monseigneur de Bruny of Marseilles," the council resigned itself to a new lord and appointed two notables who were instructed to pay their respects to Bruny's son, then living in Marseilles, and "to pray him to be good enough to let us know when his father will return from Paris in order that we might go to render our homage to him."[50] Bruny returned from Paris a month later and the council deputed 14 persons, including the priest, the mayor, and the *viguier,* to visit their new seigneur in Marseilles.[51]

Soon the council received word that "Monseigneur is expected to arrive in this place next Saturday. He is making his first visit to this village as our new seigneur and the community ought to receive him in a body and render to him the honors due to a person of his station."[52] Arriving at his chateau in November, 1719, Seigneur Bruny was greeted by 60 notables in uniform who presented their seigneur with his coat of arms. He was then feted at a banquet, the equal of which was not seen in Lourmarin in the eighteenth century.[53] The village leaders evidently were anxious to impress upon their new seigneur their respect and gratitude; perhaps they also were motivated by a desire to begin the relationship amicably in the hope of receiving future favors from their lord. Lourmarin's leaders certainly did not attempt to present a picture of poverty to the seigneur; the banquet menu was both elaborate and expensive. Among the various items consumed were 24 bottles of fine liqueur and a large quantity of wine as well as more than 100 pounds of assorted chocolates and other candies. Twelve turkeys, two hams, 20 young hens, seven chickens, two capons, and two rabbits were consumed. Various vegetables including cauliflower were on the banquet table along with lemons, oranges, pears, apples, and assorted condiments. Two hundred seventy-six loaves of bread were consumed. A large quantity of oats and 220 pounds of hay were provided for the horses of their new seigneur and his entourage. The seigneur and his party evidently were pleased by these marks of respect and all enjoyed the hearty food and drink of the banquet. Not until July, 1721, did "all the inhabitants of Lourmarin" gather to approve the expenditure of 684 livres to provide the

[50] *Ibid.,* August 13, 1719.
[51] *Ibid.,* September 17, 1719.
[52] *Ibid.,* November 1, 1719.
[53] The description of this reception is based on *ibid.,* November 1, 1719, January 1, 1720, July 21, 1721.

feast which celebrated the "joyous first visit" of their new seigneur.[54] Six hundred eighty-four livres was about equal to all other local expenditures together and amounted to ten percent of the village's total annual expenditure.

It was not long before the Lourmarinois had cause to be thankful for their new seigneur. They had occasionally received small gifts from their former seigneuresse, the Duchesse de Les Diguières, including an allocation of 45 livres in 1713 for poor relief, but there is no evidence that she ever donated larger sums to her village.[55] The winter of 1719–20 was very severe, grain prices had risen considerably by spring, and Lourmarin was unable to purchase amounts of grain sufficient to supply the villagers' needs. Fortunately in April the consuls received a letter from Bruny in which he offered to buy wheat in Marseilles and to re-sell it to them considerably below the market price.[56] On April 16, 1720, the seigneur loaned the village the large sum of 980 livres to buy grain and the council paid for hauling it to Lourmarin where it was "converted into bread and distributed to those who had the most need."[57] Because of the turmoil and unsettled conditions brought about by the plague, Lourmarin could not begin to repay the seigneur's loan until January, 1725, but there is no indication that the seigneur or his agent applied pressure to collect the debt earlier.

Heavy snowfall during the winter of 1727–28 caused much suffering and the seigneur donated 250 livres outright to be distributed to the village poor.[58] The large numbers of troops quartered in Lourmarin during the War of the Austrian Succession severely strained the village's finances. The baron helped alleviate the financial crisis by loaning the village 1,200 livres in 1744, interest-free. The loan was not repaid until 1750.[59] Although the amount of money loaned and given to Lourmarin was not large, the seigneur did demonstrate an awareness of, and an interest in, "his village."

Each year Lourmarin acknowledged the arrival of the New Year by sending the *viguier* and consuls to the seigneur's residence in January to pay

---

[54] *Ibid.*
[55] *Ibid.*, January 15, 1713.
[56] *Ibid.*, April 11, 21, 1720.
[57] *Ibid.*, April 26, June 9, 1720.
[58] *Ibid.*, August 1, 1728. Compared to his annual income from Lourmarin, the seigneur's gift of 250 livres does not seem extraordinarily generous.
[59] *Ibid.*, March 7, 1744, November 22, 1749, January 15, 1750.

their respects.[60] After the formality of the greeting was concluded, the village representatives reported the names of the newly elected municipal officers. Perhaps the formality of informing the seigneur about the new officers was followed because of a prior agreement or may simply have been the custom, but not once in the period after 1680 did the seigneur ever disapprove any of the newly elected municipal officers, an added proof that the village had a fair degree of autonomy in local affairs. Although the Brunys were Catholic, there is no evidence that they tried to interfere when Protestants began to filter back into the local government.

Since the Lourmarinois seldom were in direct contact with their seigneur, relations between the village and Bruny were limited to certain well-defined situations, such as births, marriages, and deaths in the seigneur's family or when a legal conflict between them developed. Jean-Baptiste de Bruny, who had purchased the seigneurie of Lourmarin in 1719, died in 1723.[61] It cost the village 30 livres to send the *viguier*, mayor, and second consul to Marseilles to pay their respects while the council spent 20 livres for candles for "a great mass and prayers for the repose of the soul of our seigneur."[62] His son, François, was to be Lourmarin's seigneur for 49 years. Three sons were born to the new seigneur, but it was the birth of the second in 1728 that occasioned the most celebration because Bruny's second son was titled M. de Lourmarin.[63] Writing to inform the village of the birth, the baron expressed his thanks to God for his new son and his gratitude at the happy union with Lourmarin:

I flatter myself to think that this union will be even more perfect when we will be able to live together amicably forever as I have hoped. You will always find me eager to give you additional proofs of the perfect esteem which I have for you. I am, dear sirs, your very humble and very obedient servant,

(s) St. Cannat.[64]

The village notables went to Marseilles to celebrate the joyous occasion but "joy turned to grief" when they arrived and learned that the baby had died.[65] There would not be another Bruny child to bear Lourmarin's name.

[60] *Ibid.*, January 28, 1720, and *passim*.
[61] *Ibid.*, February 28, 1723.
[62] *Ibid.*, March 7, 1723.
[63] *Ibid.*, September 3, 1724, January 18, 1728, June 7, 1739.
[64] *Ibid.*, January 18, 1728. St. Cannat was another of Bruny's villages.
[65] *Ibid.*, February 13, 1728.

Except for Bruny's first visit in 1719, the most exciting event involving Lourmarin and its seigneur prior to 1789 occurred in 1758 when the seigneur's eldest son, Jean-Baptiste Jérôme de Bruny, who was a councillor in the Parlement at Aix, was married. The mayor, M. Vial, announced at a special council meeting that he had received a letter from the baron in which he informed Lourmarin of the impending marriage. Having been given the "honor of announcing this to the village," Vial stated that "always in the past the village has given witness to its joy and I know it will this time also," because the village should honor "a seigneur who has, on every occasion, given marks of kindness and of friendship to all his vassals [sic]."[66] The council replied that the village was indeed honored "as witness the satisfaction all his vassals [sic] have for the marriage," and said they wished for the marriage "health and prosperity and that God will give them a blessed fecundity."[67] The mayor, second consul, priest, and "twenty-four of the principal taxpayers of this place" demonstrated their pleasure at the marriage by going to the chateau of La Tour d'Aigues to pay their respects. The village also formed a company of 100 men including six sergeants, four drummers, and two fifes to meet the couple in Pertuis and "conduct them up to the chateau of the said seigneur."[68] This splendid procession cost the village 150 livres.

The council decided that since it "is the custom of all of M. le Baron's villages to give a gift on the happy occasion of marriage," the village should send Henri de Girard to Marseilles to purchase "a robe of royal manufacture."[69] Given to the groom by the village, the robe cost 1,215 livres and was "graciously accepted . . . thereby doing a great honor to the village."[70] In order to purchase this garment Lourmarin once again went into debt. Some villagers, however, argued that in view of several pressing village needs—the drafting of a new *cadastre*, repair of the clock tower, the needs of its own poor, etc.—Lourmarin's gift was a bit too generous.[71]

[66] *Ibid.*, August 6, 1758.
[67] *Ibid.*
[68] *Ibid.*, September 10, 1758. This was a trip of about four miles.
[69] *Ibid.*
[70] *Ibid.*
[71] *Ibid.*

These more practical voices were not heeded and the village presented the seigneur with a lavish demonstration of its affection.

By the terms of a contract, drawn up August 4, 1758, Jean-Baptiste Jérôme was to receive one half, or 300,000 livres, of his mother's dowry at the time of his marriage.[72] He was also to receive 20,000 livres annually for his maintenance as well as that of his mother during her lifetime.[73] In 1768 François de Bruny drafted his last will and testament.[74] Three of his four daughters had married and had already received their portions as dowries. The fourth, and youngest, daughter was to receive 80,000 livres apportioned in four annual payments. The younger son, Jean Pierre Alexandre de Bruny, an officer in the king's army, could take either a life annuity of 4,500 livres annually or a lump sum payment of 80,000 livres over a four-year period. The universal heir was the eldest son, Jean-Baptiste Jérôme de Bruny, who was to have complete control of his inheritance upon the death of his father.[75]

When seigneur François de Bruny died in 1772, several village notables went to La Tour d'Aigues to express their grief to his family over the loss "of a seigneur so good and so just."[76] As was the custom, a special mass was held in the parish church.[77] Because Louis XV had suppressed the Parlement, the new seigneur was temporarily unemployed, but upon the accession of Louis XVI two years later the baron returned to Aix and Lourmarin celebrated "his re-establishment" in his former office.[78] The council spent 102 livres to celebrate its "joy" at an event "so pleasing to the community."[79] From the municipal minutes it is difficult to tell if this was a real enthusiasm for the return of the Parlement or whether they merely felt it their duty to say so. It is very possible, of course, that they

[72] *A.Not.*, Jacquier, August 4, 1758. This was a very large dowry. Robert Forster says that the dowry of the typical Toulousan noble family, robe or sword, was between 20,000 and 80,000 livres. Even for the court nobility at Versailles a dowry over 200,000 livres was exceptional. Robert Forster, *The Nobility of Toulouse in the Eighteenth Century* (Baltimore, 1960), pp. 120–51; Henri Carré, *La noblesse de France et l'opinion publique au XVIIIe siècle* (Paris, 1920).

[73] *A.Not.*, Jacquier, August 4, 1758.

[74] *M.C.*, 4588, fo. 232, July 2, 1768.

[75] *Ibid.*

[76] *A.M.*, *D.M.*, December 26, 1772.

[77] *Ibid.*, February 21, 1773.

[78] *Ibid.*, January 29, 1775.

[79] *Ibid.*, February 21, 1775.

viewed the event as a sort of local provincial victory and a check on the despotism of the far-off monarchy.

M. le President de La Tour d'Aigues, as the new baron and seigneur preferred to style himself, seemed to regard his relations with Lourmarin as a mere distraction. Bruny was an *agronome* and in his chateau at La Tour d'Aigues he established a superb botannical garden with plants from all over Europe and the Near East.[80] His library brought the following comment from Arthur Young, an English agricultural reformer, who stayed at the chateau. "The Baron has a very fine and well filled library, and one part of it totally with books and tracts on agriculture, in all the languages of Europe. His collection of these is nearly as numerous as my own."[81] The seigneur had written several articles for the publications of the Society of Agriculture in Paris which Young had read and upon which he commented favorably.[82] He was also one of 15 charter members in the Society of Agriculture established in Provence in 1778.[83] But, as in the case of many French *agronomes*, there is no evidence that the seigneur ever attempted to improve practical agricultural methods in Lourmarin.[84]

Several areas of conflict between the seigneur and his village occurred after 1750. One concerned repairs to the new village fountain, constructed in 1738 because water in the former fountain, adjacent to the public bath and wash house, was dangerous "for both man and beast."[85] In 1762 the council moved ahead with plans for extensive repairs to the fountain costing more than 1,000 livres. Whether he objected to the expenditure of money or to the fact that he was not consulted, the seigneur opposed the repairs claiming that Lourmarin had proceeded "without my permission."[86]

[80] Bancol, *Monographies communales*, p. 219.
[81] Arthur Young, *Travels during the Years 1787, 1788 and 1789* (Dublin, 1793), pp. 369–71.
[82] *Ibid.*
[83] *A.D., Bouches-du-Rhône*, C 93, fo. 253, April 18, 1778.
[84] See André Bourde, *Agronomie et agronomes en France au XVIIIᵉ siècle*, 3 vols. (Paris, 1967), as well as his earlier work, Bourde, *The Influence of England on the French Agronomes, 1750–1789* (Cambridge, England, 1953). In the latter work, especially pages 200–218, Bourde argues that real, measurable progress occurred from 1750 to 1789; however, many obstacles to agricultural reform had not been surmounted by 1789.
[85] *A.M., D.M.*, July 11, August 2, 1762.
[86] *Ibid.*, September 19, 1762.

Not until Lourmarin appealed to Aix was the village allowed to continue with the repairs.[87] Water from the new fountain was to be used for drinking only and not for washing clothes or bathing.

Two very important and related problems were the use of the Luberon Mountain and the care of Lourmarin's olive trees. The most enduring and seemingly insoluble problem, involving much litigation, was the extent to which the villagers were allowed to use the resources of the Luberon Mountain. The mountain belonged to the seigneur but by the terms of the 1523 agreement the inhabitants had certain limited rights regarding pasturage, gleaning, and the use of wood from the mountain.[88] Scarcely a year passed without complaints from the seigneur about "damages on the mountain," while the Lourmarinois complained that their rights, guaranteed in 1523, were being violated. However, a Special Council meeting in 1719 candidly admitted that almost all of the inhabitants were guilty of long-standing offenses, such as cutting prohibited trees for firewood.[89] But before the problem could be resolved, Lourmarin was sold to Bruny.

Until 1749 there was little discussion in the minutes about the mountain except for the constable's usual complaints that stray animals were nibbling the bark and branches of the saplings. In January, 1746, during the War of the Austrian Succession, Louis XV instructed Lourmarin to furnish all of its white oak (*chêne blanc*) to the navy in Toulon for use in shipbuilding.[90] In 1749 the council complained that, because the oak trees had been removed in 1746, the heavy winter rains presented a serious erosion problem for the village.[91] Bruny attempted to alleviate the problem by informing a Special Council meeting that no holm oaks (*chêne vert*) were to be cut for the next six years and the council responded by levying fines which ranged up to 25 livres for violation. The council even forbade the firing of the ovens to bake either bread or tiles without the express permission of

---

[87] *Ibid.*, May 29, 1763.

[88] *Ibid.*, October 16, 1739.

[89] *Ibid.*, February 12, March 5, 1719.

[90] *Ibid.*, January 30, 1746. On March 7, 1730, two Commissioners of the Navy, accompanied by the mayor, had inspected Lourmarin's part of the Luberon Mountain hoping to find oak trees of sufficient size to use in the royal navy. None was cut at this time because they were judged too small. *A.D., Bouches-du-Rhône*, C 284, May 3, 1730.

[91] *A.M., D.M.*, January 12, 1749.

the *viguier* and both consuls, a regulation that was confirmed one week later by the Bureau of Waters and Forests in Aix.[92]

The restrictions and subsequent fines did not stop the depredations and in December, 1753, the seigneur intervened directly against the continuing violations "notably by the principal *bourgeois.*" He was shocked, he said, that they should be the ones violating his regulations since it was the *"misérables* who often need to cut wood in order to stay alive" and the *bourgeoisie* was "setting them a very bad example."[93] The council, made up of course of these same "principal *bourgeois,*" ordered the guards to enforce the law impartially against all violators, reminding all inhabitants that two years still remained of the six-year restriction.

The other serious problem between Lourmarin and the seigneur concerned the village's olive trees, many of which were periodically killed by frost or heavy snows. Since the olive trees were especially susceptible to severe weather, arrangements had to be made to plant large numbers of replacements for those killed. The problem was compounded because young olive trees are very delicate and it was essential that all animals be kept out of the orchards, a difficult task since Lourmarin had about 40,000 olive trees in a rather small land area. This problem concerned the seigneur because without his acquiescence, regulations concerning flocks in Lourmarin would be meaningless.

The problem had been temporarily solved in 1709 by a written agreement between the village and the Duchesse which limited the number of animals, particularly sheep which were very hard on the young shoots, that could have access to the olive groves until 1715.[94] Those who owned sheep, including the butcher and Madame's *fermier*, were required to pasture them in the meadow and to use the main roads to take their animals there, thus avoiding the young olive trees. If sheep strayed into the olive groves, the fine for the first offense was to be one livre for each animal. A fine of two livres per animal was levied for the second offense, and if it happened a third time, the animals were confiscated.[95] The village constable and other officials had difficulty enforcing the prohibition and by the summer of 1710

[92] *Ibid.*, January 14, 1749.
[93] *Ibid.*, December 23, 1753.
[94] *Ibid.*, October 27, 1709.
[95] *Ibid.*

the council had voted to increase the fine to three livres during the day and six livres after dark while levying an additional fine of 25 livres on each offending shepherd. One half of this fine was to go to the seigneur, one half to the proprietor in whose orchard the offending animals were found.[96] Enforcement of these regulations was aided in June, 1715, when the council passed a law requiring shepherds to have a bell on each tenth sheep.[97]

Another severe winter in 1765–66 caused the death of many vines and olive trees, a great blow to the village's two principal crops, wine and olive oil.[98] As in 1709, measures were taken to conserve the remaining vines and trees but without notable success so that it became necessary to convoke a General Council of all heads of family in May, 1768. The consuls announced that since the existing regulations were being ignored, the council had voted to institute a 400-livre fine plus confiscation of his flock against any shepherd who allowed his sheep to stray off the main road while taking them to pasture in the meadow. The council concluded, however, that their restrictions, which were an attempt to insure the growth of the young olive trees, would be useless unless the seigneur required his *fermier* in Lourmarin to obey them too.[99] The baron agreed and the council's regulation on the "Exclusion of Flocks" was registered by the Parlement in Aix on June 6, 1768, and was then published in all of the neighboring villages so that "foreigners will not be able to plead ignorance."[100]

Lourmarin had received royal aid because of the death of its olive trees since 1766. In 1768 the village thanked the king for his generosity while presenting a petition showing that it would be unable to pay the *dîme* that year because of the death of most of its olive trees. The disaster was compounded, stated the petition, because the assessment for the royal, provincial, and district taxes which had to be paid was too high.[101] The stringent regulations of 1768 designed to permit the development of the young trees must have had the desired effect because there were few complaints for the

[96] *Ibid.*, June 29, 1710.
[97] *Ibid.*, June 16, 1715.
[98] *Ibid.*, May 4, June 29, 1766.
[99] *Ibid.*, May 22, 1768.
[100] *Ibid.*, June 26, 1768.
[101] *Ibid.*, October 30, 1768. They had earlier asked that Lourmarin's assessment be reduced by one-quarter for at least 15 or 20 years, about the time it takes for an olive tree to reach maturity, but this was refused. *A.D., Bouches-du-Rhône*, C 1177, November 15, 1766.

next several years, although the council was able to make the situation appear so grave that the village continued to receive some royal aid until Louis XV's death in 1774.[102]

The situation became critical again in 1778 when Mathieu Caire, constable, told the council that he wanted to resign because he had been threatened by several shepherds while attempting to enforce the community's regulations.[103] A General Council meeting of August 12, 1778, decided to hold all shepherds jointly responsible for damages done by sheep in the territory of Lourmarin.[104] This deliberation, along with other new requirements such as the provision that sheeps' bells now had to be audible at 500 yards, was registered by the Parlement in Aix and was approved by the seigneur.[105] By 1786, however, it was obvious that the system was not working even though individuals who owned sheep had formed a corporation and elected a *sindic* to oversee the shepherds. Too often the guilty party either was unknown or was from outside the village while the financial burden on some of the shepherds was much too heavy.[106]

One of the difficulties was that the village had no way of forcing the *fermier* and other employees of the seigneur to observe these regulations. The council complained bitterly on two separate occasions in 1786 that the seigneur's men were not observing the restrictions regarding the grazing of sheep or the new regulations against cutting wood on the mountain.[107] As Lourmarin approached the Revolution it was obvious that these twin problems had not been solved despite the council's concern and the threat of heavy fines. The terrible winter of 1788–89 caused the death of most of those olive trees so carefully nurtured in the 1760's and 1770's. Although economic disaster was threatening the village, there is no record of any offer of aid or expression of sympathy from Lourmarin's seigneur. While momentous events were occurring in Paris, a Special Council decided once again to limit strictly the number of sheep which might be kept and insti-

[102] *A.M., D.M.*, February 23. 1772.
[103] *Ibid.*, August 2, 10, 1778.
[104] *Ibid.*, August 12, 1778.
[105] *Ibid.*, November 15, 1778.
[106] *Ibid.*, July 16, 1786, October 1. 1786.
[107] *Ibid.*, May 14, July 2, 1786.

tuted even higher fines than before. On June 30, 1789, the Aix Parlement registered this deliberation and it was published in Lourmarin.[108]

The Revolution's effects on the relations between Lourmarin and its seigneur are part of a later story. But a 70-year period under three separate Bruny seigneurs had set the pattern. Lourmarin's *cahier* of 1789 has not survived and we do not know what, if any, complaints the villagers made against their seigneur. Although the term "absentee lord" has all sorts of bad connotations, the Brunys managed the seigneurie of Lourmarin in a fair and equitable, albeit businesslike, manner. The available figures indicate that Lourmarin was a good investment and that the seigneurs received a five percent return on their capital. Possibly by chance, but more likely by design, the seigneur's agents in Lourmarin were fair, intelligent men who were interested in the village's welfare and not just the seigneur's receipts. The seigneurs, whose main interest was always somewhere else, were nevertheless kept informed about Lourmarin and displayed interest in, and sympathy for, the Lourmarinois when disaster struck. This may explain why there were no general attacks on the seigneur's property at the time of the Revolution and why, when some of his goods were seized to pay his taxes, it was done in a peaceful and legal manner. Lourmarin's seigneur never emigrated and, in fact, returned to the village in 1792, made special tax contributions to the community, and was accepted, if not necessarily enthusiastically, as citizen Bruny. One cannot help but feel that its long period of virtual self-government had prepared Lourmarin for the political changes of the Revolution.

[108] *Ibid.*, May 24, August 9, 1789.

VII

RELIGION

THE HISTORY OF PROTESTANTISM in Provence is a complex and disturbing story of religious fervor which caused both Catholics and Protestants to commit the cruelest atrocities imaginable in support of the "true faith." The number of Protestants living in Provence in the years preceding the Revocation of the Edict of Nantes in 1685 has been estimated at about seven thousand, one thousand of whom lived in Lourmarin. Lourmarin's tradition of nonconformity in religious matters can be traced back at least to the fifteenth century and was not seriously weakened by the devastations of the sixteenth century, the Revocation of the Edict of Nantes, or Louis XV's periodic attempts to enforce religious uniformity. In the final days of the *ancien régime* when the futility of the state's repressive policy was finally admitted and a measure of tolerance was accorded the Protestants, all Frenchmen who had not been married in the Catholic church were allowed to register their marriages and births with the local priest: about 80 percent of the Lourmarinois appeared at the parish church to record marriages performed "in the desert."[1]

After the Albigensian heresy was suppressed in the thirteenth century, scattered remnants of this sect settled in the isolated Alpine valleys including the basin bounded on the south by the Durance River and on the north

---

[1] For a thorough discussion of the Protestants in Provence from the 1520's to the French Revolution, see E. Arnaud, *Histoire des protestants de Provence,* I.

by the desolate Luberon Mountain.[2] In the fourteenth and fifteenth centuries other settlers, descendants of the followers of Peter Waldo, were imported into this depopulated area from Piedmont.[3] Together these two groups of religious fugitives became known as *Vaudois*.[4] Although these peoples were of diverse origins, they established amicable relationships with the inhabitants of Lourmarin and nearby villages, were conscientious and successful farmers, and by the sixteenth century spoke the Provençal language native to the region.[5] Prior to the Reformation the *Vaudois* were nominally Roman Catholic and attended mass in the parish churches, but their basic religious beliefs owed much to the medieval heresies from whence they sprang. The authorities left them alone and, at least until 1522, the *Vaudois* did nothing openly to challenge the established church.

Frightened by the religious upheaval in the German states, the Parlement of Paris in 1524 drafted legislation designed to contain and eventually destroy the Lutheran threat in France. In 1528 the campaign was aimed specifically at the *Vaudois* of Cabrières d'Aigues, located just east of Lourmarin.[6] In 1536 several *Vaudois* from Lourmarin and neighboring villages were captured and burned by the authorities in Aix.[7] The most serious conflict prior to the outbreak of the Wars of Religion occurred in 1545 when Francis I was finally persuaded by Baron d'Oppède, President of the Aix Parlement, to sanction an expedition of "several thousand men, many of them mercenaries," against the Protestants of the Luberon.[8] The importance and the strength of the *Vaudois* was greatly exaggerated and it was

---

[2] Masson, *Les temps modernes*, p. 20.

[3] Marc Bloch, *French Rural History*, p. 114.

[4] Antoine Monastier, *Histoire de l'église vaudoise depuis son origine et des vaudois du Piémont jusqu'à nos jours*, I (Paris, 1847), 165–66. *Vaudois* was the French name for the Waldensians, or the followers of Peter Waldo, who lived in twelfth-century Lyons.

[5] B. Peyre, *Histoire de Mérindol en Provence* (Avignon, 1939), pp. 54–88; Masson, *Les temps modernes*, p. 21.

[6] From this time until his death in 1547 Francis I periodically fought against any extension of the Reformation in France while for political reasons he allied France with several of the new Protestant states of northern Germany. In part because of his preoccupation with Emperor Charles V, Francis I was unable to do much to destroy Protestantism in France.

[7] Masson, *Les temps modernes*, p. 21.

[8] *Ibid.*, pp. 23–25.

rumored, even in the highest circles at Aix, that the peasants planned to capture Marseilles by surprise and set up a republic.[9]

The expedition "against the heretics" was very bloody, particularly in Mérindol and Cabrières d'Aigues; some 800 men, women, and children were captured and transported to Marseilles where more than 200 died awaiting trial. Those men who managed to survive were sentenced to the galleys for life.[10] Lourmarin itself was set afire on April 16, 1545, but the troops did not remain long and the sturdy construction of the stuccoed houses kept the village from being completely destroyed. Most of the *Vaudois* escaped and hid in the many caves of the Luberon. Although several Protestants were murdered, Lourmarin escaped the general slaughter that occurred in many neighboring villages.[11] In all, 18 villages were burned; Peyre estimates that there were about 3,000 deaths.[12]

Many influential Catholics in Provence were shocked by the senseless blood-letting against their fellow citizens who had lived as peaceful and isolated farmers in their enclave north of the Durance, showing little interest in proselytizing. The fervor of the Catholic majority gradually abated and there were no other general religious conflicts until the beginning of the long and frightful Wars of Religion in 1562. The land along the Durance River continued to be a Protestant haven. Word of John Calvin's impassioned preaching was soon carried to Provence and the Protestants gained new adherents during the 1550's. By 1560 there were 60 churches of the "Reputed Reformed Religion" (*religion prétendue réformée*) active in Provence and representatives from all of them boldly gathered at Mérindol in 1560 to hold a general synod. When the fighting was renewed in 1562, the Protestants were strong enough to hold their own, at least temporarily, against the Catholic forces in the field.[13]

At the beginning of the conflict in early 1562 a Catholic band left Aix to attack several villages—partly for religious reasons but also for plunder.

[9] *Ibid.*

[10] Peyre, *Mérindol*, p. 123.

[11] *Ibid.*, pp. 88–140; Masson, *Les temps modernes*, pp. 23–27; Monastier, *Vaudoise*, pp. 207–20; Bancol, *Monographies communales*, p. 122; Courtet, *Vaucluse*, p. 215; Maurice Pezet, *Durance et Luberon* (*Provence inconnue*) (Paris, 1958), p. 43.

[12] Peyre, *Mérindol*, p. 113.

[13] Arnaud, *Histoire des protestants de Provence*, I, 117–42.

A rival Protestant group led by Paul de Richieu, a prominent Provençal Protestant, finally surrounded them at Barjols. From March 2 to March 6 the Catholics withstood the siege behind the village walls, but on the sixth the Protestants forced open the village gate. Nearly 600 defenders were slaughtered, the Catholic church and convent were burned, and the relics of Saint Marcel were profaned and then thrown into the street.[14] The memory of "the sack of Barjols" remained fresh in the minds of the Catholics. Other examples could be given. It is hard to draw up a balance sheet which would exonerate either side—whichever army controlled the field committed atrocities and senseless murders.

The Protestants (or *réligionnaires*) of Lourmarin were driven from their village again in 1562, taking refuge in the woods and caves of the Luberon. Not until 1567 were they finally able to return to their village.[15] Community life was temporarily disrupted, some lives were lost, but Lourmarin remained a Protestant village and its economy does not appear to have suffered any permanent damage. But the frightful atrocities committed by both sides were not forgotten after the Protestants' right to exist was guaranteed by the Edict of Nantes in 1598.[16]

Promulgated in 1598, the Edict of Nantes guaranteed freedom of conscience to the Huguenots, as Protestants were commonly called, who were thus granted most of the civil and religious rights already enjoyed by the Catholic population. Protestants could hold public office, receive public assistance, and attend public schools; they also obtained more than 100 fortified cities from Henry IV, himself a former Huguenot, and a measure of religious stability returned to France.[17] Recognition of the Protestants' right to exist meant that Lourmarin could exist legitimately as a Protestant village in the seventeenth century although some Catholics continued to live there.

Richelieu, acting for Louis XIII, sent troops into several Protestant villages around Arles in the early seventeenth century, but there is no record that the *réligionnaires* of the Luberon, who had suffered so much in the sixteenth century, were troubled. However, the government's policy began

---

[14] Masson, *Les temps modernes*, pp. 30–31.
[15] Courtet, *Vaucluse*, pp. 215–16; Pezet, *Durance et Luberon*, p. 44.
[16] Peyre, *Mérindol*, pp. 155–74; Masson, *Les temps modernes*, pp. 28–36.
[17] Warren C. Scoville, *The Persecution of Huguenots and French Economic Development, 1680–1720* (Berkeley, 1960), pp. 2–3.

to change under Louis XIV. The first half of the Sun King's reign saw the enactment of a number of restrictions, some petty in the extreme, designed to abrogate the guarantees of Henry IV's Edict. Warren Scoville has counted 300 such laws aimed at the Huguenots between 1661 and the Revocation of 1685. "All the laws were discriminatory; they stigmatized and penalized still further an already despised minority."[18]

Louis XIV framed a restrictive policy aimed at making life as difficult as possible for the Protestants in France in order to convince them that life would be so much simpler if they only would convert to Catholicism. Scoville has suggested that the toughness acquired by the Protestants during the struggles of the sixteenth century was gradually lost after they were granted toleration, which explains why they "knuckled under so readily and in such large numbers when Louis intensified his campaign against them."[19] The restrictive measures were a sort of negative inducement to convert, but Louis also attempted to sway the Protestants with promises of financial help such as a moratorium on private debts, exemptions from billeting soldiers, or outright cash grants.[20] A group of churchmen from Aix known as the "Propagators of the Faith" gave money payments to several new converts in Lourmarin, especially in 1681 and 1682.[21] On January 15, 1682, Jean-Baptiste Thomas, *travailleur*, and his wife each received 50 livres "left to the new converts by the will of the late Monsieur Louis Condoullet, *bourgeois* of the city of Salon."[22] An interesting variation of this kind of inducement was the payment in 1685 of 30 livres to "Daniel Martin, new convert to our holy faith, to learn the trade of weaver following his act of apprenticeship of last December first."[23]

The Protestants of Lourmarin were already on the defensive in 1680— when this study begins—since the king was attempting to secure their voluntary conversion to Catholicism by offering them financial assistance. "Conforming to the orders of the King" a tumultuous council meeting of August 25, 1680, was attended by twenty-one "Catholic inhabitants of this

[18] *Ibid.*, p. 35; Marion, *Dictionnaire*, pp. 462–63.
[19] Scoville, *Persecution of Huguenots*, p. 59.
[20] *Ibid.*, pp. 59–60.
[21] *A.Not.*, Chastroux, May 27, 1681, and *passim*.
[22] *Ibid.*, January 15, 1682.
[23] *Ibid.*, December 19, 1685.

place" to deal with the business of the community.[24] The council passed a significant resolution excluding "those of the Reputed Reformed Religion" from any participation in the village government and proceeded to elect a "council all Catholic in number."[25] By this action the Catholics succeeded in removing from their elected positions the second consul, half of the council, one auditor, one estimator, and one intendant of police. The Catholics' triumph was short-lived, however, because in December the Parlement at Aix ordered that the village councils be organized as they had been before the king's intervention.[26] This action may represent a struggle between the king and the provincial Parlement but the result was at least temporarily to give the Protestants a voice equal to the Catholics on the village council. This process of exclusion and then readmission of the *réligionnaires* was to be repeated twice before the final blow in 1685.

At the council meeting of August 25, 1680, the Catholics also complained that they would be handicapped in conducting the village's business since most of the "papers which belong to the community" were in the hands of Protestants. The records subsequently were returned and were placed in the village archives, established in the town hall.[27] The Catholic-controlled village council requested that Cardinal Grimaldi, Archbishop of Aix, authorize the construction of a cemetery "in which to bury Catholics."[28] On November 17, 1680, their request was approved, land was acquired, and construction of the walls began.[29] It appears that this appropriation was for an additional Catholic cemetery; probably the vaults in the parish church had become filled and more consecrated ground was needed. The Catholics obviously were enjoying their newly acquired influence.

The Protestants, who had been readmitted to the council, objected in May, 1681, to a Catholic proposal for prayers for the soul of their seigneur, the Duc de Les Diguières, who had just died. Although there were six Protestant councillors, only three voted against the Catholics and the proposal was carried, an indication that divisions existed within the dominant

[24] *A.M., D.M.,* August 25, 1680.
[25] *Ibid.*
[26] *Ibid.,* January 1, 1681.
[27] *Ibid.,* August 25, 1680.
[28] *Ibid.*
[29] *Ibid.,* November 17, 1680.

Protestant community.[30] In 1683 the Duchesse de Les Diguières, who was to be Lourmarin's seigneuresse until 1716, observed that it was her wish that all of her inhabitants profess Catholicism. But realizing that the majority were not Catholic, she hoped that all of her villagers would live together peacefully. The adherents of the "Reputed Reformed Religion," however, were not to interfere in any way with the "new converts" to Catholicism. She also promulgated a set of puritanical regulations which ordered *cabarets* and taverns to close at night and prohibited games and dances on Sundays and other Holy Days.[31] In April, 1684, the council, now made up entirely of Catholics, appointed two intendants to enforce the "correct observance of our Holy Sundays and other festivals" and to report those "who hold illicit assemblies," that is, Protestants.[32] Three separate disputes in 1684 alone dealt with the utilization of various properties purportedly appropriated by the Protestants prior to 1680.[33] All of these differences indicate that the Catholic minority in the months before October, 1685, knew that they had a powerful champion in Louis XIV and thus were becoming more belligerent and more determined to enforce their will on the Protestant majority.

Louis XIV's repressive policy culminated in the signing of the act formally revoking the guarantees of the Edict of Nantes on October 17, 1685. The king, professing to believe that "the best and greater part" of the Protestants in France had converted, decided to deal a final blow to the Protestants and added new restrictions to the repressive measures already enacted. Thus he ordered the destruction of all Protestant churches, forbade lay Protestants to leave the kingdom, and ordered all Protestant ministers to convert within seven days or leave France. Already foreshadowed in pre-1685 edicts, the Edict of Revocation ordered that all children of Protestant parents were to be baptized and raised as Catholics, either by relatives or by Catholic institutions. Louis seemingly guaranteed to those few who persisted in their heresy freedom of conscience, but this guarantee rang hollow because they were now bereft of minister and church build-

---

[30] *Ibid.*, May 18, 1681.
[31] *Ibid.*, August 17, 1683.
[32] *Ibid.*, April 23, 1684.
[33] *Ibid.*, April 23, June 18, July 9, 1684.

ing and were harassed by the hundreds of measures aimed at Protestants before 1685.[34]

Burdette C. Poland has observed that "this concession [that is, freedom of conscience for Protestants] had scarcely any meaning."[35] No one could logically argue with this statement, especially since we know that the direction of Louis' policy in the next 30 years was climaxed by his famous statement of March, 1715, that there were no longer any Protestants in France, since "they would not have been either suffered or tolerated here." But Poland's conclusion that "by virtue of the repressive measures against Protestants which the state had employed prior to the Revocation, hardly a Protestant was left in the country who had not been forced to abjure his religion" simply is not true.[36] Perhaps this was true in the larger population centers, where the nobles and *bourgeoisie* found it more practical and economically beneficial to abjure in the years before 1685, but it certainly was not true for Lourmarin where the pre-Revocation restrictions and inducements had not been particularly successful. This would corroborate Poland's assertion that the peasant had become "the most devoted and resolute element in French Protestanism," and that French Protestantism, after the Revocation, became basically a rural phenomenon. For example, between January, 1680, and October, 1685, there were only 30 new converts in Lourmarin.[37] Probably a few others occurred before 1680, although not many, since Louis' campaign did not really begin openly until 1679.[38] While these measures had been troublesome to the Protestants, it was the Revocation itself which tipped the scales in Lourmarin.

The news of the Revocation reached Lourmarin quickly and on October 21, 1685, Lourmarin's two notaries, Sieurs Chastroux and Pacot, stationed themselves in the parish church and prepared to receive a flood of abjurations. Since there were so few converts before, and because there is absolutely no evidence of pre-planned, concerted Protestant action, the most

[34] Burdette C. Poland, *French Protestantism and the French Revolution: A Study in Church and State, Thought and Religion, 1685–1815* (Princeton, 1957), pp. 20–23; Scoville, *Persecution of Huguenots*, pp. 5–8; Masson, *Les temps modernes*, p. 108; Marion, *Dictionnaire*, pp. 462–64.

[35] Poland, *French Protestantism*, p. 21.

[36] *Ibid.*

[37] *A.Not.*, Chastroux and Pacot, January, 1680 to October, 1685, *passim*.

[38] Scoville, *Persecution of Huguenots*, p. 29.

logical explanation for the large number of abjurations is that the last faint hope of the Protestants for religious toleration had been extinguished by Louis XIV. Although they decided to convert to Catholicism in order to escape from the restrictions prescribed against Protestants, for most of them their action was never more than a formality. In the notarial minutes, already filled with testaments, leases, marriage contracts, and a multitude of other transactions, the two notaries recorded the names of the new converts. This is a typical entry:

In the name of God in the year 1685, twenty-first of October, under the reign of the invincible monarch Louis XIV by the grace of God the very Christian King of France, in the parish church were present messire Philip, *vicaire général* of his Eminence, Cardinal Grimaldi, Archbishop of Aix; and Suzanne Roussier, widow of André Anastay, and André and Suzanne, her children, who of their own accord and free will have abjured and renounced the heresy of Calvin and the Reputed Reformed Religion which they have professed up until today; For which they have received absolution of their excommunication and have been received back into the mother church Catholic, apostolic, and Roman (*mère église, Catholique, apostolique et Romaine*). They have made public profession of their faith in which they have promised to live and to die.[39]

The majority of abjurations took place on October 21, although there were a considerable number of entries for October 22 and 23; a few occurred during the next several weeks.[40]

When the notaries finished recording the abjurations, there were 887 new Catholic converts in Lourmarin. This is a minimum figure for the Protestant population since the notaries recorded simply that in many abjuring families there were children "below the age of puberty" without indicating the number of children or their ages. To further complicate the situation, even when a child was specifically identified by name, his age was not given. Rather than add an arbitrary number of children to the total Protestant population figure, Table VII–1 lists only those adults and children who were actually named, that is, 887. Bancol, writing in 1896, estimated that there were approximately 250 Protestant families in Lourmarin on the eve of the Revocation. Assuming four persons per family,

[39] *A.Not.*, Chastroux, October 21, 1685.
[40] *A.Not.*, Chastroux and Pacot, October 21, 1685 to February 23, 1686, *passim.*

Bancol projected a Protestant population of 1,000.[41] An actual examination of the abjurations shows that this estimate was very accurate: the Protestants converted *en masse*.[42]

TABLE VII–1. ABJURATIONS IN LOURMARIN, 1685

Converts	Men	Women	Total
Adults	275	303	578
Children	—	—	309
Total			887

SOURCE: *A.Not.*, Chastroux and Pacot, October 21, 1685 to February 23, 1686.

As we have seen in Chapter II, the first relatively accurate estimate of Lourmarin's population was made in 1765 by Abbé Expilly, who projected the village's total population at 1,389. Lourmarin did not suffer the severe depopulation experienced by other Provençal communities during the plague in 1720–21, nor was there any large-scale emigration after the Revocation; therefore, one may assume some population growth from 1685 to 1765. Although it cannot be claimed that any of these figures, including Expilly's, are precise, Lourmarin's Protestant population in 1685 may conservatively be estimated at 80 percent of the total.[43]

The total population in Provence prior to 1685 was approximately 670,000, of which it is estimated that no more than 6,000 or 7,000 were Protestant. This figure is based on the Intendant's reports in 1682 which listed 6,042 *réligionnaires* village by village in all of Provence. Because of the general tendency to underestimate the number of Protestants in official reports in order to please Louis XIV, this figure may be too low. Arnaud thinks 7,000 to be closer to the true number of Protestants. In this 1682 census Lourmarin's Protestant population was larger than any community's

[41] Bancol, *Monographies communales*, p. 122. Using 1682 figures supplied by the Intendant, Arnaud also estimated that 250 families, or 1,000 Protestants, were living in Lourmarin on the eve of the Edict of Revocation. Arnaud, *Histoire des protestants de Provence*, I, 402.

[42] *A.Not.*, Chastroux and Pacot, October 21, 1685 to February 23, 1686, *passim*. Because of the number of entries which simply recorded "children below the age of puberty" it is impossible to arrive at a more exact figure.

[43] Arnaud says there were only 20 Catholic families in Lourmarin in 1661. If this figure is accepted, the Protestants may have constituted as much as 90 percent of the population. Arnaud, *Histoire des protestants de Provence*, I, 401.

in Provence.[44] If the number of Protestants is correct, they thus represented only about one percent of the total population in Provence. Lourmarin had a Protestant population of about 1,000; several thousand more were living in Mérindol, Cabrières d'Aigues, and other villages of the Luberon. Marseilles and Aix, the major population centers, were almost totally devoid of *réligionnaires*.[45] The concentration of the Protestant population in a single geographic area remote from the mainstream of Provençal life was a decided advantage for the royal government. Geographic concentration permitted the authorities to exercise strict supervision of the Protestant minority during those times when legal or practical circumstances dictated accommodation with the heretics.

After the Revocation of the Edict of Nantes was promulgated in 1685, measures were taken in Lourmarin to insure execution of the king's order. The Protestant church had already been demolished in 1663 and was not rebuilt until early in the nineteenth century, although the Protestants began to hold worship services by the mid-eighteenth century.[46] In 1688 Louis XIV forbade Protestants and new converts "to have any sort of weapons or ammunition."[47] This security measure was taken at the start of the War of the League of Augsburg and was supposed to last two years. Successive renewals of this ordinance, however, kept it in force in France until 1734.[48] The renewed ban on arms was announced in Lourmarin every two years and was also posted "in a public place so that no one can plead ignorance."[49] The prohibition was not mentioned in the minutes of Lourmarin's

[44] For the village-by-village census in 1682 see "Fragments de statistique officielle, 1682" in *Bulletin de la Société de l'histoire du Protestantisme français*, VII (1859), 22–24; Arnaud, *Histoire des protestants de Provence*, I, 389–448, 481–82. For a further discussion of this question see Scoville, *Persecution of Huguenots*, p. 8; Masson, *Les temps modernes*, p. 108.

[45] Marseilles had only 270 Protestants and Aix one hundred. "Fragments de statistique officielle, 1682," p. 23.

[46] The Archbishop of Aix ordered Lourmarin's Protestant church torn down in 1663 on the grounds that, since there had been no Protestant worship in the village in 1596 or 1597, the Lourmarinois Protestants were not protected by the Edict of Nantes. Arnaud says that, on the contrary, ample evidence showing that Protestants were worshiping in Lourmarin in 1596–97 was presented to the Archbishop's commissioners but was ignored. Arnaud, *Histoire des protestants de Provence*, I, 401–2.

[47] *A.M., D.M.*, November 17, 1688.

[48] Scoville, *Persecution of Huguenots*, p. 91.

[49] *A.M., D.M.*, November 4, 1706, and *passim*.

village council after 1712 and it may be assumed that it was no longer enforced.[50]

No accurate count of the Lourmarinois who emigrated as a result of the Revocation is available; the evidence indicates that few persons fled. Jean-Baptiste Jérôme de Bruny, seigneur of Lourmarin after 1772, stated that 33 Protestant families, originally from Lourmarin and four of his other villages, had "fled the realm" after the Edict of Revocation.[51] Afraid of persecution, a few families from Lourmarin did leave France, forfeiting their property when they did so. Although legislation governing the property of those Protestants who emigrated changed during the years after 1685, the general outlines remained constant: If a *"fugitif réligionnaire"* returned and converted to Catholicism, his property was returned; if he did not return, his property could be claimed by those relatives who were his legal heirs provided they were good Catholics; if his legal heirs were not "good Catholics" or if he had none, his property was expropriated by the state and was to be administered by the Intendant.[52]

The property of Pierre Rouvet, "abandoned" when he fled to Holland after the Revocation, was returned to him in 1688 when he reappeared in Lourmarin and "abjured his heresy."[53] Jean Monestier, one of the most prominent Protestants, fled in 1685. The government immediately confiscated his property, which was transferred in 1702 to his brother-in-law, Pierre Sambuc, *bourgeois*, upon presentation of a certificate from the local priest averring that Sambuc "had always professed the Catholic religion."[54] The priest's authority in such cases was also evidenced when Pierre Aguitton was refused a portion of his father's inheritance because "he has never fulfilled any of the duties of Catholicity."[55]

[50] *Ibid.*, December 27, 1712.

[51] There is no date on this document, but it must have been written between 1772 and 1789. As discussed below, we know that there were some Lourmarin Protestants who did leave France, but there is no evidence that the number was substantial. In this memoir, Bruny valued the real property of the Lourmarin *émigrés* at 3,197 livres, or slightly more than one percent of all *roturier* property in Lourmarin according to the 1770 *Cadastre. M.C.*, 4588, fo. 204, n. d.

[52] Scoville, *Persecution of Huguenots*, pp. 111–15; Marion, *Dictionnaire*, pp. 128–29; *A.M.*, *D.M.*, February 3, 1690, and *passim*.

[53] *A.D.*, *Bouches-du-Rhône*, C 2207, fo. 85, December 24, 1688.

[54] *Ibid.*, C 2210, fo. 39, May 18, 1702.

[55] *Ibid.*, C 2210, fo. 13, September 18, 1701.

Property confiscated from emigrating Protestants was administered by the "Director General of the Administration of the Property of *Réligion-naires* of this province who have left the kingdom because of religion." Such property was rented, usually for six-year periods, to the highest bidder.[56] The income from confiscated property was used for cash payments to those abjuring their heresy, for Catholic charities, and for the general administrative costs of winning more converts.[57] Some of this money was used to help newly converted families, particularly those with young children. Payments were also made to individual children of *réligionnaires* to further their secular and spiritual education, since these children were to be raised in the Catholic faith. Before allocating funds the authorities always stipulated that the recipient had been "reunited in the bosom of the church for . . . years, fulfilling with edification all the obligations of Catholicity."[58]

Litigation involving the disposition to be made of property belonging to *réligionnaires* who emigrated often dragged on for years. Some time after 1772 Seigneur Bruny addressed a memorandum to the Intendant in which he complained that his "feudal rights" had been violated.[59] Bruny claimed that a *lods* payment of one-sixth its value was due on all land in Lourmarin which had been confiscated. Not only had the *lods* never been paid, complained Bruny, but the land was now being administered by royal officials who knew little about agricultural methods. Their neglect caused the harvest to decline; consequently, the payment of the *tasque* (one-eighth of all grain) was lower than it might otherwise have been.[60] There is no record that the government took any action on Bruny's request.

The official view, especially after 1715, was that a "Protestant problem" no longer existed in Provence. Writing in 1724, the Intendant of Provence said there were so few Protestants or new converts in the province that he did not pay much attention to them, a situation which he applauded since he had "seen the caprice exercised by some Catholic churchmen."[61] A certain repugnance on the part of the local authorities to ferret out any re-

---

[56] *A.Not.*, Jacquier, July 22, 1723, and *passim*. The local notary recorded the leases.

[57] Scoville, *Persecution of Huguenots*, p. 114.

[58] *A.D., Bouches-du-Rhône*, C 2298, *passim*.

[59] *M.C.*, 4588, fo. 204, n. d.

[60] *Ibid.*

[61] Intendant Hébret, quoted in Masson, *Provence*, p. 571.

maining Protestants was also evident. Nor did they exert much pressure on the much larger group of new converts who remained Protestant at heart, showing "no mark of Catholicity."[62]

The decades of the 1730's and 1740's saw much vacillation between indifference to and strict enforcement of the laws against Protestants. On the night of March 30, 1735, a group of 152 Protestants gathered at Cabrières d'Aigues for a service conducted by a minister from Languedoc. The service began with readings from the New Testament by Jacques Murat of Lourmarin.[63] When Louis XV was informed of this meeting he instructed the Intendant in Provence on May 22, 1735, to take action against those present at this meeting.[64] Eighty-four of those persons attending the assembly, which was "strictly outlawed by ordinances of the King," were arrested and on March 24, 1736, eleven of these, including Murat, were convicted.[65] Begging for clemency, Murat and two friends from Cabrières d'Aigues swore that they had not understood what they were doing. In 1737 the subdelegate, who had been given authority to review the case, accepted their feeble excuse and released the men with a fine and a reprimand.[66] Arnaud credits the Intendant with "remarkable moderation" in this case.[67]

In 1741 the Intendant received complaints that Protestants were living together "as if they were legitimately married," although the marriage rite had been performed by a Protestant minister instead of by the Catholic priest. Two couples in Lourmarin had had the audacity to have marriage contracts drawn up with the local notary but had not been married in the parish church. One of the couples lived in a house next door to the priest and "caused him great chagrin, being daily under his eyes."[68] It was suggested that if the Intendant wished to make an example of a Protestant couple, he might start with these two.[69]

---

[62] This phrase was often used in the Catholic parish registers to explain why a person was denied burial in consecrated ground.

[63] A.D., Bouches-du-Rhône, C 2298, 1735; Arnaud, Histoire des protestants de Provence, I, 498–500.

[64] Arnaud, Histoire des protestants de Provence, I, 501.

[65] Ibid.; A.M., D.M., April 15, 1736; Masson, Provence, pp. 572–73.

[66] A.D., Bouches-du-Rhône, C 2298, 1737.

[67] Arnaud, Histoire des protestants de Provence, I, 503.

[68] A.D., Bouches-du-Rhône, C 2298, February 21, 1741.

[69] Ibid.

Early in 1744 the Intendant was informed that a new Protestant minister had arrived in the "valley" and that the number of clandestine services was multiplying. The military commandant of Provence sent four detachments of the Queen's Regiment to occupy Lourmarin, Cabrières d'Aigues, and Mérindol, with instructions to gather evidence against anyone who had officiated at these illegal assemblies.[70] When the troops and the subdelegate arrived in Lourmarin, they encountered a classic example of passive resistance. The subdelegate wrote to the Intendant at Aix on February 3, 1744, to assure him that the people had been cooperative, the troops had been billeted, and that there was no sign of a Protestant service anywhere. For good measure the subdelegate added that he had delivered a lecture to the Lourmarinois on the dangers inherent in disobeying the edicts of the king regarding heretical practices.[71] The next day the military commander dispatched a similar letter which recorded another warning delivered to the "principal inhabitants who have received me very well and who have appeared entirely submissive to me," but also noting that the inhabitants had been careful "to have no assemblies" while he and the troops were in Lourmarin.[72] By February 14, 1744, the commander was convinced that the minister was gone from Lourmarin, although he suspected that he had not journeyed far. The subdelegate was also pessimistic about discovering any damaging evidence concerning the Protestants. After talking to one of the "principals" of Lourmarin as well as to a peasant, he was forced to report that in his opinion the Protestant services would resume just as soon as the troops were removed.[73] The troops departed Lourmarin on March 1 without the Protestant minister and, so far as is known, without arresting anyone suspected of assisting at the services. Later evidence clearly demonstrates that the troops' attempt to frighten the Protestants back into the Catholic fold was a total failure.

Paul Masson observed that although the rigorous laws against the Protestants remained in force, the authorities in Provence "closed their eyes on their execution."[74] We know that a permanent minister was operating in

---

[70] *Ibid.*, C 2298, February 3, 1744; Masson, *Provence*, p. 573.
[71] *A.D., Bouches-du-Rhône*, C 2298, February 3, 1744.
[72] *Ibid.*, February 4, 1744.
[73] *Ibid.*, February 14, 1744.
[74] Masson, *Provence*, p. 578.

the valley by March, 1747, because the pastor began again to keep the parish register which had ended abruptly in October, 1685. Services were held openly, and soon Lourmarin had its own minister. Although the Protestant and Catholic registers did not record "relapsers," it is obvious from an examination of both registers that the number of professing Protestants increased regularly until the Revolution. By the mid-eighteenth century in Provence, as well as in France as a whole, the authorities showed little taste for enforcing the laws against the Protestants and *de facto* tolerance was granted them.

The Protestants continued to support the Catholic church, principally by their payment of the *dîme*, throughout the period prior to the Revolution. The *dîme* was paid to the tithe-collector who, as we have noted earlier, paid the salaries of the village priest and his vicar from his receipts.[75] The village was also responsible for paying a portion, usually two-thirds, of the cost of repairs to the parish church, the parsonage, and other church property. That portion not paid by the village was donated by the tithe-collector, as occurred when the new Catholic cemetery was built in 1680.[76] The priest always prefaced his requests for community funds with a justification of the church's general usefulness and the public need for the proposed repair.

Renewed Protestantism in Lourmarin was met head on by a new, assertive priest in 1759, and led to several conflicts between the priest and the village council in the 1760's. *Curé* Jean Gaspard Fauchier was elected as one of the auditors in 1760 and immediately became involved in a dispute with the treasurer, Sieur Antoine André Ailhaud, a prominent Protestant, because Fauchier refused, for a variety of reasons, to accept Ailhaud's annual financial report. Ailhaud was supported by 13 Protestant notables who held the opinion that the priest's actions were detrimental to the community. The conflict spread outside the village, the *Cour des Comptes* in Aix siding with Ailhaud while the Archbishop of Aix supported the priest. Many serious accusations were hurled back and forth until the council, after consulting lawyers in Aix, decided to accept Ailhaud's report, to dismiss the priest from his position as auditor, and henceforth to appoint three auditors each year, as required by the community rules. The seeds of a future feud were

[75] *A.Not.*, Chastroux, July 1, October 30, 1686, and *passim*. See also Chapter IV.
[76] *A.M.*, *D.M.*, November 17, 1680, and *passim*.

planted when the priest was replaced as auditor by Joseph Janselme, also a Catholic.[77]

There had been minor conflicts before among those who supervised the funds over how best to allocate the 40 livres from the Girard legacy, but no serious problem occurred until 1761. *Curé* Fauchier was once again involved. Janselme, also a Catholic and second consul in this year, initiated the 1761 dispute by charging that the priest was administering the Girard legacy too exclusively in the interest of the Catholic church. Janselme complained that of the 49 vouchers authorizing the butcher to give free meat to the poor and sick, the priest alone had signed 44.[78] A bitter exchange followed, with the priest denying any wrongdoing and wondering at the "secret motive" of Janselme.[79] Janselme, having been called a liar in public by Fauchier, responded by demanding that the regular procedure for authorizing free meat be reinstituted, claiming that the priest was taking too much authority upon himself since he had acted without the consent, and sometimes even the knowledge, of the two consuls.[80] A General Council examined the Girard bequest and decided that henceforth all authorizations would be signed by the priest and both consuls.[81]

All of the animosities between *curé* Fauchier and the council and, to a lesser extent, between Catholics and Protestants, climaxed in a 1766 dispute brought about because the bell in the church would not ring. On December 14, 1766, the priest laid before the council a letter from the Archbishop of Aix who asked that an agreement be reached to use the community's bell tower "to announce divine services."[82] The council said that most *réligionnaires* and "even a number of Catholics" were opposed, arguing that the bell was needed to announce the time of official council meetings and the two fuctions, one religious and the other secular, should not be confounded.[83] The dispute continued until March, eventually involving the Intendant as well as the Archbishop. After additional pressure from the

[77] *Ibid.*, March 9, 16, April 20, May 4, June 8, August 24, 31, 1760.
[78] *Ibid.*, April 5, 1761.
[79] *Ibid.*, August 16, 1761, and *passim*.
[80] *Ibid.*, September 6, 1761.
[81] *Ibid.*
[82] *Ibid.*, December 14, 1766.
[83] *Ibid.*, December 26, 1766, February 22, 1767. This is the first admission in the council minutes since 1685 that there were, indeed, *réligionnaires* in Lourmarin.

subdelegate, on March 3, 1767, the council agreed under duress to allow the priest to use their bell, although it was "against all rights of this community."[84] The victory was an empty one, however, because three weeks later the priest handed back the keys, saying that the bell tower was in such poor condition he was afraid to use it.[85]

In his study *French Protestantism and the French Revolution* Burdette Poland has observed a sense of fraternity between Protestants and Catholics in the years before the French Revolution despite "the guarded attitude of the Catholic clergy." He finds evidence of this in the indifference to religious matters shown by the Third Estate in their *cahiers* to the Estates General in 1789; *cahiers* drafted by the Third Estate contained few complaints about the Edict of 1787, also known as the Edict of Toleration.[86] Like the Edict of Revocation of 1685, the Edict of Toleration pledged the state to continue to work for the religious unity of all Frenchmen. But unlike the former, the Edict of Toleration was intended to guarantee the freedom of conscience apparently protected, but actually abrogated, by the 1685 Edict. The Edict of Toleration also contained a provision for civil marriage; those who had contracted marriages "in the desert" could appear within one year before the priest to have the marriages and their children legitimized.[87]

This spirit of fraternity and cooperation between Catholics and Protestants was evident after mid-century in Lourmarin. The disputes described above were initiated primarily by the priest and do not reflect any deep-seated conflict between the Protestant and Catholic segments of the population because the two factions cooperated in the village council and seemed much more concerned with defending their common interests against crown and seigneur than with religious bickering. The Edict of Toleration was greeted with a sense of relief, but since the Protestants in Lourmarin had practiced their religion openly after 1747, there was no great necessity for elation.

Beginning in April, 1788, and continuing for almost a year, the Protestants presented themselves to a chagrined priest who recorded their marriages and children in the Catholic parish register. Most of these vital

[84] *Ibid.*, March 3, 1767.
[85] *Ibid.*, March 22, 1767.
[86] Poland, *French Protestantism*, pp. 99–100.
[87] *Ibid.*, pp. 79–82.

statistics, of course, were already included in the Protestant parish register which had been kept since 1747. All of the entries followed this form:

The year 1788 and the first of April in execution of the edict of the King of the month of November last, registered in the Parlement of Aix February 13, 1788, concerning those who do not profess the Catholic religion appeared in front of me, the undersigned *curé*, Sieur Pierre de Corgier, son of the late Antoine, *bourgeois*, and the late Madame Anne Bonnafoy of this parish, aged 50 years, on the one hand and Madame Anne Sambuc, daughter of the late Sieur Louis de Sambuc, former captain, and the late Dame Anne Martin, also of this parish, aged 52 years, on the other. They have declared to me that they have been united in a true and indissoluble marriage since October 28, 1759. From this union have come two boys—the elder born January 21, 1761, baptized and named Antoine Louis; the younger born May 5, 1763, baptized and named Pierre Guilhaume. After this declaration I have recognized this act and have registered them according to the law.

(s) Fauchier, *curé*[88]

By February 10, 1789, the priest had registered 1,175 Protestants (see Table VII–2).

It is possible that this figure is too high because some couples recorded births which had occurred as much as 40 years prior to 1788, and many of the children so recorded might have died in the interim or left the vil-

TABLE VII–2. REGISTRATION OF PROTESTANTS IN LOURMARIN, 1788–89

Age of Registrant Years	Number Registered
0 to 9	232
10 to 19	194
20 to 29	229
30 to 39	192
40 to 49	136
50 to 59	106
60 to 69	65
over 70	21
Total	1,175

SOURCE: *A.M., R.P. Cath.*, 1788–89, *passim.*

[88] *A.M., R.P.Cath.*, April 1, 1788. For a discussion of the near-unanimous registration of this edict in the Parlement of Aix see Arnaud, *Histoire des protestants de Provence*, I, 539–41.

lage. It is therefore impossible to determine how many Protestants were actually alive in Lourmarin in 1788. The figure of 1,175 probably represents the maximum number of Protestants. If deaths were recorded or if a place of domicile other than Lourmarin was given, the individual was not included in the total of 1,175. The total population of Lourmarin in 1790 was between 1,450 and 1,500. Although no claim to precision can be made, it is obvious that the relative number of Protestants in Lourmarin was about the same as it had been in 1685.

The Edict contained no provision guaranteeing the status of the Protestant minister. In fact, the civil authorities were instructed not to recognize certificates of marriage, birth, or death signed by Protestant pastors.[89] As one might expect in a community that had made no attempt to hide its Protestant worship since 1747, this provision had no effect and the number of entries in the Protestant parish register show no change after the Edict of Toleration was promulgated.

In another edict of November, 1787, Louis XVI ordered that each community "designate a decent and proper piece of land for the interment of those who do not profess the Catholic religion."[90] Since the new Protestant cemetery was to be established at the community's expense, it was a matter of general concern. Several pieces of land were considered and rejected before *bourgeois* Pierre Ginoux offered to donate two *éyminés* (about one-third acre) of land to the community on condition that an amount equal to the fair market value of the land would be used to establish a fund for poor relief.[91] Ginoux's land was evaluated at 300 livres which was "placed at the disposal of the poor of this place in accordance with the charitable intentions of the donor."[92] The gravedigger, who was given specific instructions regarding the size and spacing of graves, was paid two livres for each adult (*grande personne*) and one livre, ten sous for each child. At the very outbreak of the Revolution, the Protestants in Lourmarin were granted civil recognition.

An examination of the religious life in Lourmarin strikingly demonstrates the tenacity of Protestantism which began with the sturdy *Vaudois* of the

---

[89] Poland, *French Protestantism*, p. 81.
[90] *A.M., D.M.*, April 20, 1788; Masson, *Provence*, p. 578.
[91] *A.M., D.M.*, March 28, 1789.
[92] *Ibid.*

fifteenth century and continued to the French Revolution. Although it is difficult to generalize, those who were more than nominally Catholic in Lourmarin, and who remained so throughout the eighteenth century, can be divided into three categories: a few *bourgeois* who were Catholic either on grounds of faith alone or because their professional position demanded it; artisans with small incomes; and many of the poorer peasants. The Protestants encompassed all occupational levels and included most of the large landholders. From the inception of the Reformation there had been religious disputes in Lourmarin, but in every instance these difficulties seem to have been initiated by outside forces or by the priest and not by the local inhabitants themselves. When not goaded or given incentives for intolerance, such as in the 1680's, the Catholics showed little inclination to force the Protestants to conform to their faith. The Protestants, who had shown so much religious fervor in the sixteenth century, had become surprisingly docile by the eighteenth. Michel Vovelle has noticed this at Lacoste, an isolated community about 10 miles from Lourmarin, where he sees a marked decline in the former religious zeal of the Protestants accompanied by an increase in the number of mixed marriages. "Lacoste appears to be an area already well advanced toward dechristianization." Vovelle also feels that it is more than coincidence that Lacoste was the seigneurie of the Marquis de Sade.[93]

This religious toleration—indifference perhaps is a better word—might have been related to the decrease in family size observed earlier, presumably the result of birth control by both Protestants and Catholics.[94] Since both the Catholic and Protestant churches disapproved of sexual relations prior to marriage, Lourmarin's high (16 percent for the eighteenth century) rate of pre-marital conceptions may reflect this same indifference to religious teachings. Thus the theme of the eighteenth century in Lourmarin was not one of religious conflict but rather one of mutual accommodation in defense of the interests of the village, although the spirit of fraternity which existed in Lourmarin before 1789 was to be partially, albeit temporarily, shattered by the events of the 1790's.

[93] Michel Vovelle, "Sade, seigneur de village," in *Actes du Colloque Sade tenu à Aix en 1966* (Paris, 1969).

[94] See Emmanuel Leroy-Ladurie, "Démographie et 'funestes secrèts': Le Languedoc (fin XVIIIe début XIXe siècle)," *Annales Historiques de la Révolution Française*, XXXVII (July–September, 1965), 385–99.

VIII

REVOLUTION

TIME PASSED SLOWLY IN Lourmarin and change came gradually as one season gave way to another. There were years of good harvest and years of bad, babies were born, grew to adulthood, propagated themselves and died, young men went away to serve in the army and some returned—in short, village life changed little in the century before 1789. Religious differences separated the Protestants and Catholics, but most villagers shared a common existence and the divisive tendencies engendered by the Revocation of the Edict of Nantes eventually gave way to a strong communal feeling. There was little litigation between the seigneur and his village, perhaps due as much to the fact that the Brunys rarely visited Lourmarin as to the seigneurs' reasonableness. The political structure of the community, established in the mid-seventeenth century, had matured and was operating tolerably well as the 1700's drew to a close. Community life was severely interrupted only once—by the plague—during the eighteenth century and, even in 1720–22, due to luck and the village's preventive measures, Lourmarin emerged from the crisis relatively unscathed. The events during the five years after 1789 provided the most severe test faced by Lourmarin in the eighteenth century. Buffeted by the contrary winds from Paris, Lourmarin struggled to adapt to the successive regimes. And yet beneath the seeming confusion and internal division in the village an element of stability, provided by Lourmarin's leaders, permitted the village to chart its way through the tumultuous changes in France with a minimum of dislocation and conflict.

Loménie de Brienne, Comptroller-General, announced in May, 1787, that the provincial assemblies were to be re-established. Suspended in 1639, the Estates of Provence had been a stronghold of the aristocracy, and the privileged orders were anxious to assert their former importance.[1] The "Estates General of the *Pays* and *Comté* of Provence" met in Aix from December 30, 1787 to February 1, 1788, and the privileged orders, accustomed to a free hand in running the province, managed to exclude most of the lower clergy from the deputation of the First Estate.[2] Although the Third Estate was granted 16 more votes than the first two orders combined, many of its delegates were village mayors who, because they were noblemen or owned fiefs, were subservient to the leaders of the second order.

In Provence the focal point of the deliberations was France's critical financial problems. The Provençal notables were no more willing than were their counterparts elsewhere to admit their responsibility to support the government with taxes unless they received reciprocal political concessions from the crown. Before adjourning on February 1, 1788, the Estates affirmed "the fundamental immunity of their noble possessions" although the delegates offered to share in the expenses of road construction and the upkeep of foundlings in Provence and to continue to pay the local charges they had already assumed.[3] No substantive fiscal reforms had come from the convocation of the Estates and the position of the nobility apparently had been strengthened.

The Third Estate in Provence, having been led to believe that they would be given a voice in provincial government, soon realized that they had been deceived since they had not even been allowed to elect their own deputies to the Estates of Provence. Instead, those who were chosen from among the districts merely echoed the sentiments of the first two orders and dissatisfaction with the treatment of the Third Estate was now voiced on all

[1] Jean Egret, "La prérévolution en Provence, 1787–1789," *Annales Historiques de la Révolution Française*, XXVI (1954), 98.

[2] *Ibid.*, pp. 102–3.

[3] *Ibid.*, pp. 102–5; Masson, *Les temps modernes*, pp. 525–28. This "conciliatory gesture" was almost meaningless since in many communities they already contributed toward these expenses and, in any case, the charges represented a relatively small sum.

sides. Mayors of eighteen Provençal villages gave their support to the representatives of the Third Estate and asked for a General Assembly of the Communities.[4]

Lourmarin supported this position and at a Special Council meeting on April 20, 1788, the village decided after "the most impartial deliberation" to vote unanimously to reject the system of electing deputies to the Estates.[5] They also voted that each district should be allowed freedom in choosing its delegates to the General Assembly of the Communities, scheduled to meet at Lambesc on May 5, 1788. In order to prepare for the General Assembly, the district (*viguerie*) of Apt decided to convoke a preliminary meeting of village mayors on April 27. Sieur Dominique Henri de Savornin, Lourmarin's mayor, said that his health would prevent him from attending and therefore a Special Council chose as his replacement Sieur Pierre Henri Bernard, another *bourgeois*.[6] The General Assembly of the Communities, which had met periodically at Lambesc throughout the eighteenth century, passed several mild resolutions asking for the free election of Third Estate delegates within each district and for a more equitable distribution of the tax burden.

Agitation on behalf of the Third Estate was centered in Aix during the second half of 1788. To the dissatisfied commoners were added those Provençal nobles who did not hold fiefs and who, because of the Provençal constitution, were thus excluded from sitting with the Second Estate. Finding themselves without an effective voice in government, these noblemen without fiefs found a champion in the Comte de Mirabeau, himself a member of the nobility and fief-holder of a village near Lourmarin. The Estates of Provence met again in January, 1789, and Mirabeau renewed the demand for an assembly of the three orders.[7]

By 1789 the rural population in Provence began to evince its dissatisfaction with a status quo which gave dominance to the church and nobility while little attention was paid to the problems of the Third Estate. Seventy-

---

[4] Egret, "La prérévolution en Provence," p. 106; Masson, *Les temps modernes*, p. 529.

[5] *A.M., D.M.*, April 20, 1788.

[6] *Ibid.*; *A.D., Bouches-du-Rhône*, C 1177, April 21, 1788.

[7] Egret, "La prérévolution en Provence," pp. 119–20. For a complete discussion of the preparations in Provence for calling the Estates General, see Jules Viguier, *La convocation des états généraux en Provence* (Paris, 1896).

seven heads of family were present at a significant General Council held in Lourmarin on February 15.[8] Jean Egret believes that Lourmarin's meeting is an example of the agitation in the rural areas and also demonstrates the popular participation in such assemblies.[9] The General Council voted to ally Lourmarin with the district at Apt in protesting the voting of royal and provincial taxes that had taken place in the Estates meeting in January and protested specifically against

. . . the illegitimacy of the Estates. We do not in any way regard the measures taken by the first two Orders as representing our wishes. We demand a General Convocation of the three Orders in order to proceed to a true and legitimate formation of the provincial estates and for election of deputies to the Estates General . . . in order to give a character of equality to this deputation.[10]

At the same meeting Mayor Corgier and the second consul, François Artaud, drafted the following resolution:

The citizens of Lourmarin are deeply impressed by His Majesty's gracious intentions. Let us, messieurs, offer up prayers that individual interests may be sacrificed to the general interest, and that all loyal subjects will contribute equally according to their wealth, their ability, and their labor to the glory of a true Monarch, to the prosperity of his empire, and to the general welfare of his people. Let us offer to the best of Kings as a pledge of our gratitude and our inviolable attachment to him, our property and our lives. Let us live and let us die perpetuating these sentiments and let us follow the lead of his virtuous Director General of Finances.[11]

Lourmarin's General Council ordered Corgier to send extracts of the February 15 deliberations to "Monsieur Necker and to the elected deputy of the district."[12] The above appeal demonstrated the confidence the village government had in Necker and more especially in Louis XVI, realizing that the only real hope for the Third Estate in Provence rested with the king at Versailles. But as the time for drafting *cahiers* and electing deputies to the

[8] *A.M.*, *D.M.*, February 15, 1789.
[9] Egret, "La prérévolution en Provence," pp. 119–21.
[10] *A.M.*, *D.M.*, February 15, 1789.
[11] *Ibid.*
[12] *Ibid.*

Estates General approached, it was uncertain whether the king's officials could, or would, intercede.

On March 2, 1789, a royal edict decreed that deputies to the Estates General were to be elected by the assemblies of the districts rather than by the Estates of Provence.[13] The king's decision was warmly greeted by the Third Estate, but the fief-holding nobility, fearing their control was slipping away, refused to accept it, thus triggering demonstrations and rioting in many Provençal villages. In order to stem the violence a meeting of 60 fief-holding nobles in Aix on March 27, 1789, promised under duress what they had refused for two years: the nobility agreed to relinquish their special tax privileges and accepted proportional taxation of their possessions, both noble and common.[14]

Meanwhile, the Third Estate's delegates to the district assemblies were elected in the towns and villages of Provence during the last ten days of March. Conforming to the royal instructions of March 2, 1789, "all native-born and naturalized Frenchmen over 25 years of age who are listed on our tax rolls and who are inhabitants of this place" were invited to a General Council meeting on March 29, 1789, convoked in the village church.[15] One hundred seventy-six of the 334 household heads attended, representing the largest assembly of all heads of family ever held in Lourmarin to that time. The main order of business was the drafting of a *cahier*, which has since disappeared, and the election of deputies. Given a free choice and with no obvious electioneering, the Lourmarinois chose three wealthy *bourgeois*, Sieurs Jean Paul Corgier, mayor, Antoine André Bernard, and Antoine Abraham Goulin. These three men and their ancestors had played an important role in Lourmarin's municipal government throughout the eighteenth century, and all three were among the village's ten largest property holders.[16]

The spring of 1789 posed problems for Lourmarin only peripherally related to the coming meeting of the Estates General. Two successive hard winters and the poor harvest of 1788 put real pressure on the local council

[13] Egret, "La prérévolution en Provence," p. 122; Masson, *Les temps modernes*. pp. 530–31.
[14] Egret, "La prérévolution en Provence," pp. 122–25; Masson, *Les temps modernes*, p. 531.
[15] *A.M., D.M.*, March 29, 1789.
[16] *Ibid., passim*; *A.M., Cadastre*, 1770.

to provide food for the villagers. Of course the food shortage was not unique to Lourmarin and most of France experienced it to some degree. The problem of a scarcity of grain combined with inflated prices thus occurred at the same time as the agitation which preceded the Estates General.

Because of the food crisis, the council took little note of the events transpiring in Paris until late summer. Meanwhile, on March 27 the local grain tax was suppressed in order to ease the burden on "the most indigent class."[17] The next day Mayor Corgier told a hastily convened Special Council that this measure would not really afford much relief to the poor.[18] He therefore appointed three *ménagers* to buy rye and to sell it to the poor at two livres less per *charge* than the community paid for it. Three *bourgeois*, including Mayor Corgier, agreed to loan the community 600 livres without interest to purchase grain, and on the same day Pierre Ginoux donated to the poor the 300 livres he had received for the land he sold to the community for the new Protestant cemetery.[19]

The king, "having been informed of the scarcity of grain in Provence," established grain storehouses throughout the province during the emergency.[20] It soon became obvious that despite the good intentions of the royal officials, there was not enough grain for all those who needed it. As the crisis deepened, a letter was received from the Intendant on April 19 saying that a large shipment of wheat had arrived in Marseilles. The Intendant authorized Lourmarin to buy its grain directly from Marseilles and to borrow the necessary money.[21] Pierre Henri Joseph de Girard, present at the council meeting, "begs the council to agree to an interest-free loan which he offers to the community."[22] The council gratefully accepted Girard's offer. By May 24 Girard and eight other *bourgeois* had loaned the village a total of 9,248 livres to be used to purchase 200 *charges* of wheat, or about 1,000 bushels.[23] This grain was either sold to the poor at a low price or to the bakers, who then baked it into bread and sold it to the villagers for two sous, six deniers per one-pound loaf. Lourmarin's price was

[17] *A.M.*, *D.M.*, March 27, 1789.
[18] *Ibid.*, March 28, 1789.
[19] *Ibid.*
[20] *Ibid.*, April 14, 1789. See also Chapters III and V.
[21] *Ibid.*, April 19, 1789.
[22] *Ibid.*
[23] *Ibid.*, April 19, May 10, 24, June 7, 1789.

almost one-third below that of Paris as well as Aix and Marseilles, where bread sold for three sous, eight deniers per pound.[24]

Ernest Labrousse has estimated that on the eve of the Revolution a floating pool of unemployed, propertyless peasants made up as much as 40 percent of the population.[25] Although times were hard in the winter of 1788–89, a maximum of ten percent of Lourmarin's adult male population was unemployed as compared to Labrousse's figure of 40 percent. There was no violence in Lourmarin and the village managed to raise sufficient money to feed the poor.

In a document sent to the royal officials in Aix on May 30, 1789, Mayor Corgier detailed the losses suffered by the community, caused primarily by the death of about 85 percent of the olive trees. The loss of this income, combined with the high grain prices, had increased the economic pressure on the village. As a result, the report continued, "the love of bread and the desire to insure public tranquillity have necessitated the suppression of the municipal *fermes.*"[26]

Lourmarin had been forced to borrow heavily and prospects for the future certainly were not bright, but Corgier ended his report on a hopeful note: "The weight of its [Lourmarin's] burdens is exceedingly heavy, but the consoling prospect of obtaining aid from the best of kings raises our hopes and allows us to bear with firmness the weight of our calamities."[27]

The early summer of 1789 differed from other years only because the grain shortage was unusually severe. Most villagers were busy in the fields and, although there was occasional news from Paris, no particular notice was given to the momentous events of June and July. The council met early in September to consider a letter addressed to them by the "deputies of the Third Estate of Provence to the National Assembly" who asked that Lour-

---

[24] George Rudé, *The Crowd in the French Revolution* (Oxford, 1959), p. 251; George Rudé, "Prices, Wages and Popular Movements in Paris during the French Revolution," *The Economic History Review*, VI (April, 1954), 247; Masson, *Provence*, p. 652.

[25] Ernest Labrousse, *Origine et aspects*, pp. 49–53.

[26] A.D., *Bouches-du-Rhône*, C 1177, May 30, 1789. By May 30, 1789, the local taxes on grain, wine, and fresh pork had been temporarily suppressed. The idea was to afford temporary relief but not to eliminate the *fermes* as a source of village income. Actually, of course, these *fermes* were never reinstituted. A.M., D.M., March 26, 28, 1789.

[27] A.D., *Bouches-du-Rhône*, C 1177, May 30, 1789.

marin "ratify the actions taken by the National Assembly on August 4, 6, 7, and 11."[28] Mayor Corgier, having read this letter to the council, added that "no good citizen could help but perform his duty and render homage to them [the deputies] because of the deep gratitude of all the villagers."[29] The council said that it admired all acts emanating from the National Assembly, "especially those of the famous night of August 4."[30] Sieur Pierre Henri Joseph de Girard was therefore directed "to draft an address in the name of the community in order to express, if possible, our sentiments of patriotism, love and admiration for the King and for the National Assembly." Girard's address was printed and sent to the President of the National Assembly and to all the deputies from Provence.[31] The same day the council authorized a civic celebration "in memory of the important decisions made by the National Assembly in August, 1789."[32]

One must note that in this heady atmosphere of celebration, it was not the end of noble privileges that the Lourmarinois applauded most but rather "the sacrifice that our deputies have made of the dangerous privilege which isolated this province from the rest of France. To be called a Frenchman is the first and most beneficial of all national rights and the most fertile source of liberty, of equality and of social well-being."[33] The Provençal deputies renounced these special rights, including the fiscal privileges of a pays d'état, as being "contrary to the system of equality and of uniformity which is the basis of the French Constitution."[34] Only those who were "enemies of la patrie" would oppose such a worthwhile change.[35] This endorsement seems to be an unusually broad-minded position for a rural village, almost overwhelmed by local problems, to take. The really surprising thing about Lourmarin's approval of the action taken by their deputies was that they were apparently willing to accept equality with the amorphous body of "Frenchmen." In concrete terms this meant the acceptance of fiscal equality with Frenchmen from formerly less-favored provinces.

[28] A.M., D.M., September 10, 1789.
[29] Ibid.
[30] Ibid.
[31] Ibid., September 10, 1789, February 14, 1790.
[32] Ibid., September 10, 1789.
[33] Ibid.
[34] Ibid.
[35] Ibid.

To guard against the brigands in the countryside "who devastate every-thing in their path" and to insure the "security and public tranquility" of the village, the council immediately authorized the expenditure of 257 livres for powder and balls.[36] In a move reminiscent of the extraordinary measures taken during the plague in 1720, a special committee of ten was organized to supervise the "continual surveillance" of the village and to form a *Garde Bourgeoise*. The ten included the mayor, second consul, and eight prominent *bourgeois*.[37] Shortly thereafter the council authorized the purchase of 36 guns at 20 livres each.[38]

Lourmarin's reaction was matched by security measures taken throughout Provence as a result of the "Great Fear" that began in the last days of July. Georges Lefebvre and others who have examined this phenomenon have concluded that there was never any real threat in Provence, but rumors coming from Aix and neighboring villages convinced many that hordes of brigands were loose and that the villages of Cadenet and Cucuron, adjacent to Lourmarin on the south and east, had been put to the torch. There was some trouble in Aix and Marseilles, but this had been going on since the preceding winter. The village committees organized to meet this supposed threat were generally conservative in outlook and were disbanded by late fall.[39]

The village's political organization, codified in 1648, was altered by de-crees of the National Assembly with the result that new elections were to be held in early 1790.[40] The most pressing question was the eligibility requirement for the electorate, since "all active citizens" were allowed to exercise their franchise in village elections as well as others.[41] The National

[36] *Ibid.*

[37] *Ibid.*

[38] *Ibid.*, November 5, 1789.

[39] Georges Lefebvre, *La grande peur de 1789* (Paris, 1932), pp. 198–99, 215; M. A. Pickford, "The Panic of 1789 in Lower Dauphiné and in Provence," *English Historical Review*, XXIX (April, 1914), 276–301.

[40] When France was reorganized, Lourmarin (District of Apt) was placed in the Department of the Bouches-du-Rhône, which included Marseilles and Aix. After the events of summer, 1793, the District of Apt was placed in the new Department of the Vaucluse.

[41] Jules Viguier, *Les débuts de la Révolution en Provence* (Paris, 1894), p. 74. See Frank M. Anderson, ed., *The Constitutions and Other Select Documents Illus-trative of the History of France, 1789–1907* (New York, 1967), pp. 24–29 for a copy of the decree of December 14, 1789, which discussed the reorganization of the local governments. See also a copy of this decree in *A.M., D.M.*, January 16, 1790.

Assembly defined an "active citizen" as one who paid direct taxes equivalent to three days' labor.[42] Because the payment for day labor varied greatly, each community was to use the prevailing local rate to determine which citizens were eligible. There was also the question of defining direct taxation. To answer these two questions, Mayor Corgier wrote the royal officials in Aix, who responded by setting the price of a *"journée de travail"* in Lourmarin at 20 sous, or one livre. Thus an individual who paid three or more livres in direct taxes would qualify. In answer to the second question, the *capitation* was considered a direct tax and those who made a three livres *capitation* payment were considered "active citizens."[43]

In December, 1789, Sieur Trophime Borrelly, a Catholic and Lourmarin's only notary at the time, appeared before the council. As the seigneur's *viguier*, Borrelly had formerly authorized the village deliberations, but now that "the rights of the seigneurs over municipal deliberations have been abolished by *arrêt* of the National Assembly on August 4" he requested the council not to call him in the future to authorize its meetings.[44] Instead Borrelly, who had lived in Lourmarin for 15 years and was nearly blind, asked "to be admitted to the number of active citizens on the basis of my talents and my zeal for my adopted village."[45]

Borrelly soon decided to write the officials at Aix to clarify (and justify) his position in Lourmarin and also to inquire whether the *capitation* was a direct tax.[46] Having served as *viguier* and notary, Borrelly hoped that he would be eligible for election to the municipal government, but eligibility for office-holding was set at ten days' labor, or ten livres, and his *capitation* was only seven livres, four sous. He was, however, eligible to vote. Borrelly expressed pleasure at being able to vote because, while exercising his dual function in Lourmarin, he had "acquired the affection of all the inhabitants, having used my authority only to keep peace in families in order to maintain the public good, never to serve the caprices of a seigneur, never to oppress my fellow citizens. I flatter myself to think that this opinion is shared in the village."[47] It is interesting that this former royal and seig-

[42] *Ibid.*
[43] *A.D., Bouches-du-Rhône*, C 1083, January 17, 1790.
[44] *A.M., D.M.*, December 13, 1789.
[45] *Ibid.*
[46] *A.D., Bouches-du-Rhône*, C 1045, January 17, 1790.
[47] *Ibid.*

neurial official, understanding the direction in which events were developing, moved so quickly to dissociate himself from the past and to ally himself with the forces of the future. The fact that he was a Catholic in a Protestant village probably also played a part in his attempt to ingratiate himself with the villagers.

One hundred eighty active citizens, or about 50 percent of the adult male population, met in the parish church at noon February 7, 1790, to elect a new municipal government.[48] The election was by secret ballot. Less than one-quarter of the heads of family were ineligible to vote despite the fact that the payment of three livres required to qualify as an active citizen was actually more than three days' wages for a day laborer in Lourmarin.[49] Each voter cast a separate ballot for every office, placing his slip of paper in a vase at the front of the church, while three officials were elected to tabulate the results. The process consumed so much time that the balloting was adjourned and concluded the next day.[50]

The most interesting aspect of Lourmarin's first revolutionary election was that the same men were elected who had previously served under the rather restrictive system of co-option. Pierre Henri Joseph Girard (the "de" had been dropped) was elected president of the council and Pierre Ginoux was chosen secretary. The new mayor, one of the largest landowners in Lourmarin, was Antoine Abraham Goulin.[51] Goulin and the other municipal officers were required, by decree of the National Assembly, to wear "marks of distinction," including a "scarf with the three colors of the nation—red, white and blue."[52]

Mayor Goulin is enshrined in the memory of the Lourmarinois even today as the result of an event which allegedly occurred during his administration. A group of angry peasants marched on the chateau in 1790 in-

[48] A.M., D.M., February 7, 1790.

[49] See ibid., October 5, 1790, which discusses those eligible to vote. This high participation reinforces the belief that, at least relatively, Lourmarin was a prosperous community.

[50] Viguier, Révolution en Provence, pp. 74–78; A.M., D.M., February 7, 8, 1790. See also a copy of the decree of the National Assembly explaining the duties and responsibilities of the various officers, A.M., D.M., December 16, 1789. The administrative responsibilities of the village officers remained virtually the same as under the ancien régime.

[51] A.M., D.M., February 7, 8, 1790. The office of mayor was still the most important position in the village government.

[52] Ibid., April 20, 1790.

tending to burn it. Goulin intercepted them and from the steps of the chateau persuaded the mob that it would be foolhardy to destroy the chateau and much wiser to turn it into a hospital, thereby benefiting the entire village. Evidently his persuasive powers were great because the chateau was spared.[53] An extensive examination of many documents concerning Lourmarin's activities during the Revolution unearthed no mention of this event. The story may be true, but perhaps it is just a pleasant myth originated to explain why the chateau was not destroyed after 1789 as was Bruny's chateau at La Tour d'Aigues.

It was not for a lack of provocation that Bruny's chateau was spared. In the years after 1789 there were several areas of conflict between Lourmarin and its seigneur. The first confrontation was caused by an argument over the scales used in the seigneur's mill. In April, 1789, the council had decided to check all weights and measures being used in public commerce.[54] On August 20 the specially appointed committee reported that the scales in the seigneurial mill were inaccurate and that the villagers were being cheated.[55] A debate about whether the council had the authority to check the miller's scales caused a two and one-half month delay, but when the measures were finally inspected, it was determined that the miller's charge for grinding exceeded the amount stipulated. The council did not hesitate to request that the seigneur immediately furnish his miller with correct scales.[56]

Jean-Baptiste Jérôme de Bruny, seigneur of Lourmarin, lost more than a set of scales as a result of the Revolution. Arthur Young, visiting the Baron at La Tour d'Aigues on September 1 and 2, 1789, said he already was "an enormous sufferer from the Revolution."[57] Less than a month after the legislation of August 4, Young saw that the compensation payments due the lords "are falling to nothing, without a shadow of recompense."[58]

---

[53] Varille, *Lourmarin*, p. 18; Bancol, *Monographies communales*, pp. 121–22; Robert Bailey, *Dictionnaire des communes, Vaucluse* (Avignon, 1961), p. 45.
[54] *A.M., D.M.*, April 14, 1789.
[55] *Ibid.*, August 20, 1789.
[56] *Ibid.*, December 13, 1789.
[57] Young, *Travels*, pp. 370–71.
[58] *Ibid.*, p. 371.

On March 13, 1790, the National Assembly abolished the *banalités* on ovens, mills, and presses. These *banalités* in Lourmarin were governed by the 1523 transaction between the seigneur and the village.[59] "The general interest requires that the most efficacious and prompt measures be taken so that people can enjoy the benefits of this salutary action and to free them from a servitude which increases their public misery."[60] Seigneur Bruny, however, gave no indication that he intended to relinquish these rights and the council instructed the mayor to inform him immediately of the National Assembly's action. If the baron declined to set a date for ending the *banalités*, the council said they would regard his silence as formal acceptance of suppression without compensation.[61]

Bruny fought against the elimination of other seigneurial rights, most especially that of the *tasque* from which he claimed one-eighth of the harvest. It appeared to many Lourmarinois that the National Assembly had abolished payment of the *tasque* when it declared that the "National Assembly destroys the feudal regime in its entirety," but Bruny demanded either that it be continued or that he receive compensation.[62] The resolutions of August 4, 1789, and later had provided for redemption of "manorial fees" including the *tasque*, but since the peasant was required to pay between 20 and 25 times his annual payment, it appeared that few peasants could afford such capital sums and that this source of noble income would continue.[63]

It began to appear that the apparent victories of the early days of the Revolution might prove hollow. The council minutes throughout 1791 are filled with reports from various council members who had been designated to contact Bruny regarding his remaining seigneurial rights. On at least two occasions they consulted attorneys in Aix.[64] Their attempts to communicate with Bruny were usually met by silence or by demands for continued payment. Exasperated, and probably a little afraid, the council finally decided on December 15, 1791, to address a plea directly to the National Assem-

---

[59] For a discussion of this agreement see Chapter VI.
[60] *A.M., D.M.,* May 11, 1790.
[61] *Ibid.*
[62] *Ibid.,* March 25, 1791.
[63] Georges Lefebvre, *The French Revolution from Its Origins to 1793,* trans. by Elizabeth Moss Evanson (New York, 1962), pp. 127, 129–30, 141, 164.
[64] *A.M., D.M.,* February 13, April 1, 1791, and *passim.*

bly.[65] Although Lourmarin's seigneur was never mentioned specifically, the address depicted the good intentions of the Constituent Assembly as being subverted by the nobles and by representatives from the cities, who did not understand or care about the seigneurial exactions.[66] "The countryside, tortured by *tasques, champarts, cens, agents, fermiers,* etc., has been forgotten. No one speaks for them. It is these former seigneurs, their agents and *fermiers* who, uniting with the non-juring priests and fanatics of all sorts, . . . kill the revolutionary zeal of the simple and ignorant peasant," and who are "keeping the country in irons."[67] Hoping to prevent the return of the "old order of things" the Lourmarinois concluded their address on an optimistic note:

We declare to you with a *douce joie*: The destruction of the feudal regime will be the death blow for the aristocrats. It is in the hope of reestablishing it that they are emigrating, conspiring and agitating everywhere. . . . You must believe more than ever that liberty and feudalism cannot go together; that half of the Empire is groaning under this hideous regime. This portion, since it nourishes the other, is the most precious; therefore, the achievements of the Revolution will be only partially maintained and the Constitution will be unstable if you do not make it easier than it has been up until now for citizens to redeem their feudal dues. . . . Only when you will have banished the monster of feudalism will the aristocracy be forever destroyed, and the countryside, so desolated today, will become the strongest bulwark of the Republic.[68]

Correspondence between the seigneur and the village continued until finally in July, 1792, after reading yet another letter from "citizen" Bruny in which the seigneur refused to surrender his right of the *tasque*, the council made a curious announcement: "Since there is no law which prohibits the payment of the *tasque*, the council invites all citizens to pay citizen Bruny the *droits féodaux* which have not been suppressed."[69] The negative tone of this announcement makes it appear very unlikely that many villagers availed

[65] For a copy of this address see P. Sagnac, *La législation civile de la Révolution française* (Paris, 1898), pp. 400–402.
[66] *Ibid.*, p. 401.
[67] *Ibid.*
[68] *Ibid.*, pp. 401–2.
[69] A.M., D.M., July 8, 1792.

themselves of the council's "invitation." The Terror soon abolished all such seigneurial payments without compensation.

In addition to losing the income from most of the seigneurial dues, the former seigneur now found himself liable for taxes on his real and personal property. As the result of a decree of the National Assembly passed September 26, 1789, such property was to be evaluated and entered on the local tax rolls.

All the *privilégés* who possess real or personal property will be added to the tax roll and their assessment will be made in the same proportion and in the same form as the ordinary impositions of the same year vis-à-vis others liable to contribution.[70]

Mayor Antoine Abraham Goulin was chosen by Lourmarin to meet with an expert named by the seigneur, and the two "jointly evaluated, surveyed, and registered" Bruny's property.[71] This task was completed by the spring of 1790 and Bruny paid taxes for the last half of 1789.[72]

Early in 1791 Lourmarin began preparations to draft two new tax books, the *Contribution Foncière* and *Contribution Mobilière*. The only major change was that Jean-Baptiste Jérôme Bruny replaced Girard as the largest single taxpayer.[73] In 1792 the village was charged 12,420 livres for the two new taxes; of this amount Bruny paid 1,771 livres, or 14 percent.[74] Although he lost his seigneurial dues and found his property now taxed, Bruny did adapt, albeit begrudgingly, to the new state of affairs. In January, 1800, his real property, including extensive meadowland, was virtually the same as it had been in 1789 although his income, of course, was considerably less.[75]

Lourmarin's finances, as well as those of France in general, were in chaos by 1790 because when the seigneurial payments were ended, some people decided they would pay no taxes at all. In conformance with "a proclama-

---

[70] *Ibid.*, September 26, 1789. Copy of decree of National Assembly.

[71] *Ibid.*, November 5, 1789.

[72] *Ibid.*, November 22, 1789, January 5, May 11, July 19, December 12, 1790; *A.D., Bouches-du-Rhône*, C 1177, September 25, 28, 1789, January 3, February 8, 1790.

[73] *A.M., D.M.*, February 13, 20, March 6, 1791.

[74] *Ibid.*, December 23, 1792; *M.C.*, 4580, fo. 43, September 16, 1792.

[75] *M.C.*, 4580, fo. 132, January 12, 1800.

tion of His Majesty" of September 25, 1789, the village set about trying to collect a *contribution patriotique* from its citizens.[76] The proportion for the *contribution patriotique* fixed by the National Assembly was 25 percent of one's income after all other taxes were paid plus two and one-half percent of the value of an individual's silver and jewelry. All of those with net revenue of less than 400 livres were not required to pay any set proportion, but rather were to contribute "according to their conscience." Artisans and day laborers without property were not required to contribute at all "but we will not, however, reject the free and voluntary offering of any citizen."[77]

By late 1790 the collectors named by the council had amassed 12,633 livres, but they were unable to get Bruny to pay.[78] Finally in May, 1791, the exasperated council ordered Mathieu Colletin, acting in the name of the village, to seize the wine and grain in the storehouse and wine cellar of the chateau. Before he could carry out his commission, however, Pierre Paul Cavallier, Bruny's agent (*procureur fondé*), appeared and said that Bruny would pay. The council accepted Bruny's payment and rescinded the order to Colletin.[79]

The most serious threat to Bruny's property came in late 1793 while the Committee of Public Safety was in charge of the government in Paris. The department of the Vaucluse was still suffering the aftereffects of the struggle between the central government and the Federalist forces from Marseilles. Acting in accordance with a law of September 11, 1793, aimed at "counter-revolutionaries," the justice of the peace, Pierre Bertin, affixed official seals to the door of Bruny's storehouse, as well as to his two wine cellars and both seigneurial mills.[80] There is, however, absolutely no evidence that Bruny supported the Federalist movement in Lourmarin in 1793.

[76] *A.M., D.M.*, November 8, 1789; *A.D., Bouches-du-Rhône*, C 1177, January 3, 1790.

[77] *A.M., D.M.*, October 19, 1789.

[78] *Ibid.*, August 29, October 10, 1790. By referring to Table I–2, which lists revenue from real property for 1791, and Appendix A for income from the textile industry in 1790, we can estimate Lourmarin's income for 1790 at about 63,000 livres. Their payment for the *contribution patriotique* thus represented a tax amounting to about 20 percent of the village's income, or about the same amount that they had paid for direct and indirect taxes under the *ancien régime*.

[79] *Ibid.*, May 1, 2, 1791.

[80] *A.D., Vaucluse*, 2 Q 7, October 12, 1793.

Bruny was ordered to appear within one week, thereby proving he had not left the country, or his wine, oil, and grain would be confiscated.[81] When Bruny failed to appear by October 9, the council branded him an *émigré*, broke the seals on the mills, and removed the grain, which was either given directly to the poor or to the bakers who made bread for the poor.[82] The action was completed on November 7, 1793, when the council appointed an official to break into the storehouse and inventory Bruny's olive oil.[83]

When Pierre Paul Cavallier, the seigneur's agent, appeared before the council on December 14, 1793, the villagers' real motive became clearer. On July 17, 1793, Robespierre and the Montagnards, in an effort to appease the peasants, had abolished without compensation all remaining seigneurial rights.[84] In view of Bruny's previous delays and having received no direct confirmation that he would honor this newest test of his Republican sentiments, the council decided to move against him. Representing Bruny, Cavallier presented an official "certificate of residence" from the department of the Vaucluse certifying that the seigneur's residence in the Vaucluse, if not in Lourmarin, had never been interrupted.[85] Having received no satisfaction from the council, Cavallier returned ten days later and presented a second letter from Bruny in which he argued that he had paid his village taxes and any seizure of his property was unwarranted.[86] The council listened patiently and decided that "the commune ought not to give up that which it has seized unless it is given an express guarantee that it can never again be held liable for the *tasque.*"[87] The district court at Apt twice decreed Lourmarin should return the seigneur's property, but the council refused to comply until they finally obtained the requested guarantee from Cavallier, whereupon the oil and wine were returned, the wheat having long since been consumed.[88] This dispute was not over the value of the goods confiscated, which was small, rather it occurred because of the seigneur's failure to declare his intention to honor the July decrees.

[81] *A.M., D.M.,* October 17, 18, 1793.

[82] *A.D., Vaucluse,* 2 Q 7, October 19, 1793.

[83] *Ibid.,* November 7, 1793.

[84] Georges Lefebvre, *The French Revolution from 1793 to 1799,* trans. by John Hall Stewart and James Friguglietti (New York, 1964), p. 56.

[85] *A.M., D.M.,* December 14, 1793.

[86] *Ibid.,* December 24, 1793.

[87] *Ibid.*

[88] *Ibid.,* January 1, 4, 30, February 10, 1794.

Pierre Henri Joseph Girard was the only *bourgeois* Lourmarinois whose property was seized during the Revolution, probably because Camille, one of his four sons, was a leader of the abortive Federalist movement in Lourmarin who was forced to emigrate and because he himself was implicated in this movement.[89] Like Bruny and other members of the Lourmarin *bourgeoisie,* Girard submitted a "certificate of residence" from Nîmes in the department of the Gard in December, 1793.[90] But because his son was an *émigré,* Girard *père's* furniture, clothes, linen, grain, and other commodities were seized in February, 1794.[91] In December, 1794, the revolutionary officials at Apt acknowledged they had received goods valued at 2,303 livres "belonging to Pierre Henri Joseph Girard, father of an *émigré,* seized this year."[92] The animosity displayed toward Girard probably occurred because he was the wealthiest man in Lourmarin and because of his involvement in the Federalist movement. The villagers conveniently forgot that his gifts and loans before, during, and after 1789 had provided bread for the poor.[93] Girard *père* returned to Lourmarin from Nîmes in 1795, but his son's name was not removed from the list of *émigrés* until 1801.[94] Girard never received any compensation for his personal property, but since no real property had been confiscated, his income remained unchanged.

Because Bruny did not emigrate and instead reluctantly decided to embrace the Revolution, the villagers did not receive any of the former seigneur's land. Five other pieces of land were, however, declared *biens nationaux*; three belonged to the tithe-collector and two to the *curé.* Antoine André Bernard, *bourgeois,* evaluated the "landed property in Lourmarin belonging to the former tithe-collector of Lourmarin in execution of decrees of the National Assembly."[95] The three pieces were valued at 2,690 livres and amounted to less than one percent of the total value of property in Lourmarin. The largest piece of land accounted for 90 percent of the total

---

[89] *Ibid.,* October 26, 1793. See below for a discussion of this event. Girard *père* was mayor during the period of Jacobin-Federalist conflict in 1793.

[90] *Ibid.,* December 11, 1793.

[91] *Ibid.,* February 19, March 13, May 15, 1794.

[92] *Ibid.,* December 11, 1794.

[93] There is no evidence of animosity toward Girard prior to this time.

[94] *A.D., Vaucluse,* 1 Q 114, no. 165, September 5, 1801.

[95] *Ibid.,* 2 Q 9, March 24, 1791.

and included both grain land and meadow adjacent to the Aigue Brun, the only creek watering the territory of Lourmarin, as well as an old, abandoned chapel that had not been used in the eighteenth century. Bids on these three properties were accepted on April 24, 1791, with at least three persons bidding on each. The highest bids were announced on May 9. Jean Ginoux, *ménager*, was awarded the large property (five acres), while the two smaller pieces of about one acre each went to Jean Cavallier, shoemaker, and Elzead Giraudon, baker. The total purchase price was 4,600 livres or about 650 livres per acre.[96] This figure is misleading, however, since more than 90 percent of the purchase price came from Ginoux for the largest piece. At least part of Ginoux's payment must have been for the chapel which he possibly intended to use for storage or as a house for a tenant farmer. The property belonging to the *curé* was evaluated at 275 livres in 1794 and consisted of less than one-sixth of an acre of meadow and one-half acre of grain land. These two pieces were sold to citizens Daniel Cavallier, *négociant*, and Jean Roman, *agriculteur*.[97]

On April 5, 1794, following orders from the national agent in Apt, the mayor and municipal officers, upon "the invitation of the former *curé*," went to the little Catholic church located in the center of the village to inventory its contents.[98] The council appointed Joseph Janselme and Pierre Sambuc to conduct the inventory and also "to remove all signs of royalty and *féodalité*."[99] The contents were those one might expect to find in any small village church at the time.[100] When fighting had broken out in 1793 between the Jacobin army and the "Marseilles rebels" the silver from the church was taken to the chateau in Cadenet, three miles to the south, for safekeeping.[101] The council decreed on April 22, 1794, that wives and parents of volunteers for the national army were to be aided in every possible way and that they were to be given "all the silver from the church."[102] Despite the religious differences and the overwhelmingly Protestant compo-

---

[96] *Ibid.*, 2 Q 5, 2 Q 20 bis, no. 110, May 9, 1791.
[97] *Ibid.*, 2 Q 9, April 4, 1794, 2 Q 20 bis, no. 213, June 29, 1795.
[98] *Ibid.*, 2 Q 6, April 5, 1794.
[99] *A.M., D.M.*, January 12, 1794.
[100] For a complete inventory of the contents of the Catholic Church see *A.D., Vaucluse*, 2 Q 6, April 5, 1794.
[101] *Ibid.*, 2 Q 6, April 20, 24, 25, June 17, 1794.
[102] *A.M., D.M.*, April 22, 1794.

sition of the village, this was the first recorded action taken against the Catholic church and, even then, it was done on orders from Apt. In the last analysis, the policy of dechristianization, especially in rural areas, depended more on the local authorities than upon decrees from Paris or the district.[103]

The stages of the Revolution in Lourmarin after 1789 differed little from the course of events occurring in the rest of France, although they tended to be more muted. Although the "Great Fear" touched the village at about the same time as it received news of the National Assembly's legislation of August 4, the most pressing problem in 1789 was how to find food to feed the population. Just before the elections of 1790 Lourmarin established an *Association Patriotique*, a moderate organization whose main function was to help the *classe indigente* and "to continue aid as in the past," either by direct grants or by providing public works.[104]

In answer to a departmental questionnaire of October, 1790, the council said that there were 75 heads of family living in Lourmarin who paid less tax annually than the three livres necessary to qualify as an "active citizen"; 34 of these 75 paid no tax at all.[105] The council estimated that 216 persons, or about 14 percent of the entire population—children of the poor, the aged, infirm, and the "unemployables"—needed assistance.[106] The council then analyzed the cause of mendicity and suggested how it might be alleviated.

The cause of mendicity in our community is the debauchery and irreligion which is caused entirely by the *cabarets*; the impiety and disorder occasioned by *fête* days which are too numerous, alms given to beggars who could work, laziness masquerading as mendicity, prolonged illnesses, the misery of the children of the poor, and most especially their ingratitude.

The solution to this problem would be rigorous police measures against the *cabarets*, and the suppression of several *fêtes* or at least the requirement that men work every day of the year except Sundays.

The alms should be verified and given only to those *pauvres malades* who cannot work. Others should work on the roads or be established in work-

---

[103] Lefebvre, *French Revolution from 1793 to 1799*, pp. 80–81.
[104] *A.M.*, *D.M.*, January 30, 1790.
[105] *Ibid.*, October 5, 1790.
[106] *Ibid.*

shops of charity, which would be cotton mills for the manufacture of cotton handkerchiefs.[107]

This report says more, of course, about the outlook of the village leaders than it does about the underlying causes of poverty. The tone of this indictment was certainly more harsh than anything in the minutes since 1680 and it is not immediately clear why their attitude seemingly changed so abruptly. The only previous complaint about the *cabarets* occurred during the threat of the plague and did not associate them with corruption. The 1790 report was drafted by the first truly elective council in Lourmarin's history. It is possible that the newly elected officials felt an added sense of fiscal responsibility and an increased expectation that every man should pull his weight now that the Lourmarinois had become "citizens." Whatever the cause, the attitude toward the poor had definitely hardened. The suggestion that workshops for the poor be established was an innovation, but the times were not propitious for this reform in 1790. This idea, however, was to be popularized in the nineteenth century by social reformers.

In February, 1791, Lourmarin received 130 livres from the National Assembly for poor relief. The council decided to use this money to repair its roads, stipulating that the daily wage paid to those working on this project was to be less than the prevailing day rate so that no able-bodied Lourmarinois would be tempted to abandon his bench.[108]

The year 1791 was fairly quiet in Lourmarin; there was little revolutionary agitation, the harvest was good, and most citizens readily accepted the changes made in Paris. The villagers participated in choosing the Archbishop of Aix and in naming electors to the Electoral Assembly for the department of the Bouches-du-Rhône, which in turn elected deputies to the Legislative Assembly.[109] Sometimes the silence of the villagers says a great deal. There was absolutely no discussion in the village minutes of the new Civil Constitution of the Clergy, which caused heated debate in other places. Likewise there was no opposition to the election of a new *curé*, who was simply chosen and installed. This would appear to be another indication of the lack of religious enthusiasm in Lourmarin as both Protestants and

---

[107] *Ibid.*
[108] *Ibid.*, February 13, 1791.
[109] *Ibid.*, March 6, June 13, September 18, 1791.

Catholics appeared content to forget the religious disputes of earlier days. Vovelle argues that the whole area of the Luberon and the valley of the Durance River demonstrated this same indifference to religious matters and showed little inclination to resist the Civil Constitution, accepted by most priests in the region.[110]

In the spring of 1791, Lourmarin's recently established Society of the Friends of the Constitution presented the council with a petition requesting that the local guard be reorganized so that no distinction was made as to a soldier's social position.[111] The council responded to this egalitarian request by agreeing that all active citizens would be included on the rolls of the guard.[112] The outbreak of war in 1792 meant that men were badly needed at the frontiers. The minimum age for soldiers was reduced from 18 to 16 and plans were also made to recruit the Battalion of the Luberon, including ten companies from the district of Apt.[113] For the next three years a considerable number of Lourmarin's youth served in the armies of France, although it is impossible to know precisely how many.[114]

From a reading of the village minutes one gets the very definite feeling of panic in the late summer and fall of 1792. On July 11 the Legislative Assembly had declared that *"la patrie* is in danger."[115] Lourmarin's regular council met henceforth in permanent session and no official was allowed to leave his post. Until the end of the year the council met three or four times a week and they often met daily. All citizens who were physically capable of carrying arms were put on permanent alert and the council inventoried all the guns and ammunition in the village, while money was donated to buy material and buttons for uniforms.[116] One company of 80 soldiers, formed mostly of Lourmarinois, was sent to Paris in September "to come to the aid of the fatherland."[117] While they were gone the village assumed

[110] Michel Vovelle, "Prêtres abdicataires et dechristianisation en Provence," in *Actes du 89ᵉ Congrès National des Sociétés Savantes* (Lyon, 1964), pp. 63–98.

[111] *A.M., D.M.*, March 20, 1791.

[112] *Ibid.*, July 10, 1791.

[113] *Ibid.*, August 4, 21, 1792.

[114] See, for example, *ibid.*, September 24, October 24, 1792, January 28, 1793, and *passim*.

[115] *Ibid.*, July 22, 1792.

[116] *Ibid.*, July 22, September 15, 1792, and *passim*.

[117] *Ibid.*, September 14, 1792.

the responsibility of aiding the families of these "good patriots."[118] On September 23, just as the new Republican government in Paris was being organized, all municipal officers swore an oath "to be faithful to the nation and to do everything within my power to maintain liberty and equality or else to die at my post."[119]

Jean François Artaud, 22, a local carpenter and son of the second consul in 1789, was wounded "fighting for liberty on that memorable day of August 10" while attacking the Tuileries with the *Fédérés*, and was later given a bonus by the National Convention.[120] This attack on the Tuileries marked the beginning of the radical phase of the Revolution and was to lead, in less than six months, to the death of Louis XVI. After a six-week period of terror and confusion the monarchy was abolished and the first French Republic established. Would it not be reasonable to assume that as Lourmarin's young men, such as Artaud, marched north, they underwent a process of radicalization that reached a peak as they entered Paris?

The disruption caused by the absence of so many able-bodied men and the fear that France was about to be invaded affected the harvest in 1792 and the council was forced to ask for voluntary contributions to buy grain throughout the fall months. Twenty-seven persons donated over 11,000 livres, much in *assignats*, in November alone. Pierre Henri Joseph Girard once again donated the most—2,000 livres in paper.[121] During the fall and winter the council met several times a week, often daily. Invariably the major subject of discussion was the shortage of grain combined with the mounting cost of bread. One joyful occasion in an otherwise dismal fall occurred on Sunday, October 28, 1792, when Lourmarin held a glorious *fête* and sang republican hymns to celebrate the French victory at Valmy.[122] When the last strains of the Marseillaise had faded, it must have been discouraging to return to the hard reality of how to survive the coming winter.

Because the regulatory authority of the community *fermes* had been ended, the council began to receive numerous complaints about the high

---

118 *Ibid.*, September 22, 1792.
119 *Ibid.*, September 23, 1792.
120 *Ibid.*, February 14, 1793.
121 *Ibid.*, September 9, November 7, 18, 1792.
122 *Ibid.*, October 29, 1792.

prices of bread and meat.[123] The Patriotic Society, generally made up of the more radical element in Lourmarin, intervened twice in behalf of the lower classes.[124] The Patriotic Society demanded and subsequently received a price ceiling, established for bread in both cash and *assignats*, as well as regulations controlling the quality of bread sold in the village bakeries.[125] On December 26, 1792, several persons were arrested by the constable for cutting wood.[126] The next day Jean Paul Corgier, commander of the guard, and two commissioners of the Patriotic Society appeared before the council because they had "learned with sadness" of the arrests. Although they praised the constable and the council for their diligence, as representatives of the Patriotic Society, they recommended clemency. Those arrested must be given "the reproaches which they merit" and "next time the council should prosecute to the fullest extent of the law." The council meekly acquiesced and released the violators.[127]

The most difficult year for the Lourmarinois, at least in terms of conflict, was 1793. A General Council was called January 28, 1793, to announce that the "head of Louis Capet has fallen under the sword of the law." The council wrote that "we hope that this will contribute to the prosperity of the French Republic and spread terror among its enemies." All villagers were invited to meet that evening in the parish church to celebrate the king's execution and "to renew the oath to live free and to nourish our belief in the principles of republicanism and fraternity."[128]

It was after this event that Lourmarin's close relations with Marseilles assumed great importance because of the impending Federalist revolt. The events of 1793 significantly affected Lourmarin's relationship with Mar-

---

[123] These *fermes* had performed several functions for the village. Payments made by the *fermiers* produced a considerable income for the village, while the detailed leases of the *fermes* controlled the quality, size, weight, etc., of various products sold in the village. These leases also governed prices, which immediately rose when the *fermes* were suppressed.

[124] Although no membership roll has survived, the names of the leaders were recorded when they appeared before the council and in the Society's correspondence. The leaders included a fairly broad cross-section of the "better" people of Lourmarin and it was from the Patriotic Society that the Jacobins came. Membership of the Patriotic Society fluctuated and the same names also appear in connection with the *Société Républicaine* and the later Popular Society. For more on this, see below.

[125] *A.M., D.M.*, February 18, March 26, 1793.

[126] *Ibid.*, December 26, 1792.

[127] *Ibid.*, December 27, 1792.

[128] *Ibid.*, January 28, 1793.

seilles. An alliance reached with Marseilles in May, 1790, seems to have been little more than an agreement on revolutionary principles, although the pledge was renewed in April, 1792, in a letter addressed to "our brothers and friends of Marseilles."[129] The situation in France steadily grew more tense, however, and in January, 1793, a General Council had once again affirmed its solidarity with its "friends of liberty and equality" in Marseilles.[130]

To your patriotism all the citizens of Lourmarin render homage. All of us desire, as do you, brothers and friends, the reign of liberty. Your attachment to it, your courage in defending it, your zeal for the public good, which has served our glorious revolution so well, will render to Marseilles its ancient splendor and will contribute to the triumph and the prosperity of the French Revolution as they have contributed to its establishment.[131]

It was not long until Marseilles tested the sincerity of Lourmarin's sentiments.

It became obvious within a few weeks after Louis XVI's death that France would be forced to wage war on two fronts. Already engaged in a foreign war against a coalition that included most other European countries, in March, 1793, the Convention was faced with the revolt in the Vendée. Lourmarin responded to the danger by sending 18 volunteers to Apt while the *Société Républicaine* donated 12 pairs of shoes to the cause of *la patrie*.[132] The *Société Patriotique* provided 18 rifles and ammunition.[133] Lourmarin received a letter from the directors of the district in Apt ordering the municipal council to disarm all former nobles, seigneurs, and priests along with any others who opposed the Revolution. Indicating that there was no opposition to the course of the Revolution in the village, the council replied that "there is no one in this place who can give the least umbrage to the patriots" and the order thus "will not be executed in this commune."[134]

[129] *Ibid.*, May 24, 1790; *A.D.*, *Bouches-du-Rhône*, L 2036, April 20, 1792.
[130] *A.M.*, *D.M.*, January 22, 1793.
[131] *Ibid.*
[132] *Ibid.*, March 23, April 13, 14, September 14, 1793.
[133] *Ibid.*, April 22, 28, May 3, 1793.
[134] *Ibid.*, April 9, 1793.

The National Convention, soon faced with the secessionist movement of the Federalists, sent representatives into the provinces in an attempt to assure loyalty to the central government. The village council, aided by the Patriotic Society, erected an *arc de triomphe* at the northern gate of the village through which the commissioners were escorted by a detachment of the guard as the villagers shouted *"vive la nation."*[135] Future events, however, demonstrated that the villagers were by no means committed to this concept of "nation."

Less than a month after lending at least passive support to the central government, Lourmarin's municipal council received a warning from Marseilles that several commissioners from the government in Paris were traveling through the departments of the southeast "slandering" the Marseillais as "counter-revolutionaries which is diametrically opposed to the truth" because in that "city one asks only for liberty, equality, and the republic one and indivisible."[136] The council replied that it "did not doubt the true patriotism and republicanism" of the citizens of Marseilles and promised to write immediately "to assure them of our adhesion."[137]

It is difficult to reconstruct the events of the summer months of 1793 as the Jacobin-Federalist struggle became most intense. One major problem is that incriminating evidence in the council minutes, showing adherence of some Lourmarinois to the "Marseilles rebels," was subsequently crossed out so completely that the entries are impossible to read. But from an examination of the context in which these remarks occurred and from other surviving documents it is obvious that there was very real conflict in the village. Such conflicts between adherents of the two factions occurred, to a greater or lesser extent, in most Provençal villages, and in some of them entire pages were torn from the municipal council minutes to protect those who had supported Marseilles.[138]

It would be convenient if one could divide those supporting the Jacobins or Federalists neatly along ideological lines. Georges Lefebvre has said that

---

[135] *Ibid.*, April 10, 1793.
[136] *Ibid.*, May 6, 1793.
[137] *Ibid.*
[138] For a fuller treatment of this subject and the Federalist movement in Provence in 1793 see the unpublished Ph.D. dissertation, John B. Cameron, Jr., "The Federalist Movement in the Department of the Bouches-du-Rhône in 1793," University of North Carolina, Chapel Hill, 1970.

the Federalists in 1793 tended to attract "the bourgeoisie worried about property, the Feuillants hostile to universal suffrage, the Catholics attached to the refractory clergy, and the partisans of the Old Regime" along with democrats indignant at the outrages perpetuated by the government in Paris.[139] Unfortunately it is impossible to identify all of those in Lourmarin who supported one faction or the other. However, a close reading of the council minutes as well as correspondence permits the identification of 32 Lourmarinois, 21 as Jacobins and 11 as Federalists. Those Lourmarinois who can be identified were, in almost every case, the leaders of the two factions and may not be entirely representative of the total membership. Furthermore, even among the 32 political activists who can be identified, there are unresolved questions about the degree of their attachment to one side or the other or about the intensity of their participation in the struggle during the spring and summer of 1793. However, given these qualifications and doubts, these 32 men are worthy of examination and Table VIII–1 presents an analysis of their age, religion, and income from real property. Table VIII–2 shows the occupations of these same 32 men.

TABLE VIII–1. IDENTIFICATION OF 32 LOURMARINOIS IN 1793

| | | Age | | Religion | | Average income from real property |
	Number	Ave.	Med.	Prot.	Cath.	
Jacobins	21	48	49	18(86%)	3(14%)	284 livres
Federalists	11	31	28	7(64%)	4(36%)	980 livres

SOURCE: *A.D., Bouches-du-Rhône*, series L, 1792 and 1793, *passim; A.M., D.M.*, 1792–93, *passim; Cont.Fon.*, 1791.

The most striking feature about Table VIII–1 is the age difference—the median age of the Jacobins was 49, that of the Federalists 28, or a difference of 21 years. Seven of the 11 Federalists were under 30; the only adherent over 40 was Pierre Henri Joseph Girard, 64.[140]

[139] Lefebvre, *French Revolution from 1793 to 1799*, p. 56.
[140] The youngest was Camille Girard, Pierre Henri Joseph's son, at 21. Girard *père* was mayor when the Federalist section controlled the village and evinced no strong support for the Federalist cause whereas Camille was definitely a leader.

TABLE VIII-2. OCCUPATIONS OF 32 LOURMARINOIS IN 1793

	Jacobins	Federalists
bourgeois	6	5
négociant	0	2
notary	1	0
greffier	0	1
Protestant minister	2	0
ménager	6	1
travailleur	1	1
artisan	5	1
Total	21	11

SOURCE: *A.D., Bouches-du-Rhône*, series L, 1792 and 1793, *passim*; *A.M., D.M.,* 1792–93, *passim*; *Cont. Fon.,* 1791.

The difference in religion does not seem significant, since the proportion of Protestants and Catholics who were Jacobins was probably about the same as for the general population of the village as a whole, while it is ·difficult to draw any conclusions from the small Federalist sample. Camille Girard and his father were both Catholics, of course, but it is difficult to see this as a major factor determining their adhesion to the Federalist cause. An examination of occupations in Table VIII–2 shows that the composition of the Federalist party was slightly more aristocratic. The figure for income in Table VIII–1 requires additional analysis. For one thing, four of the eleven Federalists had no income from real property since they were still living at home, but feeling that it would be misleading to consider them propertyless, they have been assigned the income of their fathers.[141] According to the revolutionary tax rolls, four Jacobins in Lourmarin had no income, but two of them were *bourgeois*, one from Marseilles and one from Languedoc, while the other two were Protestant ministers. Of course the greater number of artisans attached to the Jacobins meant that their income was not derived from real property. If the Federalists had the Girards and Sambucs, the Jacobins had the Corgiers and Ailhauds.

How then does one explain the division within the village? It may have been partly economic, with the poor generally supporting the Jacobins and the more wealthy the Federalists, but it would be difficult to prove this. Religious reasons do not seem to have motivated either side, although

[141] For one thing this means that the large income of the Girards was counted twice.

Camille Girard was a leader of the Federalists and both Protestant ministers were Jacobins. The most striking difference between the two groups is the age factor. The Jacobins were considerably older; most of them had guided Lourmarin since the early days of the Revolution. With the very significant exception of Girard *père*, the Federalists were young men who had not yet had a voice in administering village affairs. Camille Girard, at 21, was both a Catholic and a potentially wealthy *bourgeois*, and like his brothers, had been educated in Marseilles. It is possible that Girard was ideologically motivated, at least in part, by the fear that the Jacobins would move against the property of the wealthy, but his following was more personal than ideological. The Federalists must have had at least the passive support of a goodly segment of the Lourmarinois in order for them to control the village as long as they did. Certainly the proximity of Marseilles, whose leaders apparently were successful in their defiance of the government in Paris, must have convinced some that they were joining the winning side.

In imitation of its more populous neighbors to the south, by early June Lourmarin was organized as a section in the Federalist movement.[142] On June 10 Lourmarin's section sent a greeting to the "brave republicans of the city of Aix."[143] Like the citizens of Aix, the Lourmarinois declared war on the Parisian "anarchists," under whom they now were suffering from "the cruelest despotism."[144] After enduring so long in silence, "the time has finally come when the voice of the honest man can make itself heard," declared the Lourmarinois and they lent their support to Aix and Marseilles.[145]

On June 23 a committee of the Lourmarin section wrote to the sections of Aix, who had joined "their brothers in Marseilles," to compliment them on "showing the way to a new regime of peace and law."[146] Four prominent Lourmarinois carried this letter to Aix where it was countersigned by

---

[142] The sections had been created in 1789 when the new municipal governments were organized. In villages such as Lourmarin the section encompassed the entire village although there were 24 urban sections in Marseilles and six in Aix. The Federalists controlled the sections and hence the local governments during the summer of 1793.

[143] *A.D., Bouches-du-Rhône*, L 1891, L 1975, June 10, 1793.

[144] *Ibid.*

[145] *Ibid.*

[146] *Ibid.*, L 1898, June 23, 1793.

all six sections of Aix. The Aixois then accorded recognition to Lourmarin's patriotism.[147] The Committee of Correspondence of the Lourmarin section evidently expected more leadership and advice than it subsequently received because on June 30, 1793, it wrote to the General Committee at Marseilles to ask why it had received no instructions.

If, among the great affairs which occupy you, our memory is lost as a single point is lost in the universe we pardon you for it, but if you do not believe that the inhabitants of Lourmarin are worthy of participating in your glorious work, they are anxious to prove to you by their conduct that they do not merit your unjust suspicions.[148]

This indignant letter was signed by Camille Girard, Dominique Sambuc, a prominent *bourgeois*, and Daniel Michel, secretary of Lourmarin's section.

Upon the invitation of Camille Girard, Citizen Jean-Baptiste Pascal Mejean came from Marseilles to investigate those in Lourmarin who were opposing federation with Marseilles. Mejean arrived on July 3, 1793, and was informed that "the principal author of the troubles [opposition to Marseilles] in this commune is Sieur Bassaget, minister of the Protestants."[149] Mejean advised the section to collect evidence against Bassaget, who had supported the Jacobins for the past year, and to present it to the General Committee of Marseilles, who "would take the necessary measures to silence this intriguer."[150] But the confrontation between the Jacobins and Federalists was approaching a showdown and there is no evidence that Lourmarin's section ever actually moved against Bassaget.

In an attempt to unite the cities and villages of Provence in the Federalist cause, the General Committee of Marseilles, consisting of representatives of all of the sections of the city, invited the "sections of all communes in this area to assemble and to begin their meeting by swearing the following oath":

We swear not to recognize the decrees made by the National Convention since the 31st of May last until such time as liberty will be restored, to

---

[147] *Ibid.*
[148] *Ibid.*, L 1975, June 30, 1793. Judging by Lourmarin's past conduct, there were grounds for this "suspicion."
[149] *Ibid.*, L 1960, July 2, 1793.
[150] *Ibid.*, July 3, 1793.

maintain the Republic one and indivisible in liberty and equality, to respect persons and property, and to recognize the popular tribunal of Marseilles.[151]

Lourmarin's section discussed the oath and their warm feelings for their brothers in Marseilles and voted unanimously to support the resolution. Then each member raised his right hand as they solemnly pledged in unison *"je le jure."*[152] It must be emphasized that Lourmarin's section and its municipal government were not the same, although they shared some of the same members and sentiments. The most damaging evidence against Lourmarin's Federalists can be found in the correspondence with other sections rather than in the council minutes.

The Federalist army from Marseilles was forced out of Avignon on July 27, 1793, and the Jacobin forces pressed southward until they entered Marseilles on August 25.[153] After the fall of Avignon it was obvious that the Federalist cause was doomed and on July 28 Lourmarin's council voted to send a deputation to the National Convention pledging its support of the government in Paris.[154] Two days later they announced that decrees of the National Convention would be recognized as the only legitimate authority.[155] The new constitution was accepted in Lourmarin on August 1 and the following decree was published: "Vive la constitution, vive la république, vive la convention nationale, vive la montagne, et à bas tous les traîtres et les conspirateurs."[156] After the victorious Jacobins had passed through the area, the council asked for volunteers to march with them "against the rebels" to protect *"la patrie."*[157] Lourmarin had quickly adapted its policies to the new realities.

A deputation from the Popular Society, as the local Jacobin club led by Bassaget was now called, demanded that new elections for all local offices

---

[151] *Ibid.*, L 48, July 7, 1793. This oath was designed to be a formal part of the *fête* of July 14, but some communities, such as Lourmarin, took it earlier.
[152] *Ibid.*
[153] Lefebvre, *French Revolution from 1793 to 1799*, p. 58. Some leaders of the sections had asked that English grain ships be allowed to provision the city, but several sections vehemently opposed this request. This debate was ended with the entry of the English into Marseilles.
[154] *A.M., D.M.*, July 28, 1793.
[155] *Ibid.*, July 30, 1793.
[156] *Ibid.*, August 1, 1793.
[157] *Ibid.*, August 17, 1793.

be held immediately, replacements to be chosen by popular vote.[158] New elections were held on August 23. The newly elected mayor was Antoine André Bernard, a wealthy Lourmarinois, and the national agent was Jean Paul Corgier, who had been mayor in 1789 and, except for Bruny and Girard, was the largest landholder in Lourmarin.[159] Daniel Michel, secretary since January, 1791, and one of the leaders of the former Federalists, was re-elected.[160]

Except that the rules governing elections had become more democratic and their duties were less circumscribed, the officers chosen in Lourmarin's annual elections after 1789 were similar to those of the *ancien régime*. Alfred Cobban points out that throughout France "the administrative personnel of the *ancien régime* was taken over with little change by the Revolution, and the same personnel seems to have survived generally in local administration up to the summer of 1793."[161] The village government's police and judicial functions were considerably strengthened by the annual election of three police officers. In addition, three men were elected to staff the new local Police Tribunal "to hear the cases of those who violate the regulations."[162] In the year of the Terror at Paris, some leveling was seen in Lourmarin when 12 notables and five other municipal officers, at least eight of whom had never served before, were elected. Two or three of the new officers were *travailleurs* of modest means.[163] At the next year's election a few more *travailleurs* were elected.[164] The composition of the municipal officers showed a leveling tendency in 1793 and 1794; that is, a few artisans and *travailleurs* were elected, but not as much change occurred in Lourmarin as Cobban has found elsewhere in France under the Jacobins.[165] Bernard and Corgier were re-elected in 1794, and the wealthier and more

---

[158] *Ibid.*, August 21, 1793. The Popular Society had about the same personnel and program as the earlier Patriotic and Republican Societies.

[159] Bernard, 67 years old, had managed to stand aloof from the Jacobin-Federalist conflict and was acceptable to both factions as a replacement for Pierre Henri Joseph Girard as mayor.

[160] *A.M., D.M.*, August 23, 1793.

[161] Alfred Cobban, "Local Government during the French Revolution," in *Aspects of the French Revolution* (London, 1967), p. 117.

[162] *A.M., D.M.*, November 20, 1791.

[163] *Ibid.*, August 23, 1793.

[164] *Ibid.*, November 24, 1794.

[165] Cobban, "Local Government," p. 117.

influential men continued to lead the village.[166] Thus they retained control of village affairs even in the most radical time of the Revolution.

The events of the tumultuous summer of 1793 have a twofold significance. Politically Lourmarin had moved slightly to the left and participation in village government had been broadened. Except for *émigré* Camille Girard, most members of Lourmarin's section were allowed to adhere to the Jacobin cause as the villagers overlooked past indiscretions. Secretary Michel volunteered in the Battalion of the Luberon and was appointed surgeon major.[167] In January, 1794, a certificate sent to the village council praising his efforts included that highest of compliments: "He has the esteem of all *sans-culottes*."[168]

After the defeat of the Federalists, the Department of the Vaucluse was organized, and on September 21, 1793, an order concerning the areas of the Vaucluse still in revolt was sent to the villages of the new department.[169] Only a few Federalist enclaves remained in the Vaucluse, but to the south, Toulon had allied itself with the Anglo-Spanish forces at war with the Republic and the Jacobin army had not yet conquered it. In addition to joining France's enemies, the Federalist leaders in Toulon went so far as to proclaim the re-establishment of a constitutional monarchy under "King Louis XVII."[170] Lourmarin, whose section movement had never contemplated such treasonous action, copied the new decree in the municipal minutes. It was directed against "the frightful hydra of Federalism which by its hypocrisy has poisoned the public spirit in the district of Apt. We must have administrators free from all suspicion of royalism or of federalism, not those like that horde of Marseilles aristocrats."[171] The decree included a long list of specific measures to be taken against those "involved in the Federalist plot" in order to "prevent the birth of a new Vendée," but except for the seizure of property belonging to Camille Girard's father, Lourmarin did little more than register the decree. Nonetheless, the departmental administration seemed satisfied that Lourmarin

---

[166] *A.M., D.M.*, November 24, 1794.

[167] *Ibid.*, December 19, 1793.

[168] *Ibid.*, January 25, 1794.

[169] *Ibid.*, October 6, 1793. Henceforth Lourmarin was in the Department of the Vaucluse.

[170] Busquet, Bourrilly, and Agulhon, *Histoire de la Provence*, p. 91.

[171] *A.M., D.M.*, October 6, 1793.

had turned its back on Federalism. Upon orders from the local representatives on mission, Lourmarin furnished one-eighth of the grain from the 1793 harvest and one-half of its hay to the army besieging Toulon.[172] On December 19 Toulon fell to the besieging Jacobin troops, supported by artillery commanded by Captain Napoleon Bonaparte, and the English fleet retired. The "good news of the fall of the infamous city of Toulon" was announced to the assembled Lourmarinois, who then held a general celebration.[173]

Life in Lourmarin from the fall of 1793 to the summer of 1794 tended to reflect in a pale way the events occurring in Paris where Robespierre and the Committee of Public Safety attempted to end the civil war while simultaneously fighting the invading armies. At the insistence of the local Popular Society, Lourmarin established a Committee of Public Surveillance, but it was not very active and the regular municipal officers continued to manage village affairs.[174] Indeed, the "Terror" hardly had any meaning in Lourmarin. There was no guillotine and no violence and the village notables retained control of the village. Thus in the most radical period of the Revolution, Lourmarin was quiet. Lourmarin tried to apply the price controls emanating from Paris. The maximum was promulgated in the name of the revolutionary government and was applied particularly to the charge for grinding grain in the mills and to the price of bread.[175] The imposition of price controls in Lourmarin was not new, of course, and there was no real opposition to the maximum. When the bakers began baking bread almost exclusively from rye flour, the council ordered that the bread was to contain at least one-half wheat and was to be sold for two sous, three deniers per pound.[176] Lourmarin also elected members of the *gendarmerie nationale* for the Vaucluse brigade.[177]

---

[172] *Ibid.*, November 9, 1793. It is worthy of note that this grain requisition was just about the same as Lourmarin had been accustomed to paying for the *tasque* before 1789.

[173] *Ibid.*, December 20, 1793.

[174] *Ibid.*, October 6, 11, 1793. On May 21, 1794, the Committee of Surveillance wrote the village of Rognes (about ten miles to the south) trying to locate an errant army volunteer from Lourmarin. *A.D., Bouches-du-Rhône*, L 1838, May 21, 1794. This is one of the few bits of evidence that the Committee of Surveillance was active during the Terror.

[175] *A.M., D.M.*, October 15, 21, 1793.

[176] *Ibid.*, February 18, 1794.

[177] *Ibid.*, December 11, 1793.

Early in June, 1794, the council began to make plans for a glorious celebration on July 14. The political divisions of 1793 had been reconciled, Bruny had returned to the village and had redeemed his property, there was no fighting in the immediate area—in short, as the Lourmarinois prepared for this *fête* it must have seemed to them that the Revolution had run its course. As we have already pointed out, the notables who had guided Lourmarin before 1789 managed to keep control of the village through the most radical stages of the Revolution. The village and its leadership had shown once again the lack of deep political or ideological commitment and thus the adaptability that we have witnessed throughout the eighteenth century.

On July 14 all citizens were urged to decorate their doors with verdure and the Popular Society joined with the National Guard in decorating an altar to *la patrie*.[178] Mothers and daughters were encouraged to participate, with the mothers bearing oak boughs while the young girls, dressed in white, carried wild flowers and the tricolor. The public school was dismissed and all the pupils assembled at the Catholic church, which had been transformed into a temple for the worship of the Supreme Being.[179] Because of its central location, the council decided to build the altar in the *Place de la République*, the small square in the center of town adjacent to the former Catholic church.[180] On July 14 the villagers, carrying busts of the Goddess of Liberty as well as Marat, marched to the newly planted tree of liberty near the town hall. As the young girls in their white dresses danced around the tree of liberty, all citizens "waved the tricolor and sang patriotic songs."[181] The cortege then wound its way through the narrow streets to the temple where several municipal officers made patriotic speeches that were warmly greeted by the throng. More patriotic songs were sung as the busts were solemnly placed on the altar. The rest of the day was devoted to a *fête* with a general illumination in the evening.[182]

This 1794 celebration was undoubtedly the high point of revolutionary sentiment in Lourmarin. On the national scene, the Thermidorean reaction

[178] *Ibid.*, July 15, 1794.
[179] *Ibid.*
[180] *Ibid.*, June 27, July 3, 1794.
[181] *Ibid.*, July 15, 1794.
[182] *Ibid.*

was imminent; locally, the harvest had to be gathered. Gradually the enthusiasm of the Lourmarinois ebbed away and as months gave way to years, as the Directory was replaced by the Consulate and then by the Empire, as more and more young men left home to fight in faraway places unknown to the Lourmarinois, a sort of apathy set in. Gone was the altar to *la patrie* and the temple dedicated to the Supreme Being, the celebrations of July 14 and August 10 became perfunctory, and fervor appeared to be missing from the old hymns. Indeed, to most Lourmarinois their revolution was over by 1794. For the next 20 years they merely waited out the end of the storm, hoping to keep their family and their property together, but with no real interest in *la gloire nationale* generated by the martial exploits of a young Corsican general.

At first glance, it appears that Lourmarin experienced, on a reduced scale, the various stages of the Revolution. This view is strengthened because the villagers so quickly adopted the verbiage and the forms of the Revolution. A galaxy of words that the Lourmarinois had never used before—*bon patriot, constitution, république, patrie, nation*—began to appear in the council minutes. The impression persists, however, that this was all superficial. Moreover, this impression is reinforced when one looks at the actual effects of the Revolution in Lourmarin. Religious changes, although momentous in France as a whole, caused hardly a stir in Lourmarin. The few pieces of church land were sold and a new *curé* was elected, but in a community where indifference was far advanced, the Civil Constitution of the Clergy hardly caused a ripple. The largest landholder in Lourmarin became citizen Bruny, stripped of his seigneurial rights and dues, to be sure, but retaining his land intact. Decrees of the National Assembly and the National Convention had changed the structure of the local government, but the same men continued to govern the village. In these and many other ways Lourmarin emerged from the Revolution little changed from 1788. The villagers showed that they were not necessarily wedded to the past and thus were willing to accept changes made, in the name of the people, by the government at Paris. But neither were the Lourmarinois in the revolutionary vanguard, and they demanded no radical legislation from their representatives. In short, the effects of the Revolution in Lourmarin were short-lived and superficial, and one is led to conclude that not much had really changed.

CONCLUSION

THE STUDY OF A SINGLE RURAL French village cannot pretend to be representative of a history of rural France or even rural Provence in the eighteenth century. But it can suggest a number of generalizations about the nature and tempo of rural life, the impact of the Revolution, and the more subtle and perhaps more profound trend toward secularization in the French countryside in the century before 1789. Until more village studies are completed, any claim to typicality or atypicality must be resisted. Nevertheless, this study should serve as a warning against facile generalizations. One need not choose between the "schools" of Tocqueville or Lefebvre, Cobban or Soboul.

In terms of social composition little changed; the village was divided into about the same social groups after 1800 as it had been in 1680. The number of weavers and others dependent upon the rural textile industry increased during the period studied, but Lourmarin remained essentially an agricultural community and the textile industry continued to be tied to the shops, apartments, and farm houses of the artisans and *travailleurs,* as well as to the schedule imposed by the agricultural seasons. The hierarchy in the village evident after 1800 continued to be based primarily on land ownership, as it had been throughout the eighteenth century. The "new aristocracy" of the nineteenth century of whom Alfred Cobban writes, as well as the rural aristocracy of the pre-revolutionary period, was one of landed proprietors.[1]

Eighteenth-century agricultural terms—*travailleur* and *ménager*—were replaced in the nineteenth century by *cultivateur* and *agriculteur*, but the structure of society remained essentially the same and there was still very strong pressure on a son to follow his father's profession. This is not to say, however, that the classes were closed and that there was no social mobility. Several examples of upward mobility have been chosen to illustrate this. In the early 1700's Pierre Tertian was the proprietor of the *Auberge de la Croix d'Or*, but by mid-century his son, a *ménager*, served on the municipal council. Still later in the century his grandson Pierre had become a *bourgeois* and married his only child, a daughter, to the son of Denis Sambuc, one of the wealthiest men in the community. The Roman family also demonstrates upward movement. Jacques Roman, *ménager*, was born in 1725. His son, Etienne (b. 1754), married Marie Suzanne Cavallier, daughter of Pierre Paul Cavallier, the seigneur's *procureur fondé* and a wealthy man in his own right. Etienne Roman, a *négociant*, was a Protestant while the Cavalliers were Catholic. Another son of Jacques Roman was Jacques (b. 1765), who in 1808 married Jeanne Sambuc, the daughter of *bourgeois* Denis Sambuc mentioned above. The younger Jacques, a *propriétaire*, was thus the brother-in-law of Denis Sambuc *fils*, one of the leaders of the Federalist movement, and also of Daniel Michel, who had been secretary of the Lourmarin section in 1793. Mathieu Colletin, a carpenter born in 1734 in the neighboring village of Sivergues, married Jeanne Clot, daughter of a *travailleur*, in 1760. One of their sons, Jean Albert (b. 1766), was married to Jeanne Anastay, whose father Jacques was a *négociant*. Jean Albert's son, Joseph Caliste, born in 1797, was a *négociant* and married the daughter of Pierre Ginoux, who was the schoolteacher in Lourmarin during the 1790's. The Colletins, Romans, and Tertians had certainly made social and economic advances over three generations.

The only *privilégié* in the village at the time of the Revolution was the seigneur, although none of the Brunys had ever lived in Lourmarin. The

---

[1] Alfred Cobban, *The Social Interpretation of the French Revolution* (Cambridge, England, 1964), pp. 81–90. See also Pierre Bouyoux, "Les 'six cents plus imposés' du département de la Haute-Garonne en l'an X," *Annales du Midi*, LXX (July, 1958), 317–27.

Lourmarinois had always been ready to defend their interests, respectfully to be sure, when they felt the seigneur was infringing upon them. Thus it is not altogether surprising that the village should institute legal action after 1800 against the heirs of Jean-Baptiste Jérôme Bruny over the ownership of the wood on the mountain. The dispute concerned the rights of the villagers to cut firewood on the mountain because, although technically it belonged to the seigneur, the wood had been used by the Lourmarinois since the sixteenth century. The dispute was finally resolved in 1832 when the village and Bruny's heirs agreed to divide the wood "in order to put a stop to this litigation."[2] One infers from the tone of the proceedings that the Bruny *mystique* had disappeared and that the villagers were dealing not with their seigneur but simply with another French citizen.

The seigneur's agent (*viguier*), although he owned little or no land in Lourmarin, was an important person in the village in the eighteenth century. Until his position was abolished by the Revolution, the *viguier* sat in on council meetings and was on the best of terms with the village notables. It is noteworthy that most of the *viguiers* were concerned not only with the seigneur's interests but on occasion acted to protect the villagers. The *viguier* was not the object of village hostility as often pictured by Lefebvre and others.

It is impossible to measure with any certainty the degree to which the Lourmarinois were influenced by events outside the village. However, it does seem that many villagers were becoming increasingly aware of events elsewhere in France through travel to Aix and Marseilles and from newspapers and journals, a development that seemed to reach a peak at the time of the Revolution. Lourmarin had always sent its young men to the militia, but never in such large numbers or to such faraway places as after 1789. It is impossible to measure the impact the returning soldiers had on Lourmarin, especially since there is scant mention of events in France or Europe in the village minutes after 1800; but because so many young men served in Napoleon's armies, the course of the war and of events in Paris must have been discussed by the villagers.

The most important economic change resulting from the Revolution was the elimination of seigneurial dues and the *dîme*. Although no firm evi-

[2] *A.M., D.M.,* May 16, 1808, to November 16, 1832, *passim.*

211

dence is available, it does not appear that the Lourmarinois spent this additional income to improve the land they already owned. It is probable that the villagers simply decided to consume the surplus they no longer were required to give to the seigneur, thereby increasing their standard of living slightly. This judgment must not be applied only to the small and middle sized farmers, however, because even the largest landholders showed little inclination to experiment or innovate, either before or after the Revolution. In fact, neither agricultural nor textile production showed much growth during this period. Little land changed hands in Lourmarin in the eighteenth century aside from the traditional processes of inheritance or inclusion in a dowry. Furthermore, there was little national land to sell because of the Revolution and Lourmarin remained primarily a village of small landowners and artisans.

Lourmarin was not poor by eighteenth-century standards although ten to fifteen percent of the population always required some assistance. One of the themes of this study has been how the Lourmarinois in the eighteenth century took care of their own poor, even though the system was haphazard and crisis-oriented. The attitude of the village, as seen in the 1790 report quoted in Chapter VIII, had changed by the end of the century. The villagers continued to care for their poor, but help was given more grudgingly and a certain stigma was attached to those who were forced to accept aid. Although evidence for the nineteenth century in Lourmarin is too sketchy, Alfred Cobban may very well be correct in saying that "for the poor, possibly a harsher governmental climate was inaugurated. Whoever won the revolution, they lost."[3]

Supporting the view that Lourmarin was not a poor community is the fact that prior to the Revolution, community indebtedness was rare. When the village was forced to borrow, as it did from the seigneur during the War of the Austrian Succession, they quickly repaid the loan. Lourmarin's local expenses remained about the same in the early nineteenth century as they had been before the Revolution. In lieu of the community *fermes* abolished in the early days of the Revolution, the council, in order to meet current expenses, levied a local toll (*octroi*) on most products bought and sold within the village. Like the *fermes*, the *octroi* provided sufficient income for

[3] Cobban, *Social Interpretation*, p. 170.

local expenses; however, the paternalistic features of the *fermes* had completely disappeared and there was no agency in the village to guarantee quality or price. When the regulatory features of the *fermes* were removed, the activities of the village merchants were governed only by the actions of their competitors, and it is hard to imagine that competition in Lourmarin was very keen. For better or worse, the buyer, no longer protected by the local authorities, found himself subjected to the vicissitudes of a policy of *laissez-faire*.

Politically the most significant conclusion of this study is that the notables of Lourmarin (*bourgeois* in the eighteenth century, *rentiers* in the nineteenth), men whose wealth and position came primarily from the land, guided the village throughout the entire period. Oligarchic in structure, the group of notables in Lourmarin was neither excessively small nor concerned exclusively with its own interests, but it was an oligarchy nevertheless. The municipal government was not a closed corporation and some artisans and *ménagers* served as officers, but almost invariably they followed the lead of the Girards, the Sambucs, the Bernards, the Savornins. Even in the heady days of the 1790's when many Lourmarinois who had been disenfranchised under the *ancien régime* participated in relatively free elections, the pre-revolutionary notables managed to maintain control and thus insured a certain continuity of local government.

The paternalism exercised, at least in the eighteenth century, by these notables tended to shield the poorer classes from the various echelons of government as well as from the seigneur. They fought battles for the less fortunate in Apt, Aix and La Tour d'Aigues, although not without realizing that the community's welfare coincided with the welfare and security of the village leaders. The pragmatic approach to local problems adopted by the notables was also evidenced in their ready acceptance of changes at the national level. For example, they believed that changes in the government in Paris would have little effect on them. They therefore applauded with equal enthusiasm the death of Louis XVI, the defeat of Napoleon and the accession of Louis XVIII, the subsequent return of Napoleon, and the "glorious July days" of 1830.[4] The 1793 Jacobin-Federalist controversy

[4] *A.M., D.M.*, January 28, 1793, April 22, 1814, September 30, 1815, August 15, 1830, July 20, 1831.

which divided the village was a definite exception to the pattern of acquiescence and occurred in part because Lourmarin was geographically so close to Marseilles, the leader of the Federalist movement in the Midi. Regional loyalties were not dead in 1793.

Continuity of government in Lourmarin was very real and also very important: The great-grandsons of the village officers in the 1680's and 1690's led Lourmarin in the 1790's. In fact, the same names continued to appear as mayor and councillors through the first third of the nineteenth century. Among Lourmarin's municipal councillors today can be found many of the same family names so prevalent in the seventeenth and eighteenth centuries. One obvious drawback to this system of inbreeding and co-option was that new personalities and new ideas were effectively excluded from village life; this along with emigration may have contributed to the stagnation of the nineteenth and twentieth centuries.

The points of continuity in village political life are obvious; the changes which led to political atrophy are more subtle. From 1680 to the mid-1790's the village council meetings, at least 15 to 20 annually, served as a sort of public forum where local issues were discussed, courses of village action were planned, and where the average villager could be heard if not always heeded. Occasional General Council meetings afforded all heads of family the opportunity to come together and discuss issues vital to the village. One cannot claim that the average villager exercised any real voice in his government, but important issues were discussed in a quasi-formal manner and an impression of village vitality emerges from reading the municipal deliberations for more than 100 years before the Revolution. After reading the minutes for the first one-third of the nineteenth century, when the council often did not meet for months, one definitely feels that the village council had become a mere figurehead, an administrative body used primarily to channel instructions and information to and from cantonal, district, and departmental officials. Political, economic, social, and religious discussions were now brief and perfunctory, and many questions that consumed so much time in the eighteenth century were not discussed at all. The council had ceased to be a forum for conflicting views. These issues were still discussed, of course, but the forum had been transferred to the street, the café, and the field.

There is much we do not know about population patterns in eighteenth-century France, but the available information suggests that Lourmarin's illegitimacy rate of just over two percent was not unusual for rural France. Yet the rate of pre-marital conception in Lourmarin, averaging at least 16 percent during the eighteenth century, was higher for a rural village than the scattered studies have suggested it to be. We also know that three inter-related developments occurred in the years 1686–1815—women were marrying at an earlier age, were bearing their first child sooner after marriage, and yet were having fewer children in a completed family—indicating that at least by the last quarter of the eighteenth century the Lourmarinois were practicing some sort of birth control, probably *coitus interruptus*.

The most significant religious trend was the growing toleration in the eighteenth century. The Edict of Revocation of 1685 was never very enthusiastically enforced; it was generally ignored after mid-century. The minor religious problems in the early 1760's were instigated by the new *curé*, Messire Fauchier, and the evidence indicates that even some Catholics were upset by his tactics. The major religious changes of the Revolutionary and Napoleonic eras, the Civil Constitution of the Clergy and the Concordat, caused not a trace of trouble in Lourmarin.

Since Lourmarin had not had a formal Protestant church after it was destroyed in 1663, the Protestants decided to build the present church just down the road from the chateau. Begun in 1805, the church was finally completed in 1816 at a total cost of more than 23,000 francs. About 60 percent of the construction cost was paid by the congregation, the other 40 percent came from general community revenue.[5] Thus the Protestant church was constructed at least in part by the money of the village Catholics and there is no indication of any resentment over the expenditure.

Lourmarin's school, operating continuously since well before 1680, was only slightly affected by Guizot's education bill of 1833.[6] The village government decided to follow its previous policy of not including religious instruction in the curriculum of the new school established in the chateau in 1833. The council supported this arrangement by saying "that by this

---

[5] *Ibid.*, May 9, 1813, December 7, 1816, and *passim*.

[6] It is worthy of note that of the 38,000 communes in France in 1833, 15,000 of them had no school of any kind. Gordon Wright, *France in Modern Times: 1760 to the Present* (Chicago, 1960).

reunion the children will learn at an early age to live together on good terms without bothering to examine the differences in their religions. This, of course, has never been a problem in this commune because of the good relations which have always existed between the two communions."[7]

Both the Catholic and Protestant churches taught that sexual relations outside marriage were wrong, and yet the rate of pre-marital conception among those women whose marriage date could be established was high (about one-sixth) throughout the eighteenth century, increasing to more than one-third in the 1790s and then leveling out at about one-quarter from 1801 to 1830. Both churches also denounced the practice of birth control, but circumstantial evidence indicates that by the 1770's many couples were disregarding their church's teachings. This assumes that the Lourmarinois knew that by practicing birth control they were sinning: Leroy-Ladurie has found evidence in northern France of the circulation of a book by *Père* Feline denouncing "the crime of the infamous Onan."[8]

In many French rural villages the Catholic church had played an important role in helping to create a feeling of community. This was not true in Lourmarin since the *Vaudois* had introduced an element of religious disunity. Lacking the religious unity provided by one single village church, the inhabitants of Lourmarin early learned to accept their neighbors and not to dwell on religious differences. This was a very enlightened approach for an isolated rural community to take. Despite the government's severe laws, *de facto* recognition of the Protestants had existed since the 1740's. All evidence that I have examined indicates a very definite atmosphere of toleration, and even indifference, to religious matters in Lourmarin. Fortunately for the peace of the village most inhabitants looked upon their neighbors as fellow villagers and not as Catholics or Protestants. It would seem that this spirit of religious indifference, definitely observable by mid-century, also manifested itself in the practice of birth control as well as in the increased rate of pre-marital conception. The precise time in the eighteenth century when this spirit of religious indifference appeared depends on whether one looks at the pre-marital conception rate, the circumstantial evidence for birth control, or the decline in religious conflict. It is probably impossible to date this phenomenon. What does seem certain is that secular-

---

[7] *A.M., D.M.*, August 12, 1833.
[8] Leroy-Ladurie, "Funestes secrèts," p. 390.

ization was implanted in village mores well before 1789 and definitely was not a result of the Revolution.

The question of Lourmarin's atypicality as an eighteenth-century village must be raised but probably cannot be satisfactorily answered. Certainly some of the conclusions reached earlier seem to be at variance with many generalizations about the eighteenth-century countryside. Among the many factors which seem to set Lourmarin apart from other villages of eighteenth-century France were its good government, low unemployment rate, practice of birth control, high rate of pre-marital conception, interest in education, and religious toleration. Why was Lourmarin apparently different? Was it because of the predominantly Protestant composition of its population? It is possible that there is a connection between the presence of a large number of Protestants and the remarkable degree of mutual aid witnessed in Lourmarin. However, until more village studies are completed I am hesitant about ascribing these features of Lourmarin's life exclusively, or even primarily, to the Protestant ethic. Additional village studies may demonstrate that Lourmarin was not so unusual after all.

As the eighteenth century progressed the Lourmarinois were made to feel the presence of the royal government more and more in their daily lives as the Intendants at Aix requested an ever-increasing number of reports about such subjects as crops, soil, and occupations. In this sense, Tocqueville was correct in asserting that centralization in France developed in the *ancien régime* and was merely taken over by the Revolution which, once it had swept aside the old seigneurial and monarchial institutions, felt it needed centralization to defend its achievements. But it is a mistake to say, as does Tocqueville, that "the population was little more than a horde of ignorant, uneducated peasants, quite incapable of administering local affairs."[9] In eighteenth-century Lourmarin some peasants, as this study has demonstrated, would have fit this pattern, but the village also contained a large number of men who were literate, intelligent, aware of the world around them, and quite capable of decision-making on the local level. If the village council did not initiate any major programs, neither was it completely submissive to outside authority. It was Lourmarin's political vitality, relatively broad participation in village affairs, and its continuing

[9] Alexis de Tocqueville, *The Old Regime and the French Revolution*, trans. by Stuart Gilbert (Garden City, N.J., 1955), p. 49.

concern for all its inhabitants, that were hallmarks of the *ancien régime* in Lourmarin. This vitality and excitement were gone after the Revolution and Lourmarin became in the nineteenth century what Tocqueville believed most villages had become in the eighteenth—a mere cog in the administrative machinery of the central government. The municipal council discussed only those matters referred to it, made very few decisions itself, and functioned primarily to administer laws and orders channelled to it by the prefect. Bureaucracy and centralization had come to Lourmarin, but the village paid heavily for such modernization.

APPENDIX A

ÉTAT OF THE COMMUNITY, 1790

<small>COMMUNITY OF LOURMARIN</small>

Grains

Number of *charges* of grain sown in this *terroir* each year:

wheat	108	*charges*
maslin	90	"
rye	115	"
oats	2	"

Number of *charges* of grain harvested each year:

wheat	640	*charges*
maslin	465	"
rye	492	"
oats	12	"

Number of *charges* of grain necessary for the subsistence of the inhabitants:

wheat	1,072	*charges*
maslin	800	"
rye	1,077	"

Summary value of the vegetables harvested in this place—600 livres

Fodder

Quantity of *quintaux* (hundred-weight) of hay produced:

	4,500
average price per *quintal*	2 livres, 15 sous

Quantity of *quintaux* of straw furnished: 4,989
average price per *quintal* 1 livre, 5 sous

Oil

Number of *quintaux* of oil which was produced in this commune before
the death of the olive trees: 600
today: 12
average price per *quintaux* 43 livres

Number of *quintaux* consumed in this place: 300

Wine

Number of *milléroles* of wine produced in this *terroir*: 1,800 *charges*
(each *charge* weighs 240 pounds)
average price of wine per *charge* 7 livres

Amount of wine consumed in this place: 1,500 *charges*

Fruits

Number of *panaux* of almonds produced in this *terroir*: 20 *pan*
average price per *pan* 3 livres

Number of *charges* of almonds *dures* produced in this *terroir*: 50 *charges*
average price per charge 19 livres

Textiles

How many *quintaux* of wool is produced by the flocks of this
terroir: 30
average price per *quintal* 36 livres

How many *quintaux* of silk are produced each year in this
    terroir: 12
    average price per *quintal* 1,700 livres

What is the value of the flax produced: 850 livres

Livestock

Number of cattle and cows in this *terroir*: 4
Number of cattle and cows consumed in an average year: 6
Number of calves consumed in an average year: 0
Number of sheep and ewes consumed in an average year: 900
Number of sheep and ewes in this *terroir*: 600
Number of lambs which are consumed: 150
Number of pigs in this *terroir*: 120
Number of pigs which are consumed: 230
Number of goats in this *terroir*: 25
Number of goats which are consumed: 30
Number of kids in this *terroir*: 14
    average price of each goat: 120 livres
Number of mules which are in this *terroir*: 74
    average price of each mule: 150 livres
Number of asses in this *terroir*: 113
    average price of each ass: 25 livres

Wood

Sum of the average annual value of wood which is cut in
    this *terroir* for firewood: 8,000 livres

Manufacturing

What is the value of woven serge and other cloth which is manufactured
    in this place for exportation:
    Heavy and light woolen serge 2,880 livres
    Woolen hats 750 livres
    Silk stockings or silk floss 12,050 livres

221

What is the value of linen manufactured in this place for consumption
within the village: 3,600 livres

What is the value of lace made here: 600 livres

Distilling

Number of *quintaux* of brandy produced in this *terroir*: 6
average price per *quintal* 15 livres

Number of *quintaux* consumed in this place: 7

Number of artisans of all professions that there are in this
place: 65

Number of inhabitants there are in this place including
the artisans: 1,500

Drawn up and signed March 1, 1790 according to our knowledge and
conscience at Lourmarin.

(s) BERNARD
BERNARD
AGUITTON
RICHARD

APPENDIX B

INVENTORY OF THE POSSESSIONS AT DEATH OF
PIERRE VIAL, BOURGEOIS, WHO DIED OCTOBER 4, 1685

In the Kitchen:

One cupboard of walnut with shelves and two drawers still in good
   condition
one round wooden table nearly new
one wooden bench well used
one wooden pastry table partly used
one small pine cupboard partly used with lock and key
one small bucket of mulberry wood used to carry water, well-worn
6 walnut chairs in good condition
one iron warming pan in good condition
one small iron polishing tool
one small iron ladle
one iron pitcher which holds about one quart
one iron frying pan and one iron spit
one horse's bit and bridle, new
one iron cooking pot with lid in good condition
one small cooking pan
one cooking pot holding about 2 quarts in good condition
dishes valued at 73 livres
14 *panals* of wheat
5 *panals* of rye

In the Salle:

One walnut chest with lock and key in good condition in which was found 7 lengths of red woolen serge in good condition, a cloak of gray material and cloth of the same color in good condition, 10 *pans* of white serge, one garment of black serge partially worn

one mirror hanging on the wall, the glass of which is 1 *pan* high and ¾ *pan* wide with a border of olive wood, nearly new

one walnut table nearly new with lock and key in which was found 5 *cannes* of material, 18 *cannes* of woolen material, leaf-green in color, 4 men's shirts of linen, another man's shirt, new, and another partially worn, 1 pound 8 ounces of thread

one bed, nearly new, with mattress, a covering of India cloth with two ruffles, another covering of lace

22 white napkins, partially worn

5 table cloths—one large and the others of medium size, all partly worn

9 men's shirts partly worn

one cradle blanket of red wool bordered with silk, partially used

2 pairs of iron andirons 4 *pans* high

Room next to the Salle:

one pair of goatskin shoes in good condition

one pair of wooden shoes, partly worn

one gown of gray wool, partly worn

one blouse of white wool, worn

one blouse of white wool, worn

one small walnut table, well-worn

one walnut bench in good condition

one bed with mattress and mattress cover

one small woolen window hanging

one pair of pistols with holsters

two woolen garments more than half-used

one fire bucket in good condition

Second Floor:

6 *quintaux* of hay

one walnut cradle

6 pounds of wool

Salle:

2 small chairs of walnut

one small woven carpet

one medium-large table in which was found:

11 30-sous pieces and one *écu*, total of 19 livres, 10 sous

marriage contract of 7 June 1680

division of property with his brother, Jacques Vial

obligation of 27 December 1675 in favor of Anne Aubin with Jean
  Rouvet and Paul Meynard, 315 livres

promesse privé in favor of Vial 4 May 1684 by Jean and Daniel
  Mille, 18 livres

promesse privé in favor of Vial 27 November 1684 by Michel
  Giraudon, 750 livres

promesse privé in favor of Vial 5 February 1685 by Jean Michel,
  marchand, 67 livres, 10 sous

promesse privé in favor of Jean Vial, his father, 1656 by Pierre Bail
  of Lacoste, 11 *écus*

promesse privé in favor of Vial 6 June 1684 by Pierre Sambuc, 200
  livres

promesse privé in favor of Vial 4 October 1684 by Pierre Sambuc,
  100 livres

plus other *promesses privés* amounting to 147 livres, 10 sous

Source: *A.Not.*, Chastroux, October 4, 1685.

APPENDIX C

FIVE-YEAR AVERAGES OF LOURMARIN'S VITAL STATISTICS

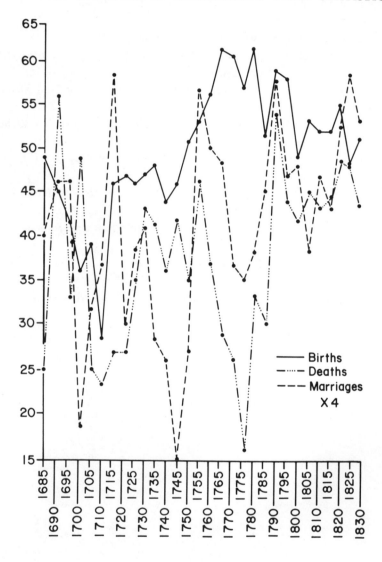

APPENDIX D

ANNUAL VITAL STATISTICS FOR LOURMARIN, 1681–1830

Year	Baptisms	Marriages	Burials
1681	53	8	25
1682	57	19	13
1683	40	2	20
1684	53	15	38
1685	42	6	31
1686	43	10	85
1687	49	3	30
1688	42	14	59
1689	51	21	76
1690	42	10	32
1691	45	9	25
1692	39	7	31
1693	49	18	35
1694	34	11	38
1695	43	12	36
1696	41	8	28
1697	32	4	22
1698	41	2	54
1699	27	5	62
1700	38	3	78
1701	41	12	21
1702	30	2	17
1703	44	7	22

Year	Baptisms	Marriages	Burials
1704	35	12	36
1705	45	7	31
1706	29	10	24
1707	27	1	25
1708	30	16	24
1709	28	7	15
1710	26	13	25
1711	40	18	45
1712	49	16	23
1713	53	10	20
1714	30	15	19
1715	59	13	27
1716	51	8	29
1717	44	7	21
1718	51	10	17
1719	48	7	49
1720	42	6	20
1721	41	9	17
1722	49	10	46
1723	44	5	44
1724	46	10	39
1725	51	14	31
1726	47	7	39
1727	55	14	33
1728	36	8	55
1729	40	11	43
1730	57	11	46
1731	49	8	39
1732	51	4	51
1733	50	5	40
1734	44	12	43
1735	47	6	30
1736	45	7	32
1737	43	10	45
1738	42	10	21
1739	46	3	42
1740	43	3	40

Year	Baptisms	Marriages	Burials
1741	39	1	32
1742	30	4	45
1743	51	2	60
1744	54	7	40
1745	58	3	35
1746	46	2	51
1747	45	15	34
1748	55	7	16
1749	60	6	39
1750	51	4	33
1751	54	14	34
1752	43	6	60
1753	43	14	38
1754	51	15	61
1755	72	22	38
1756	59	13	40
1757	48	17	50
1758	66	11	42
1759	56	13	29
1760	50	9	23
1761	68	7	34
1762	56	12	44
1763	71	20	21
1764	57	9	18
1765	60	12	23
1766	81	8	32
1767	60	7	27
1768	57	7	27
1769	57	13	21
1770	49	11	23
1771	66	5	11
1772	60	9	18
1773	57	11	19
1774	51	11	21
1775	51	8	9
1776	66	11	28
1777	64	13	30

Year	Baptisms	Marriages	Burials
1778	61	8	34
1779	53	10	35
1780	64	6	37
1781	56	12	29
1782	52	11	34
1783	40	10	10
1784	56	13	33
1785	56	10	46
1786	57	19	54
1787	71	8	56
1788	56	6	40
1789	53	25	49
1790	59	14	69
1791	68	12	32
1792	58	14	54
1793	53	8	39
1794	51	16	55
1795	60	8	40
1796	31	8	39
1797	55	11	46
1798	51	12	43
1799	47	19	34
1800	59	11	50
1801	50	10	40
1802	63	13	44
1803	56	8	48
1804	46	8	43
1805	49	8	57
1806	56	6	54
1807	58	12	46
1808	38	11	37
1809	49	16	43
1810	58	14	34
1811	53	6	33
1812	51	10	43
1813	42	31	60
1814	56	10	42
1815	57	8	40
1816	58	13	45

1817	49	10	45
1818	49	23	59
1819	62	11	53
1820	59	11	38
1821	42	17	50
1822	52	16	48
1823	44	12	47
1824	50	14	52
1825	54	14	28
1826	48	19	35
1827	62	15	41
1828	53	13	55
1829	53	10	34
1830	38	8	52

APPENDIX E

ARRENTEMENT AGREEMENT BETWEEN SEIGNEUR BRUNY AND FRANÇOIS COLLETIN, 12 JANUARY 1789

1. Colletin will make his full-time residence with his family in the apartment furnished him in the chateau.
2. He must keep a sufficient number of animals to provide manure for the said property and he must carry it into the fields which need it most. The cattle which he keeps must be lodged in the stables provided by this lease.
3. He cannot beat the oak trees to get acorns nor cut any tree alive or dead either at the base or the branches without the express consent of the seigneur; also he cannot prune any tree although he has the right to gather nuts. He may pasture some pigs in the vicinity of the trees but cannot pasture sheep there; and he will prune in the said property and the prunings which he will make from time to time will belong to him.
4. Each year of his lease he must plant 25 trees in places chosen by the seigneur. The shoots will be furnished by the Baron.
5. Colletin will do all the farming that is necessary and will leave the property at the end of his lease the same as it is now.
6. He will be permitted to work the land which he will fertilize and that land only.
7. At the end of his lease he will furnish the same capital in seeds and hay as he received at the beginning.
8. He must keep the ditches, especially the ones in the meadow, in good repair during his lease and he will leave them at the end of his lease in the same state as he finds them. He may take the water for irrigation of the meadows on the days appointed [Wednesday sundown to Monday sunrise] and in the customary manner *sans abus*.
9. The straw of the last year of his lease will be stored in the granary.

10. He must leave all the property as he finds it and must also see to the up-keep of the roofs of all the buildings included in this lease and make other minor repairs. As for major repairs (*réparations foncières*), they will be at the expense of the seigneur, but Colletin will be responsible for carting the necessary materials.

11. In the name of the seigneur there will be reserved three turkeys which will be sent to the seigneur each Christmas, three chickens and 20 dozen eggs sent each August, and a suckling pig in the proper season. The alcohol coming from the last grape pressing done in the [wine] cellar of the chateau will belong to the said lessee (*preneur*) for which he will furnish every year of his lease six *corvées* for gathering the sheaves, and finally the said Sieur Colletin promises and obliges himself to hold and to manage all the land and buildings dependent upon the properties of this lease as a good husbandman (*un père de famille*).

Source: *A.Not.*, Borrelly, January 12, 1789.

BIBLIOGRAPHY

I. PRIMARY SOURCES

In lieu of a formal listing of individual *liasses* found in the five main archives, I have elected to describe the types of sources to be found in each depot. Specific references may be found in the footnotes.

Archives Municipales, Lourmarin

These archives contain the minutes of the deliberations of the municipal council since the early seventeenth century bound in volumes, each of which covers five to ten years. In addition to the minutes these volumes include such varied subjects as leases for the village *fermes* and instructions from the Intendants. There are also the parish registers, those kept by the Catholic priest and those kept by the Protestant minister; the Catholic register begins in 1620 and continues without interruption to 1792, the Protestant register from 1620 to 1685 and from 1747 to 1792. The *État-Civil* (the lay parish register), kept by a locally elected official, begins in 1792 and is bound in volumes of ten years each. The archives include numerous tax records pertaining to the village. The most useful were the huge, two-volume *Cadastre* for 1770 and the 1791 *Contribution Foncière* and *Contribution Mobilière*. There are other more recent tax rolls but the first complete atlas for the sections of the village is for 1830. Various other documents dealing with village administration include a detailed 1685 document to regulate the village irrigation system.

Archives du Château, Lourmarin

Notarial minutes normally are not state property but are the property of the individual notary. The Foundation which administers the chateau has assembled notarial records for Lourmarin and some of the surrounding villages from the fifteenth century to the early nineteenth. For this study the following notaries were most useful: Joachim Chastroux (1680–1722), Pierre Pacot (1680–1712), Joseph Jacquier (1723–70), Pierre Ailhaud (1759–77), Jacques Rey (1774–78), and Trophime Borrelly (1778–92). The chateau also has an excellent library of local history.

Archives Départementales, Bouches-du-Rhône (Marseilles)

Series B (Judicial), C (Administration), and L (Revolution) are particularly useful for material dealing with Lourmarin. There is a considerable correspondence between Lourmarin and the Intendant, subdelegate, and other royal officials on such subjects as roads, taxes, poor relief, and requests from Lourmarin for information or assistance. There is also material about the plague in Lourmarin as well as the treatment of former Protestants after 1685 and the disposition made of their property. Valuable information on Lourmarin's community *fermes* supplements data in the council minutes and the notarial records. Since Lourmarin was incorporated into the new department of the Vaucluse in 1793, there is no pertinent material in Marseilles after this date, although there are several letters and documents illuminating the Jacobin-Federalist conflict in 1793.

Archives Départementales, Vaucluse (Avignon)

In general the same kind of documents are available in Avignon for the period after 1793, including village censuses beginning in 1804. Particularly useful were Series L and Q which include information on the evaluation and sale of *biens nationaux* in Lourmarin.

Musée Calvet, Municipal Library (Avignon)

This library has an excellent manuscript collection and was particularly valuable for information on the Bruny family and the seigneurie of Lourmarin. It also has a good library on local history and genealogy.

II. SECONDARY SOURCES

A. Manuals and Dictionaries

Bailly, Robert. *Dictionnaire des communes, Vaucluse.* Avignon, 1961.
Barjavel, C. F. H. *Dictionnaire historique, biographique et bibliographique du département de Vaucluse.* 2 vols. Carpentras, 1841.

Bresc, Louis de. *Armorial des communes de Provence ou dictionnaire géographique et héraldique des villes et villages des Bouches-du-Rhône, du Var, des Basses-Alpes, du Vaucluse, et des Alpes-Maritimes.* Paris, 1866.

Caron, P. *Manuel pratique pour l'étude de la Révolution française.* Paris, 1947.

Courtet, Jules. *Dictionnaire, géographique, géologique, historique, archéologique et biographique des communes du département de Vancluse.* Avignon, 1876.

Expilly, Abbé Jean-Joseph. *Dictionnaire géographique, historique et politique des Gaules et de la France,* vol. V. Paris, 1769.

Fleury, Michel, and Henry Louis. *Nouveau manuel de dépouillement et d'exploitation de l'état civil ancien.* Paris, 1965.

Langlois, C., and Stein, H. *Les archives de l'histoire de France.* Paris, 1891.

Marion, Marcel. *Dictionnaire des institutions de la France aux XVIIe et XVIIIe siècles.* Paris, 1923.

Martin, A., and Walter G., *Catalogue de l'histoire de la Révolution française.* 5 vols. Paris, 1936–55.

United Nations, Statistical Office, Department of Economic and Social Affairs. *Demographic Yearbook, 1966.* New York, 1967.

Walter, G. *Répertoire de l'histoire de la Révolution française. Travaux publiés de 1800 à 1940.* 2 vols. Paris, 1941–45.

B. Secondary Works

Anastay, Jacques P. "L'administration des communes au XVIIe siècle: Lourmarin." *Provincia,* VII (1927), 97–100.

Anderson, Frank M., ed. *The Constitutions and Other Select Documents Illustrative of the History of France, 1789–1907.* New York, 1967.

Arnaud, E. *Histoire des protestants de Provence du Comtat Venaissin et de la principauté d'Orange.* 2 vols. Toulouse, 1884.

Aubenas, R. "La famile dans l'ancienne Provence." *Annales d'histoire économique et sociale,* VIII (November, 1936), 523–41.

Babeau, Albert. *L'école de village pendant la Révolution.* Paris, 1885.

———. *La vie rurale dans l'ancienne France.* Paris, 1885.

———. *La ville sous l'ancien régime.* 2 vols. Paris, 1884.

Baehrel, René. *Une croissance: La Basse-Provence rurale (fin du XVIe siècle– 1789).* Paris, 1961.

Bancol, M. *Monographies communales; arrondissement d'Apt.* n.p., 1896.

Baratier, Edouard. *La démographie provençale du XIIIe au XVIe siècle, avec chiffres de comparaison pour le XVIIIe siècle.* Paris, 1961.

———. ed. *Histoire de la Provence.* Toulouse, 1969.

Barber, Elinor G. *The Bourgeoisie in Eighteenth Century France.* Princeton, 1955.

Biraben, Jean-Noël. "Certain Demographic Characteristics of the Plague Epidemic in France, 1720–1722," *Daedalus, XCVII* (Spring, 1968), 536–45.

Biraben, Jean-Noël; Fleury, Michel; and Henry, Louis "Inventaire par sondage des registres paroissiaux de France." *Population*, XV (January–March, 1960), 25–58.

Bloch, Camille. *L'assistance et l'état en France à la veille de la Révolution Généralités de Paris, Rouen, Allençon, Orléans, Chalons, Soissons, Amiens), 1764–1790.* Paris, 1908.

Bloch, Marc. *French Rural History: An Essay on its Basic Characteristics.* Translated by Janet Sondheimer. Berkeley, 1966.

Bluche, François. *Les magistrats du parlement de Paris an XVIIIᵉ siècle (1715–1771).* Paris, 1960.

Bois, Paul. *Paysans de l'ouest (des structures économiques et sociales aux options politiques depuis l'époque révolutionnaire dans la Sarthe).* Paris, 1960.

Bourde, André. *Agronomie et agronomes en France au XVIIIᵉ siècle.* 3 vols. Paris, 1967.

———. *The Influence of England on the French Agronomes, 1750–1789.* Cambridge, England, 1953.

Bourrilly, V. L. *Les protestants de Provence aux XVIIᵉ et XVIIIᵉ siècles.* Aix-en-Provence, 1956.

Bouyoux, Pierre. "Les 'six cents plus imposés' du département de la Haute-Garonne en l'an X." *Annales du Midi*, LXX (July, 1958), 317–27.

Busquet, Raoul. "Les cadastres et les 'unites cadastrales' en Provence du XVᵉ au XVIIIᵉ siècle." *Annales de Provence*, VII (April, June, 1910), 119–34, 161–84.

———. *Études sur l'ancienne Provence. Institutions et points d'histoire.* Paris, 1930.

Busquet, Raoul; Bourrilly, V. L.; and Agulhon, Maurice. *Histoire de la Provence.* Paris, 1966.

Cameron, John B., Jr. "The Federalist Movement in the Department of the Bouches-du-Rhône in 1793." Unpublished Ph.D. dissertation, University of North Carolina, Chapel Hill, 1970.

Carré, Henri. *La noblesse de France et l'opinion publique au XVIIIᵉ siècle.* Paris, 1920.

Castel, Jean-Baptiste. *Histoire de Cucuron: Period de la peste de 1720 à 1730.* Cucuron, n.d.

Chaunu, Pierre, ed. *À travers la Normandie des XVIIᵉ et XVIIIᵉ siècles.* Caen, 1963.

Cobban, Alfred. "Local Government during the French Revolution." *Aspects of the French Revolution.* London, 1967.

————. *The Social Interpretation of the French Revolution.* Cambridge, England, 1964.

————. "The Vocabulary of Social History." *Political Science Quarterly,* LXXI (March, 1956), 1–17.

Cornée, Jean. *Les débuts de la révolution aux Baux-en-Provence, 1788–1792.* Aix-en-Provence, 1957.

Dakin, Douglas. *Turgot and the Ancien Régime in France.* New York, 1965.

Davies, Alun. "The Origins of the French Peasant Revolution of 1789." *History,* XLIX (February, 1964), 24–41.

Didiée, Joseph. "Notes bibliographiques." *Académie de Vaucluse,* XVII (1917), 227–32.

Dupaquier, J. "Étude de la propriété et de la société rurale d'après les terriers." *Actes du 89e Congrès National des Sociétés Savantes.* Lyons, 1964, 259–70.

————. "Sur la population française au XVIIe et au XVIIIe siècle." *Revue Historique,* CCXXXIX (January–June, 1968), 43–79.

Egret, Jean. "La prérévolution en Provence, 1787–1789." *Annales Historiques de la Révolution Française* (1954), 97–126.

————. *La prérévolution française (1787–1788).* Paris, 1962.

Esmonin, Edmund. "L'abbé Expilly et ses travaux de statistique." *Études sur la France des XVIIe et XVIIIe siècles.* Paris, 1964. 1964.

Festy, Octave. *L'agriculture pendant la Révolution française: Les conditions de production et de récolte.* Paris, 1947.

————. *Les délits ruraux et leur répression sous la Révolution et le consulat.* Paris, 1956.

Fleury, Michel, and Henry, Louis. "Pour connaître la population de la France depuis Louis XIV. Plan de travaux par sondage." *Population,* XIII (October–December, 1958), 663–86.

Ford, Franklin. *Robe and Sword: The Regrouping of the French Aristocracy after Louis XIV.* Cambridge, Mass., 1953.

Forster, Robert. *The Nobility of Toulouse in the Eighteenth Century.* Baltimore, 1960.

"Fragments de statistique officielle, 1682." *Bullétin de la Société de l'histoire du Protestantisme français,* VII (1859), 22–24.

Glass, David V. *Population Policies and Movements in Europe.* London, 1967.

Godechot, Jacques. *Les institutions de la France sous la Révolution et l'empire.* Paris, 1951.

————. *Les révolutions, 1770–1799.* Paris, 1963.

Goubert, Pierre. *Beauvais et le beauvaisis de 1600 à 1730.* 2 vols. Paris, 1960.

————. "The French Peasantry of the Seventeenth Century: A Regional Example." *Past and Present,* X (November, 1956), 54–77.

————. "Legitimate Fecundity and Infant Mortality in France during the Eighteenth Century: A Comparison." *Daedalus*, XCVII (Spring, 1968), 593–603.

————. "Recent Theories and Research in French Population between 1500 and 1700." *Population in History*. Edited by David V. Glass and D. E. Eversley. London, 1965.

Greven, Philip J., Jr. "Historical Demography and Colonial America." *William and Mary Quarterly*, 3d Ser., XXIV (July, 1967), 438–54.

Grillon, Pierre. "L'invasion et la libération de la Provence en 1746–1747." *Provence Historique*, XII (October–December, 1962), 334–62.

Gruder, Vivian R. *The Royal Provincial Intendants, A Governing Elite in Eighteenth Century France*. Ithaca, N. Y., 1968.

Guide Michelin. *Provence*. Paris, 1968.

Hampson, Norman. *A Social History of the French Revolution*. Toronto, 1963.

Henry, Louis. *Anciennes familles génévoises: étude démographique: XVIe–XXe siècles*. Paris, 1956.

————. *Fécondité des marriages: Nouvelle méthode de mesure*. Paris, 1953.

————. "The Population of France in the Eighteenth Century." *Population in History*. Edited by David V. Glass and D. E. Eversley. London, 1965.

Henry, Louis, and Gautier, Etienne. *La population de Crulai paroisse normandie: étude historique*. Paris, 1958.

Herbert, Sydney. *The Fall of Feudalism in France*. London, 1921.

Hufton, Olwen. *Bayeux in the Late Eighteenth Century: A Social Study*. London, 1967.

Hyslop, Beatrice. *French Nationalism According to the General Cahiers*. New York, 1934.

Kaplow, Jeffry. *Elbeuf during the Revolutionary Period: History and Social Structure*. Baltimore, 1964.

Labrousse, Ernest. *La crise de l'économie française à la fin de l'ancien régime et au début de la Révolution*. Paris, 1943.

————. *Esquisse du mouvement des prix et des revenus en France au XVIIIe siècle*. Paris, 1932.

————. *Origines et aspects économiques et sociaux de la Révolution française, 1744–1791*. Vol. 1: *Les cours de Sorbonne*. Paris, 1946.

Lavoisier, A. L. *Oeuvres*. Vol. II. Paris, 1862.

Lefebvre, Georges. *The French Revolution from Its Origins to 1793*. Translated by Elizabeth Moss Evanson. New York, 1962.

————. *The French Revolution from 1793 to 1799*. Translated by John Hall Stewart and James Friguglietti. New York, 1964.

————. *La grande peur de 1789*. Paris, 1932.

————. *Les paysans du Nord*. Lille, 1922.

————. *Questions agraires au temps de la terreur*. La Roche-sur-Yon, 1954.

————. "Répartition de la propriété et de l'exploitation foncières à la fin de l'ancien régime." *Études sur la Révolution française.* Paris, 1954.

Leroy-Ladurie, Emmanuel. "Démographie et 'funestes secrèts': Le Languedoc (fin XVIIIe début XIXe siècle)." *Annales Historiques de la Révolution Française*, XXXVII (July–September, 1965), 385–99.

————. "From Waterloo to Colyton." *Times Literary Supplement* (September 8, 1966), 791–92.

————. *Les paysans de Languedoc.* 2 vols. Paris, 1966.

————. "Voies nouvelles pour l'histoire rurale (XVIe–XVIIIe siècles)." *Études Rurales*, XIII (April–September, 1964), 79–95.

Leymarie, M. "Les redevances foncières seigneuriales en Haute-Auvergne." *Annales Historiques de la Révolution Française*, XL (July–September, 1968), 299–380.

Livet, R. *Habitat rural et structures agraires en basse Provence.* Aix-en-Provence, 1962.

Lockridge, Kenneth A. "The Population of Dedham, Massachusetts, 1636–1736." *Economic History Review*, 2d ser., XIX (May, 1966), 318–44.

McCloy, Shelby. *The Humanitarian Movement in Eighteenth Century France.* Lexington, Ky. 1957.

McKeown, Thomas, and Brown, R. G. "Medical Evidence Related to English Population Changes in the Eighteenth Century." *Population In History.* Edited by David V. Glass and D. E. Eversley. London, 1965.

Martin, H. *La dîme ecclésiastique en France au XVIIIe siècle et sa suppression.* Bordeaux, 1912.

Masson, Paul. *Les Bouches-du-Rhône encyclopédie départementale.* Vol. III: *Les temps modernes.* n.p. 1931.

————. *La Provence au XVIIIe siècle.* Paris, 1936.

Maugis, E. "L'enquête du parlement sur la tenue des registres paroissiaux d'état civil dans les vingt dernières années de l'ancien régime." Vol. I. *Revue Historique de Droit Français et Étranger.* Paris, 1922.

Monastier, Antoine. *Histoire de l'église vaudoise depuis son origine et des vaudois du Piémont jusqu'à nos jours.* 2 vols. Paris, 1847.

Morineau, Michel. "Y a-t-il eu une révolution agricole en France au XVIIIe siècle?" *Revue Historique*, CCXXXIX (January–June, 1968), 299–326.

Mourre, Charles. "La peste de 1720 à Marseille et les intendants du bureau de santé." *Provence Historique*, XIV (April–June, 1963), 135–59.

Noonon, John T., Jr. *Contraception: A History of its Treatment by the Catholic Theologians and Canonists.* New York, 1967.

Palmer, Robert R. *The Age of the Democratic Revolution.* 2 vols. Princeton, 1959, 1964.

Peyre, B. *Histoire de Mérindol en Provence.* Avignon, 1939.

Pezet, Maurice. *Durance et Luberon (Provence inconnue).* Paris, 1958.

Pickford, M. A. "The Panic of 1789 in Lower Dauphiné and in Provence." *English Historical Review*, XXIX (April, 1914), 276–301.

Poland, Burdette C. *French Protestantism and the French Revolution: A Study in Church and State, Thought and Religion, 1685–1815.* Princeton, 1957.

Reinhard, Marcel. *Étude de la population pendant la Révolution et l'empire.* 2 vols. Paris, 1961, 1963.

Robert, P. Albert. *Les remonstrances et arrêtes du parlement de Provence au XVIIIe siècle.* Paris, 1912.

Rouchon-Guigues, E. C. *Résumé de l'histoire de l'état et comté souverain de Provence.* Aix-en-Provence, 1863.

Rudé, George. *The Crowd in History: A Study of Popular Disturbances in France and England, 1730–1848.* New York, 1964.

———. *The Crowd in the French Revolution.* Oxford, 1959.

———. "Prices, Wages and Popular Movements in Paris during the French Revolution." *The Economic History Review*, VI (April, 1954), 246–67.

Sade, Marquis de. *Oeuvres complètes.* Edited by Gilbert Lely. Vol. XII. Paris, 1964.

Sagnac, P. *La Formation de la société française moderne.* Vol. II. Paris, 1945.

———. *La législation civile de la Révolution française.* Paris, 1898.

Scoville, Warren C. *The Persecution of Huguenots and French Economic Development, 1680–1720.* Berkeley, 1960.

Sée, Henri. *Les classes rurales en Bretagne du XVIe siècle à la Révolution.* Paris, 1906.

———. *Economic and Social Conditions in France during the Eighteenth Century.* Translated by Edwin H. Zeydel. New York, 1927.

Slicher van Bath, B. H. *The Agrarian History of Western Europe, A.D. 500–1850.* New York, 1963.

Soboul, Albert. "The French Rural Community in the Eighteenth and Nineteenth Centuries." *Past and Present*, X (November, 1956), 78–95.

———. "Notes sur étude des documents foncières du XVIIIe siècle." *Actes du 89e Congrès National des Sociétés Savantes.* Lyons, 1964, 231–58.

———. *Paysans, sans-culottes et Jacobins.* Paris, 1966.

———. *Précis d'histoire de la Révolution française.* Paris, 1962.

———. "La Révolution française et la 'féodalité.' Notes sur le prélèvement féodal." *Revue Historique*, XL (July–September, 1968), 33–56.

Sumeire, Gabriel-Jean. *La communauté de Trets à la veille de la Révolution.* Aix-en-Provence, 1960.

Sydenham, M. J. *The Girondins.* London, 1961.

Taine, Hippolyte A. *The Ancient Regime.* Translated by John Durand. New York, 1888.

Theus, Pierre. *La fondation d'un village de Provence au XVIIIe siècle: Charleval—1741.* Aix-en-Provence, 1960.

Tilly, Charles. *The Vendée*. Cambridge, Mass., 1964.

Tocqueville, Alexis de. *The Old Regime and the French Revolution*. Translated by Stuart Gilbert. Garden City, N.J., 1955.

Valmary, Pierre. *Familles paysannes au XVIIIᵉ siècle en Bas-Quercy: Étude démographique*. Paris, 1965.

Varille, Mathieu. *Lourmarin de Provence, capitale du Luberon*. Lyons, 1967.

Viguier, Jules. *La convocation des états généraux en Provence*. Paris, 1896.

———. *Les débuts de la Révolution en Provence*. Paris, 1894.

Vincent, Paul. "French Demography in the Eighteenth Century." *Population Studies*, I (June, 1947), 44–71.

Vovelle, Michel. "État présent des études de structure agraire en Provence à la fin de l'Ancien Régime."*Provence Historique*, XVIII (October–December, 1968), 450–84.

———. "Prêtres adbicataires et dechristianisation en Provence." *Actes du 89ᵉ Congrès National des Sociétés Savantes*. Lyons, 1964, 63–98.

———. "Propriété et exploitation dans quelques communes beauceronnes de la fin du XVIIIᵉ au début du XIXᵉ siècles." *Memoires de la société archéologique d'Eure-et-Loire*, XXII (1961).

———. "Sade et Lacoste, suivi de Mirabeau et Mirabeau: Réflexions sur le déclassement nobiliaire dans la Provence du XVIIIᵉ siècle." *Provence Historique*, XVII (April–June, 1967), 160–71.

———. "Sade seigneur de village." *Actes du Colloque Sade tenu à Aix en 1966*. Paris, 1969.

Wolff, Louis. *Le parlement du Provence au XVIIIᵉ siècle. Organisation. Procédure*. Aix-en-Provence, 1920.

Wright, Gordon. *France in Modern Times; 1760 to the Present*. Chicago, 1960.

Wrigley, Edward A. "Family Limitation in Pre-Industrial England." *Economic History Review*, 2d ser., XIX (April, 1966), 82–109.

———, ed. *An Introduction to English Historical Demography*. New York, 1966.

———. "Mortality in Pre-Industrial England: The Example of Colyton, Devon, over Three Centuries." *Daedalus*, XCVII (Spring, 1968), 546–80.

Wylie, Laurence. *Chanzeaux, A Village in Anjou*. Cambridge, Mass., 1966.

———. *Village in the Vaucluse*. New York, 1964.

Young, Arthur. *Travels during the Years 1787, 1788 and 1789*. Dublin, 1793.

INDEX